THE
COMMUNITY JUSTICE
IDEAL

CRIME AND SOCIETY

Series Editor
John Hagan, *University of Toronto*

The Community Justice Ideal: Preventing Crime and Achieving Justice,
Todd R. Clear and David R. Karp

*Whistleblowing at Work: Tough Choices in
Exposing Fraud, Waste, and Abuse on the Job,*
Terance D. Miethe

*Losing Legitimacy: Street Crime and the Decline
of Social Institutions in America,* Gary LaFree

*Casualties of Community Disorder: Women's Careers
in Violent Crime,* Deborah R. Baskin and Ira B. Sommers

Public Opinion, Crime, and Criminal Justice,
Julian V. Roberts and Loretta Stalans

Poverty, Ethnicity, and Violent Crime,
James F. Short

*Great Pretenders: Pursuits and Careers of
Persistent Thieves,* Neal Shover

Crime and Public Policy: Putting Theory to Work,
edited by Hugh D. Barlow

Control Balance: Toward a General Theory of Deviance,
Charles R. Tittle

Rape and Society: Readings on the Problems of Sexual Assault,
edited by Patricia Searles and Ronald J. Berger

THE
COMMUNITY
JUSTICE IDEAL

Preventing Crime and Achieving Justice

TODD R. CLEAR
John Jay College of Criminal Justice

DAVID R. KARP
Skidmore College

Westview Press
A Member of the Perseus Books Group

Crime and Society

Copyright © 1999 by Westview Press, A Member of the Perseus Books Group

Published in 1999 in the United States of America by Westview Press, 5500 Central Avenue, Boulder, Colorado 80301-2877, and in the United Kingdom by Westview Press, 12 Hid's Copse Road, Cumnor Hill, Oxford OX2 9JJ

Find us on the World Wide Web at www.westviewpress.com

A CIP catalog record for this book is available from the Library of Congress.
ISBN 0-8133-6765-4 (hc)
ISBN 0-8133-6766-2 (pbk.)

The paper used in this publication meets the requirements of the American National Standard for Permanence of Paper for Printed Library Materials Z39.48-1984.

10   9   8   7   6   5   4   3   2   1

Contents

Tables and Illustrations

Tables

Figures

Boxes

THE
COMMUNITY JUSTICE
IDEAL

Introduction

There is disquiet in America about what is happening to community life. Americans seem to have a sense that the quality of community life is diminishing and that family life is deteriorating. There is widespread talk about the need to "restore" the community and family, and many feel that a crisis of values is occurring in both the public and the private spheres of American life. Some of this is almost certainly nostalgia and sentimentalism. To the degree that the "community movement" is a romantic appeal to an inaccurate recollection of the past, it is an interlude destined for a short life.

But other, more objective indicators suggest that community life is indeed changing in America and that many citizens' concerns are justified. Some of these changes involve distance and technology: With our growing use of computers and involvement in international markets, the world is increasingly everyone's neighborhood. Other changes appear more rooted in socioeconomic trends; the increasing inequality and structural distance between social groups, combined with fewer intact families raising children, cause many observers to worry that the infrastructure of good citizenship is deteriorating. People move from place to place, and at every turn their children are confronted by technical, social, and interpersonal change. With our society undergoing such rapid transformation, people worry about whether the foundations of democratic life are strong enough to take us very far into the future.

These changes have enormous implications for criminal justice. As people begin to feel and express their alienation from institutional life, including political institutions, their actions cannot help but spill over into the formal mechanisms of social control. In a quarter century, the size, cost, and potency of the justice apparatus has grown three to five times over, depending on how one counts the growth. Public confidence in the justice system is, if anything, less than when the growth began. Surely if the justice system were put up for a vote of confidence, the prospects would be dim. One way of interpreting this situation is that people have little confidence that the justice system supports the quality of daily life.

The movement of criminal justice toward the community initiatives described in this book is a response to the common sense of dismay about community life. Criminal justice officials, sensing that confidence in their actions is slipping away, have sought a closer alignment with community

1

members partly as a vehicle for increasing faith in justice practices. It must also be remembered that criminal justice practitioners are also members of the community. They feel some of the same disillusionment in official policies and they experience the same type of yearning for a better quality of community life.

The disquiet about community life that has translated into a community movement in criminal justice has, to date, consisted of sporadic experiences and initiatives and has lacked a philosophy and a strategic model—an "ideal." This book is an attempt to fill that void. We address three main questions:

- What is the practical case for greater community involvement in criminal justice?
- What is the philosophical basis for community-oriented criminal justice?
- What might a community-oriented justice practice look like?

In discussing these questions, we do not pretend to offer any final resolutions. The analysis that follows is an attempt to organize the issues of community-oriented criminal justice in a way that makes sense, and to consider them systematically. We hope this discussion will stimulate others to analyze more deeply and critically the territory we have outlined.

Community Justice: A Thought Experiment

There is no standard formula for a community justice program. The design of a particular community justice approach will depend upon the interlocking traditions of the neighborhood's community organizations, justice system practices, and crime problems. One way to illustrate the array of possibilities is through a description of one hypothetical neighborhood: Tocqueville Heights.

Community Justice in Tocqueville Heights

Tocqueville Heights is an old, inner-city neighborhood in the city of Megalopolis. Comprised of roughly 100 square blocks, Tocqueville Heights has three multistory public housing complexes and a small business section, and is served by a public school complex named Tocqueville Heights School. One-half of the residents have incomes under or just over the poverty line, and the area has high rates on all indicators of disorganization: single-parent families, high-school dropouts, unemployment, vacant dwellings, and public assistance. The area also is among the highest in arrest rates for drugs and street crimes.

The Tocqueville Heights Community Justice Center (CJC) is located in a renovated building across the street from the police precinct. What used to be a ma-and-pa deli now serves as an office for Miriam Bledsoe, director of the center, her staff of two, and an assortment of volunteers and interns. Bledsoe is a lawyer and community activist. Her staff includes Jethro McDowell, a former probation officer with a master's degree in social work; and Luke Wallace, a paraprofessional and ex-offender. The center is a nonprofit organization funded by government contractual fees (paid for services rendered), and has an annual budget of $250,000.

The CJC runs a number of projects, the most popular being:

- *Crimestop.* Working with the local police, the CJC convenes meetings of local residents to discuss crime problems in their areas. The CJC staffers then lead a "crime prevention" analysis of these problems and develop mechanisms for reducing the incidence of targeted crimes.
- *Victims' Awareness (VA).* Local residents who are victims of crime are brought together to talk about how victimization has affected their lives. The nature and extent of crime in Tocqueville Heights is discussed, as are the programs in existence that try to reduce crime. Opportunities are given for victim-offender mediation. Methods for preventing repeat victimization are described, and individuals are assisted in taking steps to secure their living areas from crime. The VA sessions help CJC funnel victims into appropriate services through referral to a range of concrete and counseling services the CJC may purchase for clients or send them to.
- *Too Legit to Quit (TLQ).* This is a recreational club that meets two nights a week and on Sunday afternoons in the local school. It is open to teenage male children whose fathers or mothers are incarcerated; each child is paired with two adults and another child. Adult offenders under a community justice sentence attend with one of their children, and they are teamed up with another adult who will act as a mentor for the child. The TLQ team attends workshops on parent-child relationships and engages in organized, supervised recreation with other teams. The structure is designed to strengthen ties between offenders and their children and to establish supports between offenders and other local adults.
- *Tocqueville Heights Habitat.* Squads of offenders under community justice sentences rehabilitate local buildings, which become shelters for the homeless or are rented to small businesses at advantageous rates. Habitat work crews employ local residents, who are paid wages at near prevailing rates, as well as offenders, who re-

ceive minimum wages. Private contractors for renovation must agree to employ local residents and be willing to supervise offenders as part of the crew. Offenders are required to abide by the same regulations as full-pay employees.

- *Seniorcare.* Offenders are paired with elderly residents who are otherwise without services. Formally, each offender pays weekly social visits on eldercare partners and keeps them company. Informally, deeper relationships are encouraged by having the offender accompany the senior citizen to health appointments and community social clubs. In some cases, the TLQ teams spend regular time in visits with senior citizens.
- *Afterschool.* Local adults supervise a series of after-school activities for youngsters, ranging from recreation to creative arts. The activities are age-relevant, and some of the volunteers are offenders and former offenders. The latter are always paired with other residents, who act in a supervisory capacity.
- *Resolve.* Citizens in this neighborhood who have a dispute are typically unable to afford legal assistance, and they avoid the municipal civil justice system. Resolve is a dispute resolution program that provides mediation to local residents who have a conflict they cannot resolve on their own.
- *Circles.* CJC convenes sentencing circles with offenders and members of the community, especially the crime victims. The Circles have three objectives: to reaffirm local behavioral standards; to reintegrate offenders; and to negotiate sentencing agreements that establish terms of community supervision and reparation for the harm caused by the offense.

These projects are all made possible through partnerships with existing organizations and citizen volunteers. The local probation department has assigned a unit of its staff to a special team managing the cases of approximately 1,000 probationers living in Tocqueville Heights. The state's parole department assigns two parole officers to the area as well, housing them in an office adjacent to the CJC. The two officers work in close partnership with the CJC, paying special attention to clients the two agencies have in common. By "partnership" we mean not only cooperation and information sharing but also the setting of mutual goals involving community safety and offender adjustment. The CJC shares the parole department's goals and interests, and stays aware enough of client behavior to serve as another check on client adjustment. Indications of alcohol or drug abuse are immediately reported to the appropriate justice agencies, and there is a continual attentiveness for signals of new problems in an offender's circumstances, which are immediately made known to authorities. The two correctional agencies have come to rely on the expertise and sympathetic involvement of the CJC in their clients' lives.

To support the work of the CJC, the court system has specialized its assignments. An assistant district attorney handles all cases against residents except those involving capital offenses (the city district attorney's office has a homicide division), and most criminal cases are heard by a judge whose jurisdiction is Tocqueville Heights. This geographic specialization is seen as an essential foundation for the cooperative working environment sought by the CJC. Cooperation is actively pursued also by Bledsoe in regular, formal and informal contact with members of the community and of the justice system.

The CJC uses a network of volunteers, as well. Every offender in a CJC program must have a community sponsor, and finding and maintaining these sponsors requires a substantial effort. The most common sponsorships come from three of the local churches and the local mosque, but the CJC also has received assistance from a few local businesses that have hired offenders and/or sponsored them. The most important volunteers are the Program Associates—citizens who participate in each of the three programs, teaching building-renovation skills, joining in the TLQ teams as foster mentors, or contacting and supporting seniors who participate in Seniorcare. CJC also maintains a community board made up of volunteers who provide oversight of CJC activities.

How the Program Works

Mission.   On the wall facing the front door, a four-foot sign declares the mission of the CJC of Tocqueville Heights. It says:

> The Tocqueville Heights Community Justice Center seeks to strengthen the capacity of residents of our community to manage their own affairs, solve their own problems, and live effectively and safely together. This is best achieved by giving everyone a stake in the quality of community life. Our specific focus is on people who have violated the law. We seek to reestablish their community ties and reawaken their connection to community life.
>
> We recognize that our clients are among the most important to our community harmony, because they have disturbed it in the past. Therefore, we are dedicated to improving the quality of community life by addressing the harm directly. We believe in a basic truth: Every member of our community—including offenders—has a stake in maintaining a safe neighborhood.
>
> Our commitment to the community is:
> - To ensure that offenders coming into this community are offered an opportunity to compensate the community for the costs of their crimes; and

- To ensure that offenders coming into this community receive interventions or controls that will guard against the recurrence of crimes.

Our commitment to victims of crime is:

- To ensure some compensation and reparation for the losses caused by crime, and to involve offenders in making that compensation; and
- To promise that no offenders return to this community through the CJC without a complete evaluation of the risk they pose, and the establishment of programs to manage it; and
- To include victims in every step of the community justice process.

Our commitment to the offender is:

- To provide the best set of opportunities for making reparations to the community; and
- To help create and strengthen ties to community life.

Approach.   The CJC thinks of itself as having three distinct client groups: community, victim, and offender. It operates with a community advisory board, and it maintains numerous ties to influential members of the community. The director, Bledsoe, is a dependable presence at local meetings, where she often speaks in support of a safer community and a higher quality of community life. As a steady voice for community justice, she sees herself not only as an advocate but also as an educator and conciliator. The facts, she believes, are on her side: Nearly every Tocqueville Heights resident convicted of a felony spends some time in incarceration—either in jail, awaiting trial, and/or in prison, serving terms of about two years on average—and nearly all will return to live in Tocqueville Heights. The problem of community safety, she reminds her audience, is not nearly as dependent on the period of confinement as it is on what happens when offenders return to the streets.

She sees the victims of crime as her most important ally in this effort, for they are often the most neglected. Her staff, led by McDowell, tries to contact victims as soon after the offense as possible, to prepare them for what will happen next. The focus of their efforts is on the various aspects of injury suffered by victims of crime—concrete losses as well as emotional damage. The CJC tries to build trust with victims in order to restore their faith in community life and in the potential for community safety.

With offenders, the CJC's foremost objective is to situate them in community activities and restrictions that control the risk they pose. This objective cannot be fully accomplished without the offender's making reparation to the community and the victim. Thus the CJC concerns itself with offender risk by opening the community to stronger and more effective connections with the offender, and it creates opportunities for the offender to compensate for the offense.

The CJC recognizes that it is not the only agency carrying these responsibilities. Elected leaders are responsible for community development, victims' services agencies assist victims of crime, and correctional agencies manage the offender's risk to the community. What makes the CJC unique is its concentrated focus on Tocqueville Heights; the neighborhood is its ultimate client. The CJC knows that it can use its strategic location in the community to strengthen the effectiveness of existing agencies by working in partnership with them. By the same token, the existing agencies see the CJC as helpful in accomplishing their mission in this difficult neighborhood.

Practicing Community Justice

The function that the CJC performs in community justice comprises four kinds of tasks: risk assessment and control, victim restoration, community contract, and cost sharing.

Risk Assessment and Control.   Because the CJC practices its correctional program within the environs of Tocqueville Heights, it can engage in more holistic risk management than can office-bound correctional agencies. Most of traditional community correctional practice focuses on the problems of the offender and on how those problems contribute to risk. The CJC also considers opportunities for crime and seeks to increase the environmental controls on opportunity for repeat offending. By "opportunity" we mean the factors that are essential to crime, based on the "routine activities" concept. This model asserts that for a crime to occur, two factors must be present and two absent.

Present must be:

- *A motivated offender.* A crime is committed by a person, and that person must want to gain the benefits of the criminal act.
- *A suitable target.* There must be a place or person that is desirable as a target for the offender.

Absent must be:

- *A capable guardian.* Targets, no matter how suitable, can be made safe from crime by the presence of a person or system that guards them against the offender.
- *An intimate handler.* A person with a strong emotional tie to the potential offender inhibits the offender from criminality for fear of damaging the emotional tie.

Crime prevention programs like the CJC's Crimestop focus on criminal targets and guardians, seeking to strengthen their anticrime potential. Normally such programs have little to do with offenders. However, the CJC's community focus enables its staff and community members to work to increase opportunities for legitimate activities and to decrease opportunities for crime. For example, the Too Legit to Quit program is designed to strengthen the relationship between parents who are offenders—especially the men—and their children so as to inhibit repeat offenses. People who live in contact with the offender, when properly involved in the community safety agenda, also can serve as guardians. They can observe the offender's conduct for behavioral irregularities signaling a return to criminality, and thus make preemptive interventions possible.

The CJC first conducts a comprehensive risk assessment—not only of the risk factors that are *present* in the offender's life, creating problems that need to be controlled, but also of the risk-abating factors that are *absent* from the offender's situation. It then prepares a "risk management plan" that details the tasks of offenders, their family members and associates, and formal service-delivery agencies within an overall strategy for maintaining the offender in the community with the reasonable expectation of a positive, crime-free outcome.

Victim Restoration Plan.   The establishment of a realistic risk management plan is a necessary but not a sufficient condition for the CJC to accept a case. There must also be a victim restoration plan that adequately provides for the alleviation of the damage suffered by the victim of the crime. An adequate plan to restore the victim has three elements:

- A full accounting of the costs of the crime, both in tangible losses of property, services, and income and in emotional losses, or "quality of life" costs;
- A strategy for addressing those losses, to which the victim assents; and
- Offender contribution to the overall strategy.

A *full accounting* is necessary because too often victim compensation is thought of only in terms of material property losses. To go beyond property costs is to recognize the way that crime damages the victim's sense of personal security as well as the entire community's quality of life. The CJC subscribes to the belief that there are very few truly "victimless" crimes: Even in cases where there is no specific person to be restored, there is still the community's expectation of recompense for the criminality in its midst.

Victim assent to the restoration strategy is also important. Making the plan contingent upon victim approval is a fundamental way to elevate the status of the victim to that of a full player in the process. It also confronts the offender with the very real presence of a cocitizen who has been harmed by the crime and who must be considered in response to the crime. The same principle explains why the *offender contribution* to the strategy is essential. The offender's contribution—whether in time, financial resources, or services—symbolizes the offender's resolve to treat cocitizens as people who have the right to live free of victimization.

The CJC meets with victims (or in the case of "victimless" offenses, with its community board) and develops an assessment of the full costs of the crime. It then convenes a sentencing circle open to all members of the community, especially those who are closely affected by the crime. The CJC describes the offender's risk assessment and outlines what might be done to manage the offender under a sentence to the CJC. The alternative—what the criminal justice system will do if the offender is not accepted into the CJC—is also described. The CJC works with the community to develop a restorative package that might repay the costs of the crime. Until the victim and other members of the community are satisfied, the offender cannot expect to be accepted into the CJC's programs.

The elements of a compensation plan are also negotiated with the offender. There might be several options for "paying" the community—in labor, money, services, or other specified actions. The CJC sees its goals as compiling a plan that the offender finds superior to what will happen as a result of the normal justice process. By incorporating a series of supports, positive activities, and risk reduction services (such as employment and job training), and by reducing the punitiveness of sanctions, the CJC attempts to assemble a plan the offender would prefer to "straight punishment." Its plan is more frequently accepted by offenders accused of serious offenses (those that would normally result in a year or more of imprisonment), since the potential responses of the justice system are more severe for such crimes. In addition, the greater harm suffered by victims of more serious offenses means that victims will find more of the services CJC offers attractive as alternatives to what is offered by the traditional justice process. However, extremely serious cases are almost never referred to the CJC, if only because of practical constraints. Victims of profoundly serious crimes typically find it impossible to construct a scenario that would lead to their restoration. Offenders often pose so great a risk that a satisfactory management plan is not feasible. Lastly, the community typically resists involvement with the most serious offenders.

Community justice is a three-way proposition, and each party must feel the CJC's proposal is wise before it will be acceptable. When the stakes are small for any of the actors, little basis exists for a CJC-initiated accommodation. As the stakes get larger, the room the CJC has to develop an alternative to the justice process also grows. Because of these inherent pressures, the CJC makes no blanket exclusions based on prior record or current conviction; any case may be pursued if there seems a chance of working out agreements. This is not as chaotic as it might seem; over time, Bledsoe and McDowell have developed realistic expectations about which cases they will be able to work out.

Community Contract.   The community contract is an agreement by the community to accept the offender into the CJC under the terms described in the risk management plan and the victim restoration arrangement. When the community accepts a CJC plan, it accepts the reasonable risks the plan involves and sanctions the arrangements in the risk management and restoration plans as consistent with community values. The main body CJC uses for community actions is the sentencing circle. In some cases, victims' advocates are actively recruited as participants, especially when the crime involves a class of victims, such as in family violence offenses. The CJC has often found it helpful to include advocacy groups for the class of victims in its planning; victims' support groups, family violence service agencies, and the like can provide a valuable voice and helpful input as the circle considers a case.

It is the community contract that obligates the various parties to their tasks. The offender has received permission to join in a community-sponsored justice initiative and is obligated to perform certain actions to earn this permission. The victim has accepted the offender's presence in the community as part of a broader restorative process. The CJC, in order to make the complex arrangement sensible, agrees to monitor all parties' progress through the agreement and to report to the community board, which provides oversight, any problems in the system of agreements.

Cost Sharing.   The CJC receives offender referrals from three sources: the department of corrections, the court, and the public defender's office. The first two refer traditional offenders who have been released from prison or who have been placed on probation, respectively. Referrals from the third source—the public defender's office—are especially important because they are the basis for public funding of the CJC.

Cost sharing is essential to community justice, both in concept and in practice. The conceptual basis for cost sharing is that offenders referred by the Public Defender face prison terms if they are not accepted into the CJC. Prison sentences, which average about 28 months for offenders from Megalopolis, cost the state's taxpayers an average of $45,000 in correctional costs per offender. These taxes come from communities wealthier than Tocqueville Heights, and they are used to pay for the incarceration of Tocqueville Heights residents in state prisons. When one of these offenders is accepted into a CJC program, savings are created—essentially because Tocqueville Heights citizens are assuming the responsibility for punishment and absorbing the social risk. The CJC believes the neighborhood's citizens should also accrue some of the benefits. At the same time, the CJC recognizes that none of the existing criminal justice agencies can absorb all of the CJC's operating costs; and it sees programmatic value in being fiscally independent of traditional justice agencies. Yet if existing justice agencies do not benefit from community justice (and the benefits of the CJC support services described above for traditional agencies are paramount), then community justice will be at odds with the criminal justice system. The creation of a separate funding stream for community justice alleviates this problem.

To receive funding, the CJC must guarantee that the clients it accepts are prison-bound offenders. This it does through inquiries about the prosecutor's sentencing recommendation as well as studies of past sentencing practices. For each prison-bound offender accepted by the CJC, $15,000—a third of the savings to the justice system—is set aside for the CJC to use on program development. For each offender who completes a year under CJC supervision, the full amount of $15,000 is credited to the CJC's account. The math is straightforward: Tocqueville Heights sends 500 residents a year to the state's prison system. If CJC has fifteen successful cases in any given year, its operating expenses are fully covered. Each additional success helps fund crime prevention in Tocqueville Heights: One successful offender each week generates $500,000 a year in excess of the CJC's operating budget; and a number of outside sources stand ready to provide matching funds. The community board thus has an operating budget to spend on various crime prevention projects.

And spend they do. In the Crimestop program, which has proven highly successful in reducing crime, $150,000 a year is spent on targeting locations that suffer from serious crime problems. Victims' Awareness gets $80,000 a year. The rest is used for neighborhood reclamation projects or is deposited in the bank for a rainy day: Some victims may require expensive services, and this fund ensures that those services will be available.

The Traditional Justice System

The CJC works closely with the criminal justice system. The fundamental requirement is that the system have confidence in the CJC's work, and confidence is engendered by hard work and attention to detail. The "detail" involves attending to the interests of the system—for example, keeping the judge informed of an offender's progress under CJC, especially when problems arise.

That is why the CJC works in close partnership with the probation, parole, and police agencies. This is the secret to credibility with the justice system. Judges, after all, sentence. Their willingness to send offenders to the CJC is dependent upon their perception that the CJC is a responsible agency, and this depends upon the CJC's willingness to take the justice system's interests seriously. Therefore, the CJC caters to the system's needs. It wants probation to know that probation's clients will be monitored; it wants parole to know that its clients' progress will be followed. Most important, it wants the system to know that reasonable plans will be developed for CJC offenders, and that these plans will have a chance to succeed.

Failures. The linkage to the criminal justice system becomes most significant when the CJC experiences failure. There are two types of failure: the inability to develop a three-way agreement, and the failure of an offender to live up to the terms of the agreement.

The first type of failure—the inability to arrive at an agreement—has important implications for the criminal justice system, for the case goes forward as usual in that system. The CJC takes care to ensure that the failure to accept a case does not undermine an offender's processing by the criminal justice system. Studies of nonacceptances provide the CJC with a basis for estimating the costs that might have been avoided, had the case been accepted.

The second type of failure—offender program failure—is a far more serious matter. The CJC distinguishes between two versions of offender noncompliance with agreements: new criminality, or other behavior that indicates a significant risk of new criminality, and the failure to live up to one of the requirements of an agreement (such as victim compensation or attendance at Tocqueville Heights Habitat). Though either type of program failure will result in return to court for sentencing, the CJC is particularly concerned about risk-related failures. The CJC defines community safety as a central concern for all of its programs, and it stakes its organizational credibility on its success in maximizing community safety. When an offender fails to abide by any element of the community justice agreement, reasonable efforts are made to achieve the offender's compliance. If these measures do not work, the CJC terminates its involvement and the case is remanded to the court or other appropriate justice agency.

Community Justice: Can It Work?

The scenario described here is not a blueprint; it lays out one way that a community justice model might work, but this is not the only possibility. Myriad models seem plausible, and a particular community might consider several options before identifying the arrangement that best suits its needs. The essential elements are a professional organization that sets up and operates community programs; a participating community; a sympathetic justice system; and sufficient crime to make the arrangement financially feasible. Also helpful are an imagination and a willingness to experiment with cost sharing in poorer communities.

There are obvious problems with a community justice model. Citizens will not be eager to participate, and justice officials may be resistant as well. The field of community organization and development has a history of lukewarm experiences as well as successes; it is well known that community programs present complicated operational difficulties. Some offenders will fail—sometimes dramatically so. So why do we think that community justice will turn out to be a good idea?

For three reasons: First, the criminal justice system, in its current form, has lost credibility with the public. It is a bureaucracy whose methods and perspectives seem peculiarly at odds with common sense. Any call to preserve the current criminal justice system without exploring alternatives seems blind to foundational discontent with justice today. If there is to be a rebirth of credibility in criminal justice, it will be based in greater community involvement in justice activities.

Second, there is much to be gained from community justice. Victims may receive greater benefit from community justice outcomes than from traditional justice; offenders may find a more meaningful way to repay the community for the costs of their crimes; and the community's safety and quality of life might be enhanced from its involvement in justice-related projects. The parties accept risks in pursuit of these gains, and the risks add incentive to make these programs work.

Third, the community is already becoming more actively involved in administering justice. Across the United States, criminal justice agencies are reaching out to bring community groups into the justice process, and forming partnerships with individuals and groups representing community interests. The fact that a movement is already afoot to bring the community back into justice, and that it is gaining momentum at the grass roots, is immensely meaningful. It is not just criminal justice policy makers who are embracing community justice but—more importantly—the line professionals, the everyday justice workers who are in search of better ways to deal with crime and the harms of crime. As these justice workers partner with citizens and citizen groups, a new momentum emerges for community justice initiatives including mentor programs, church programs, and neighborhood organizations. What remains is for those interested in advancing the aims of community justice to harvest the results by guiding these developments forward. We hope this book will contribute to that end.

1

The Community
Justice Movement

In recent years, there has been a rapid growth in new approaches to criminal justice that involve the community. There are literally hundreds of examples of this trend, from offender-victim reconciliation projects in Vermont and Minneapolis to "beat probation" in Madison, Wisconsin; from neighborhood-based prosecution centers in Portland, Oregon, and in New York City, to community probation in Massachusetts. The most well known version of community justice is community policing; but localized projects involving all components of the justice system have been widely encouraged (Karp 1998a; National Institute of Justice Journal 1996).

Community-oriented models of criminal justice are also being implemented in other countries. Family group conferencing for juvenile offenders is a prominent method in New Zealand and Australia. There juvenile offenders and their families meet in conferences with community members to discuss strategies for victim restitution and personal interventions to prevent further delinquency (Alder and Wundersitz 1994). Native American groups in Canada commonly use sentencing circles, in which tribal members meet together with the offender and the victim to discuss a resolution to the criminal conduct (Stuart 1996).

These developments clearly signal the early stages of a movement to make the criminal justice system more responsive to the community. The initiatives accompanying this trend are too varied to be characterized in a simple manner. They have come about not as part of a grand plan but as the disunited results of local problem-solving efforts. However diverse, these initiatives all have in common (to some degree or another) a new perspective on crime and justice. They share an ideal that the justice system ought to be made relevant (or perhaps more relevant) to the quality of community life, and that it ought to make better use of a community's individual and institutional resources in dealing with crime.

At first blush, "community justice" seems a simple, unremarkable concept that most people would automatically embrace. Who could object to a call for our justice system to more actively improve community life?

However, a deeper investigation of the idea reveals considerable complexity and no small degree of controversy: What exactly *is* "community"? How can the justice system be made relevant to all the various communities out there; indeed, should it? What is the relationship between the ideal of "equal protection under the law" and the movement toward innovation and variation at the community level? These and other questions illustrate that a community justice program, for all its apparent appeal, is a potentially profound shift away from traditional conceptions of criminal justice.

Recently, a working group at the U.S. Department of Justice began to explore the underpinnings of the wide variety of community justice programs. In one of the working group's early drafts, it listed as "principles" the following:

- The community is the ultimate customer and the full partner of the system.
- The primary goal is harmony among system components and the community.
- Community-based sanctions are worthy responses to the problem of crime.
- Work efforts must focus on the underlying causes of *crime* rather than respond only to *criminal behavior* (Working Group 1996).

These principles are offered as more than glib public relations sentiments; they are meant to guide the design and implementation of community justice initiatives. They help define a new approach to the establishment of justice that gives a prominent role to the community and its members. What is suggested by these changes is what we refer to as a "community justice ideal." This is the vision of a justice system that links its actions to the quality and safety of community life. It redefines the justice objectives away from traditional, disinterested law enforcement toward an activist, involved system that treats crime as a community problem to be unraveled. In short, the *ideal of community justice* is that "the agents of criminal justice should tailor their work so that its main purpose is to enhance community living, especially through reducing the paralysis of fear, the indignities of disorder, and the agony of criminal victimization."

Recent Innovations

The new interest in community to some degree embraces the community justice ideal. These initiatives shift the focus of the justice process from the accused and convicted to the resident and the neighbor. There are many examples of this new interest in the community that illustrate how traditional criminal justice functions of policing, adjudication, and correction are currently being reinterpreted to embrace a community emphasis, and how those reinterpretations are leading to innovations in practice. Several such examples are outlined in this chapter. What follows is not a comprehensive critique of community justice or its antecedent programs but rather an exploration of how community-driven changes are redefining the traditional justice functions. In later chapters, we will return to some of the approaches described here and consider them in more detail.

Policing

The push for community justice in many ways derives from the community-oriented and problem-solving experience of policing. In a very short time, policing has shifted from a detached professional model to an involved community model. Peak and Glensor (1996, p. 68) report that the majority of America's police departments have adopted a community policing approach. As the concept has gained nationwide popularity, there has been much variation in both the definition and the practice of community policing. Underlying all of these various approaches are the dual strategies of problem solving and community involvement (Goldstein 1990; Skogan 1997; Skolnick and Bayley 1986; Sparrow et al. 1990; Trojanowicz and Bucqueroux 1990).

Problem solving in the context of police work implies a focus on identifying and resolving the underlying causes of criminal incidents rather than on reacting immediately to a particular incident. This has not been an easy reassignment of priorities. There is a certain tension between the dedication of resources to 911 calls and the commitment of officers to a variety of in-depth problem-solving efforts. The hypothesis guiding community policing is that prevention efforts will better address the inadequacies of "911 policing" than would more aggressive cops, more sophisticated 911 technology, or shorter response times. The shift in focus has necessitated wide-ranging organizational changes in police departments, from new recruitment policies that seek well-educated self-starters to greater autonomy and authority for line officers. The paradigmatic shift is best reflected in the seemingly commonsense, everyday activities that characterize the approach:

> In Aurora, Colorado, on the eastern edge of Denver, a popular bar catering to hordes of young people was hit with a rash of purse thefts from customers' cars. Community police officers working with the bar owner and patrons determined that young women left their purses in their cars because they liked to dance and feared their purses would be stolen off tables while they danced. Police got the bar owner to install lockers where women could lock

their purses; the incidents went from hundreds per month to virtually none (Peak and Glensor 1996, p. 332).

In addition to problem solving, community policing is typified by a concern for community involvement. At a minimum, this involves a sincere effort to identify and respond to community concerns. One major outcome of this effort has been an increased emphasis on addressing social disorder—public drinking, panhandling, graffiti, prostitution, and so on—because of widespread community concern over these problems (Skogan 1990; Kelling and Coles 1996). More profoundly, community involvement means sharing the responsibility for social control with community members. Rather than being simply the "eyes and ears" of the police, the community is the more powerful agent of social control, if for no other reason than the fact that parents, teachers, or neighbors provide a level of surveillance that can never be matched by the police in a free, democratic society.

Community involvement can encompass a broad range of activities. Efforts range from police participation in community anticrime campaigns and organization of citizen patrols (Davis and Lurigio 1996) to the creation of neighborhood police "ministations," fostering closer contact and longer-term relationships between police and communities (Skolnick and Bayley 1986). Although such initiatives are now widespread, evaluations of their effectiveness are as yet few and limited in scope. Still, several patterns have emerged from the studies conducted to date (Police Executive Research Forum 1995). First, community policing strategies encounter significant resistance from line workers, especially in the initial stages of implementation. Line workers think of policing as fighting crime, and tend to see community-building and problem-solving strategies as "soft," as a retreat from their hard-won authority in return for uncertain gains. Second, no standard, proven procedure exists for the design and implementation of the idea; rather, effective community policing appears to be a product of locally conceived measures to mobilize the community against crime. Third, the move toward community policing is a long-term effort that cannot be fully accomplished in a few months—or even a year or two. Fourth, the long-term effects of community policing on serious crime are unclear, although reductions in some forms of "street" crime have been observed in some cities (Kelling and Coles 1996; Bratton 1995).

Community strategies are gradually redefining police work. Line officers are less often seen as bureaucrats caught in autocratic organizations and more often as innovators whose knowledge of the world at the street level gives them a special expertise in problem solving. Arrest rates and 911 calls are less frequently used as indicators of policing success; they are being replaced by citizen satisfaction with police services, direct solutions to citizen-articulated problems, and reductions in victimization. Police are learning to divest themselves of the traditional "us versus them" mentality and to see residents as potential partners in making localities better places to live.

Adjudicating

Examples of community-oriented innovations are also found in case adjudication, in the form of victim impact statements, victim-offender mediation, neighborhood defense, community prosecution, and community courts.

The victims' movement has called for ways to give the victim "a voice" in the criminal justice system; for the state to provide services such as legal advice, therapeutic counseling, and security enhancement assistance; and for offenders to receive tougher punishments and/or to make restitution. With regard to the victim's role, the movement to date has been rather circumscribed. At formal decision points, such as sentencing or parole, the system's officials provide an opportunity through *victim impact statements* for victims to speak about the crime's impact and voice an opinion as to the most appropriate decision. Almost nobody disputes the value of allowing victims to voice their feelings about crime and justice, but some critics of the victims' movement point out that this is a very narrow type of involvement (Elias 1983).

The victim's role in the justice process is much expanded in *victim-offender mediation* (Van Ness and Strong 1997). Victim-offender mediation programs provide alternatives to prosecution of a case in the court system: If offenders agree to participate, they can avoid going to trial and jail. The victim is given the opportunity to confront the offender with questions or statements about the impact of the crime and may negotiate terms for restitution or other community-based sanctions. These programs allow a more intensive involvement of victims in adjudication. Studies show that victim-offender meetings often lead to a stronger sense of satisfaction with the justice process for both victims and offenders (Quinn 1996; Umbreit 1994).

Community defense describes both a shift in priorities and a continuity of concern among public defenders for protecting the rights and safety of their clients. In community defense, priority is given to serving a wider array of needs of clients and their neighbors. The most important example of community defense is the Neighborhood Defender Service of Harlem (Stone 1996). A unique feature of this program is its location outside the court and inside the neighborhood it serves. Another unique feature is its active outreach to the community, fostering ongoing relationships with residents instead of functioning passively as an impersonal, default referral service of the court. A third feature of the program is that each client is assigned to a team that includes attorneys and community workers, which helps shift priorities from court activities to problem-solving efforts on the street. Perhaps the most important aspect of community defense is its central concern for the experience clients have when in contact with the justice system: It prioritizes fair and respectful treatment in a system that often drives a wedge between troubled residents and their communities.

Prosecutors also have become more involved in the community. One of the best examples of *community prosecution* is provided in Portland, Oregon (Boland 1998). There, local district attorney Michael Schrunk, troubled about crime complaints in a particular area of Portland, moved one of his central offices out to the district to provide a more localized, relevant prosecution of crime. Local prosecutors soon learned that residents were concerned not only about serious crime but also about disorder, petty disturbance, and the overall quality of life in their neighborhood.

In Portland, citizens' input into the prosecutorial function called forth changes mirroring those among police in problem-solving mode: Crime fighting became less central to the activities of the office. Instead, prosecutors (renamed "neighborhood district attorneys") took on the role of legal advisors to local police and community members who were dealing with crime problems. Instead of automatically invoking the adversarial system, neighborhood DAs found that they were often called upon to resolve disputes, restore orderly relations, and intervene in problem situations. Their role shifted from the prosecution of specific cases to the solving of crime and the restoration of order.

Community courts are yet another facet of the community approach to adjudication. Variations of the community court model, such as teen courts, drug courts, and family violence courts, specialize in particular areas in order to develop more comprehensive solutions. The underlying assumption of community courts is that communities are deeply affected by the sentencing process yet are rarely consulted or involved in judicial outcomes. An important example of such a court is Manhattan's Midtown Community Court, which specializes in misdemeanor cases (Rottman 1996). The Midtown Community Court has ready access—all within the same building—to a social services center, a community service program, community mediation services, and a sophisticated information network that tracks cases as they are relayed from one department to another. The central message of the court exemplifies the community orientation:

> Take the defendants one by one and hold them immediately accountable with swift, real sanctions. Beyond that, pay attention to who they are and ad-

dress the issues underlying the charges that brought them in. Above all, keep the emphasis on quality-of-life crimes, those pervasive low-level offenses that undermine a whole community's morale (Anderson 1996, p. 3).

This advice hints at a general observation about community justice: Communities are not necessarily looking for better crime fighting. Instead, many residents want a better quality of living, which often is not a direct product of the adversarial, war-on-crime model. The adjudication apparatus is at its most restricted in terms of the actions that can be taken when it seeks to prosecute, convict, and punish. When the legal system sets out to solve local problems and address the concerns of crime victims, it has a much wider set of available choices. A community-oriented adjudication model can be tailored to local issues and concerns more easily if one is willing to abandon the adversarial mode of interaction.

Correction

Community corrections has long been used to describe a wide variety of correctional offices and functions; therefore, one might easily assume that an active, community-oriented approach to corrections has an equally long tradition. This is not necessarily so. Although it is true that for most of this century the number of offenders under active supervision in the community has far outweighed the number of those in prison—often by two or three times—the fact that many offenders happen to reside in a community does not mean that the correctional supervision of those offenders is oriented toward community justice. *Community corrections* as commonly used merely refers to the mechanisms for dealing with convicted offenders who happen to reside in the community. Correctional institutions enter the community, but the community has little if any role to play in corrections.

But there is extraordinary promise for the development of a productive community role in corrections. It is widely known that repeat offenders contribute disproportionately to the amount of crime in a community (Wolfgang et al. 1972) and that most offenders removed from a community for incarceration will eventually be released—usually to that same community. It would seem that substantial benefits would result from making the primary goal of corrections the improvement of community life through effective offender reintegration.

A number of projects have recently been initiated with precisely that goal. In Vermont, a series of "consumer studies"—focus group interviews with citizen groups—led to a statewide overhaul of the relationship between correctional practices and the community. Community reparative boards now play an active role in restoring offenders to community life

(Dooley 1995). The boards are tasked with making the offender fully aware of the damage caused by the crime; negotiating a sanction with the offender that will make up for this damage; and charting a course that will better integrate the offender into the community. A similar approach is taken by the district attorney's office in Philadelphia, in dealing with juvenile offenders (DiIulio and Palubinsky 1997). In countless other community corrections systems, citizens are called upon to serve as volunteers, advisers, and paraprofessionals. A recent publication highlighted nearly twenty other examples of community-citizen partnerships with correctional agencies (American Probation and Parole Association 1996). The focus of such partnerships ranges from offenders to victims to ongoing neighborhood problems.

Yet, in contrast to policing and prosecution, the community movement in corrections is nascent—perhaps in part because the familiar usage of *community corrections* gives false assurance that the concerns of local residents are already taken into account. In reality, most community corrections agencies act as though they are somehow afraid of the residents who live in the areas they serve. Historically, many local leaders, far from being supportive of community corrections, have been hostile to the agency that manages what many citizens consider to be a threat: the former offender who lives among them.

The isolated examples in which correctional leaders have reached out to community members reveal the possibility of a different, more productive dynamic. Citizens can learn to understand and support the necessity—even appropriateness—of the correctional worker's job. Local leaders can take responsible roles in assisting in the supervision and reintegration of convicted offenders. Yet much remains to be done. A major impediment to offender readjustment is the suspicion and hostility of community members. A community yearning for public safety is an opportunity for justice professionals to help offenders and reduce public fears by creating links of support and supervision between community members and offenders. The task of corrections professionals is not to dismiss or attempt to placate public fears; it is to forge realistic links to community members and institutions that can help reduce the risk of repeat offenses by effectively reintegrating offenders. The community agenda, as it moves into the correctional realm, will increasingly find itself confronting these concerns.

There is, of course, one area where the community has entered the correctional world—the victims' movement. Correctional personnel, from probation officers to parole boards, are increasingly called upon to consider the implications of the victim's needs and experiences in their day-to-day correctional work. For the most part, this has been seen to date as a problem of "managing" victims and their input; but the promise of a much more active concern for victims and offenders hovers above the horizon (Van Ness and Strong 1997; Galaway and Hudson 1996). Incarcerated offenders might be actively engaged in community service even while serving their sentences. In an even more radical development, volunteer community boards could orchestrate reparative agreements between victims (often broadly conceived) and offenders (Dooley 1995). Such approaches combine formal social control with informal control, forcing offenders to confront the consequences of their actions before their community peers and to assume responsibility by writing letters of apology, making restitution, and performing community service. A number of other innovative approaches call for offenders to repair the damage of their criminal acts and to show their cocitizens that they are trustworthy and should be allowed a place in the community.

Beyond the Criminal Justice System

Community justice is not the exclusive domain of the criminal justice system. When the focus shifts from crime control to the quality of community life, the antecedents of crime become central: The activities of community justice become oriented toward prevention as well as response. Community justice may be concerned with neighborhood stability, the quality and nature of community social networks, and the community's institutional capacity—its families, schools, housing, and churches and other voluntary organizations. A community-building orientation blurs the boundaries that have traditionally compartmentalized social welfare and public safety functions.

A recent approach that is consistent with the community justice perspective—particularly noticeable among private foundations—is to support *comprehensive community initiatives* (Connell et al. 1995; Kennedy 1996; Schorr 1997). These initiatives attempt to address many different neighborhood problems at once, focusing as much on coordination and collaboration as on individual program development. Projects that focus on social or economic conditions in a neighborhood often intersect with criminal justice concerns. For example, projects with a central focus on improving public housing must also consider the criminal activities almost endemic to large, urban public housing projects (Chavis et al. 1997; Sampson 1995).

Community justice also includes community crime-prevention efforts that do not formally involve the criminal justice system. An example is the assortment of practices that fall under the heading *situational crime prevention* (Clarke 1995; Ekblom 1995; Taylor and Harrell 1996). Private security, burglar alarms, street lighting, steering wheel locks, surveillance cameras, and similar devices are direct efforts by private citizens, businesses, and municipal governments to reduce crime. Another recent trend has been the mobilization of the business community to form *business improvement districts* (BIDs). Such entities levy their own taxes to fund crime prevention and disorder reduction in order to enhance community conditions for the benefit both of employees and of customers (MacDonald 1996).

Summary

In many respects, the community justice movement reflects a radical departure from past criminal justice activity. Localized, dynamic, variable strategies replace the centralized, standardized, expert model that has been the object of most systemic innovations in recent years. The new frontier of community justice is thus on the cutting edge in the way it uses information, organizes staff, plans its activities, and responds to its environment. Programs based on the new paradigm represent initial, tentative stages in a longer-term shift toward a justice strategy that is more relevant to community concerns. Experience so far has been encouraging. Justice officials involved in these programs report that they successfully transform the justice worker into much more of a community worker. Satisfaction with these new approaches is based on a sense of greater citizen involvement, and consequently greater support among citizens for the justice process.

But it is important to emphasize that these changes are something of a spontaneous adaptation of the system to its lack of credibility and effectiveness, undertaken by some elements of the justice system, often in isolation from others. What has not occurred is a systematic, overarching conceptualization of community justice that exploits its full potential both in design and in implementation. Until an encompassing notion of community justice is established, the piecemeal and idiosyncratic nature of innovations will continue to predominate. It is our aim to contribute to community justice by providing a broader, more encompassing conceptualization of its meaning and value—a "community justice ideal." We begin by outlining the basic elements of community justice practice.

Elements of Community Justice

Recent community justice innovations are widely varied efforts to move justice into the community. In some ways, they are appropriately seen as essentially unrelated initiatives. But the surface dissimilarities obscure a foundational set of corresponding assumptions and tactics that place these initiatives within a loosely articulated common framework—a community justice ideal.

Definition

Community justice broadly refers to all variants of crime prevention and justice activities that explicitly include the community in their processes and set the enhancement of community quality of life as an explicit goal. Community justice is rooted in the actions that citizens, community organizations, and the criminal justice system can take to control crime and social disorder. Its central focus is community-level outcomes, shifting the emphasis from individual incidents to systemic patterns, from individual conscience to social mores, and from individual goods to the common good. Typically, community justice is conceived of as a partnership between the formal criminal justice system and the community; but often communities autonomously engage in activities that directly or indirectly address crime.

Community justice is an emerging perspective that is gaining attention partly as a result of setbacks in other arenas and partly on the promise of the community concept. It is not yet a coherent practice or a systematic theory, nor is it grounded in a particular tradition of cumulative empirical research. As we look at the various current trends in crime prevention and criminal justice, we see common concerns across spheres, common goals being articulated, and common strategies amid the experiments.

Four core elements distinguish the new community justice from prior policies and practices (see Box 1.1). These characteristic elements are not disclosed on the basis of abstract theory. Rather, they seem to be born of the frustrations of implementation; the practical necessities of attempts to improve community life by reducing disorder and crime; and a desire to increase the public trust.

First, attention is given to the coordination of activities at the neighborhood level. The meaning of *community* in *community justice* requires some extended consideration; but without doubt one of its core features is the sense of belonging that a neighborhood provides. This membership in a place-based community is grounded in the important set of relationships and institutions that help create standards and expectations of behavior. Community justice relies in large part on these local institutions. Second, explicit attention is given to both short- and long-term *problem solving*. Community justice activities are initiatives based on identified problems. This is a conceptual shift from traditional reactive approaches that address incidents as they occur, without attention to underlying causes. Third, community justice practices require *decentralization of authority and accountability*, which empowers communities and local agencies. In the criminal justice system, organizational changes are necessary to give line workers more decisionmaking autonomy and to facilitate collaboration among law enforcement and social service agencies. Fourth, *citizen partic-*

BOX 1.1   Elements of Community Justice

Community justice . . .

- operates at the neighborhood level
- is problem solving
- decentralizes authority and accountability
- involves citizens in the justice process

---

ipation is central. Not only do citizens participate to ensure that local concerns are addressed, but citizen participation is strategic for building community capacity so that informal mechanisms of control can gradually share or even replace much of the formal justice apparatus. Below we describe these four elements and illustrate their importance in existing programs.

Community Justice Operates at the Neighborhood Level

Community justice is experienced by members of a community. In the introduction to George L. Kelling and Catherine M. Coles's (1996) book *Fixing Broken Windows,* James Q. Wilson observes that a judge views a crime quite differently than does a community. Where judges see an isolated incident—as "a snapshot," to use his metaphor—the community views the event as one frame in a filmed documentary of community life. The crime takes place in real time and space, in a context of local relationships and institutions. Community justice takes this moving-picture view of crime, attempting to expand the partial, traditional outlook to a holistic community perspective. To do so requires consideration of natural areas and indigenous definitions of community boundaries instead of relying on jurisdictional or political boundaries.

Criminal law jurisdictions are defined by political boundaries—states, municipalities, and governments; but from the point of view of community life, these legal perimeters are often without meaning. Both Lubbock and El Paso implement Texas criminal law, but the nature of community life in these towns, hundreds of miles apart, is quite different when it comes to crime and its control. Indeed, within Lubbock and El Paso, there are local variations that have a major impact on the way crime is addressed in those areas. Differences among communities are the facts that lead to a desire for greater community-level justice; but it is the disjuncture between legal categories and neighborhoods that poses the biggest problem for community justice ideals. Some way must be found to identify and mobilize more geographically confined versions of justice system activities. Operationally, this means thinking in terms of *blocks* of space instead of cities, counties, or states. Under a community justice ideal, criminal justice activities will be tied to these delimited localities and will be free to adapt to particular manifestations of local community life.

New York City is experimenting with this conceptual shift in its creation of the Midtown Community Court (Anderson 1996). Unlike other courts, which represent much larger geographic areas, the Midtown Court is located in the center of a well-defined neighborhood—Times Square, Clinton, and Chelsea—in this case, a highly commercial area that borders residential neighborhoods well known for their high levels of disorder (prostitution, panhandling, illegal vending, graffiti, shoplifting, fare-beating, vandalism, and so on). The neighborhood focus is not simply a matter of relocating the courthouse or of redrawing boundaries. The purpose is to respond to specific problems in a comprehensive, context-specific manner. The Midtown Court does this by coordinating justice activities so that efforts are supported and intensified. It works with police in disorder enforcement strategies. It works with local residents, businesses, and social service agencies to forge creative, collaborative solutions to quality-of-life issues. It develops individualized sanctions for offenders that bring restitution to victims, community service to the neighborhood, and education and treatment programs to offenders.[1]

The focus of community justice is not individuals or individual criminal incidents. Nor is the focus on a city-, state-, or nationwide crime problem. Community justice is explicitly concerned with a pattern of relations and institutions that effectively operate at the level of the neighborhood. It is concerned with questions that loom large enough to affect crime and disorder rates over time—for example, Why does a particular neighborhood remain criminogenic long after a cohort of delinquents has moved on or passed away? But it is also concerned with questions that are relevant to the behavior of particular individuals. At the same time, community justice is not myopic with regard to neighborhood boundaries. Neighborhoods are understood in the context of larger economic, political, and social systems, systems that are subject to forces beyond neighborhood control. Thus community justice begins with a focus on solving neighborhood problems by drawing on local resources and initiatives and bolstering them with extralocal resources, which are often necessary in order to create viable local institutions and practices.

---

[1]We note in passing that many of the offenders in the Midtown Court are not local residents, since the court serves a largely commercial area. This makes for a unique version of community adjudication and sets the Midtown Court apart from more prototypical community justice, as we would define it.

Community Justice Is Problem Solving

In the public discourse about crime, "war" terminology dominates. Offenders are referred to as "them," victims are "us." Policy to deal with crime is described in terms of "combating" crime, and strategies are thought to be effective when they isolate the offender—thought to be an unusual miscreant—as an enemy of the people. This type of imagery distorts the reality of criminality and victimization. Most offenders brought into the justice system are young males; but young males are also overrepresented among victims. Almost a third of all males will experience a felony arrest (Wolfgang et al. 1972), and self-report studies show that most citizens have both committed an offense and been victimized by one (Huizinga and Elliott 1987; Dunford and Elliott 1984). In short, domestic tranquility is not a problem of warfare; it is a general problem of citizenship.

The war metaphor is inadequate in another way. It describes an attack on an external foe, whereas in crime the threat is seldom external; usually the offender is a cocitizen. Combat enemies can be "vanquished" and driven out; but offenders who are arrested, convicted, and removed from a community for a period of time nearly always return to their neighborhoods eventually.

An alternative to the war metaphor is to treat crime as a societal problem. Under this approach, the people affected by crime—offenders, victims, and their families and neighbors—are seen as afflicted by the precursors and consequences of crime. Each of these factors can be defined not as an "enemy" to be conquered but as posing problems to be solved. In community justice, a much higher priority is given to resolving public safety problems in order to improve community life, and greater emphasis therefore is placed on the potential consequences of the means taken to solve those problems.

Problem-solving approaches differ from the conflict paradigm in that they rely on information, deliberation, and mutual interest for a resolution. The belief is that citizens share a set of values and concerns, and with proper information and order, a way out of the problem can be found. When crime is approached as a problem, solutions can take various forms, from rearranging public space to providing oversight of youths. Prosecution and punishment need not be the only ways to approach a crime problem. Indeed, the search for a creative solution derived from community members' own ideas is one of the hallmarks of community justice approaches.

Information is a key to solving problems. Local areas conduct crime analyses to determine the type and nature of public safety problems that residents want to prioritize. The uniqueness of these crime problems to the specific area will set the substantive foundation for the community justice initiatives. Actual strategies will emanate from interactions between citizens and justice system officials, as they try to determine the most productive means to solve crime problems.

Kelling and Coles (1996) describe an excellent example of the problem-solving approach. The New York subway system was once well known for its high levels of disorder—one manifestation being the graffiti that covered train cars from top to bottom, inside and out. Today, the more than 5,000 train cars are virtually graffiti-free. Critical components of the successful strategy involved interviews with subway passengers, transit officials, and graffiti artists. It was discovered that a major motivation behind the graffiti was the knowledge that others would see the artists' "tags." The strategy called for entering the trains, one by one, into a program that required that each car be completely cleaned and returned to service. If graffiti appeared on a "clean car," it was immediately taken out of service and cleaned again. In time, the graffiti artists stopped their tagging because their motivation was taken away: They never saw their tags. The result of this and other efforts was a reduction in disorder and crime and a renewed public trust in the safety of the subways.

Information is used in three ways. First, geographically specific information ranks places in terms of their priority (Taylor and Harrell 1996). High crime[2] locations receive greater attention and greater investment of local resources, for not only is the problem there more difficult but the potential payoff in improved quality of life is greater. Second, residents' concerns and desires are a source of program information. Residents are encouraged to tell justice officials what factors they see as most closely tied to the problems in their community's quality of life (Kelling 1992). Third, information translates into targets that can be used to evaluate the success of a given strategy for confronting crime (Sherman et al. 1997).

The new age of community justice is made possible by the power of information. Using geographically coded data, crime control services are organized around the most frequent locations of crime events, near offenders and victims. Data drive problem solving and action: both official data about crimes and offenders and qualitative data that come from offenders, victims, and neighborhood residents. Evaluative feedback about the success of strategies comes from the same official and unofficial sources. The imaginative use (and production) of information is one of the factors that sets aggressive community safety strategies apart from the routine functions of the local cop on the beat.

---

[2]For ease of expression, we often use the term *crime*. The reader should know that in our usage, we understand the term to refer not just to illegal predatory events but to signify more broadly a range of "public safety problems"—certainly a more cumbersome phrase.

Community Justice Decentralizes
Authority and Accountability

Moving toward community justice requires a rethinking of the line-authority relations within criminal justice organizations. Traditionally, criminal justice management is hierarchical: At each level of the organization, a worker reports to an immediate superior, who in turn reports to the next level. All positions have one "boss," and each manager has a specific jurisdiction. Under community justice, this complex, highly specialized system of organization is further complicated by community involvement. A number of agencies currently are experimenting with ways to formalize the relationship between residents and professional justice workers.

Community justice approaches have nontraditional organizational alignments. Staff may report to citizen groups in addition to professional superiors. Managers in one organization (say, policing) may be "matrixed" with managers of another (say, probation or prosecution) in order to improve coordination and increase cross-fertilization of ideas and action. For example, in Wisconsin, a program titled Beat Probation links probation officers to police officers with shared, localized workloads involving offenders on probation. In Boston, Operation Night Light (Corbett et al. 1996) uses a similar approach, teaming police with probation officers to facilitate monitoring and supervision of offenders in their neighborhoods, particularly at night. In each of these cases, multiple lines of authority exist, and some involve nonemployees, such as volunteer mentors.

The communications channels in such inventive organizational structures are complicated. Lateral information sharing and short-term, ad hoc problem-solving groups may dominate. Community justice approaches have dynamic organizational models that shift and are reconstituted, based upon the problem being encountered. Community justice calls for more authority and accountability at lower organizational levels as well as for the involvement of community members and community organizations.

The decentralization of authority and accountability encourages innovative problem solving. Processes of change are based on a foundation of interaction with citizens in which new ideas are valued and new solutions encouraged (Travis 1996). In order for such interaction to be effective, new methods and strategies have to replace the old. Since the new ideas are grounded in the problem-solving process, they tend to be creative and to reflect the particular experiences and priorities of the locality. The spirit of innovation requires a transformation of the justice profession from hidebound antagonisms among citizens and across agencies to interconnected processes of problem identification, information gathering, intervention design, and evaluation.

Such innovations not only require adjustments on the part of staff who are accustomed to the traditional "command" model of their profession; they also demand dramatically different criteria of accountability. Instead of sharing accountability for operational standards of practice (as do most criminal justice workers today), community justice participants operate at the strategic level, requiring that staff implement a vision rather than a concrete set of preordained actions. Moving away from the comfort of operational standards is one of the major challenges of community justice approaches, since workers tend to be more comfortable being held accountable for their specific actions rather than for the impact of those actions on public safety.

The primary motivation for abandoning operational standards is not to reduce or diffuse responsibility but to enable stakeholders to deliver on promises to solve problems even when they fall outside the traditional purview of the particular stakeholder. For example, new line authority in community policing often enables the cop on the beat to do much more than enforce the law. He or she is often able to organize community anti-crime campaigns, mediate in ongoing disputes, and coordinate solutions to problems by collaborating with workers from other agencies. Whether a social worker places an at-risk youth in a drug treatment program or a transportation planner alters traffic flow through a highly visible drug market or "bazaar," the solution to any particular public safety problem will nearly always require interorganizational integration.

Community Justice Involves Citizens in the Justice Process

A variety of roles exist for citizens in community justice initiatives, but every role involves the capacity of the citizen to influence the local practice of justice. The least involved citizens may influence practices by attending and participating in meetings in which issues of crime and order are discussed. Others may volunteer their time to work on particular projects, provide support to victims, assist offenders in their reintegration into the community, and carry out community crime-prevention activities. Still others will take on more formal roles as members of advisory boards, providing more structured input into community justice practices.

In the traditional model, the system of justice is a professional service system of state agents who work in response to criminal events. This professional model assumes a level of personal detachment, or professional disinterestedness. It is also accountable for a set of performance standards that apply uniformly to all who are engaged in the practice of justice. Although these standards help to create a set of universal ideals, they often mitigate responsiveness at the neighborhood level. In contrast, the community model involves professionals who work in response to problems articulated by citizens. The worker is accountable to those citizens for the types of service responses taken to problems. Because of the relatively greater citizen input and activity in the latter model, professional effort tends to be judged on the basis of citizen satisfaction with justice services.

Even though this is a seemingly minor shift—criminal justice professionals will say they were *always* concerned with public satisfaction—the shift from professional to community accountability is a profound difference for the justice system. The participation of local residents in justice shifts priorities toward local problems and refocuses the attention of justice officials on the viewpoints of local residents.

The shift toward citizen participation is grounded in two important insights. First, formal social control by police and the courts is a thin layer in a much thicker foundation of institutions and cultural practices that produce social order. The "thin blue line" is buttressed by the important work of families, schools, churches, civic organizations, and other institutions involved in the creation of law-abiding citizens and safe public spaces. Community justice is an attempt to recognize, support, and expand the partnership between the community and the criminal justice system toward the common goal of improving community life. Second, the shift toward citizen participation is grounded in the basic recognition that community members are citizens in a democratic society. Each community member deserves to be treated with dignity and respect and guaranteed the autonomy necessary for creating competent, self-reliant, civic-oriented selves. This commitment to individuals extends to offenders as well as to crime victims. At the same time, it is assumed that citizens in a democracy must actively work toward the welfare of the whole society and not just look out for themselves. Thus, citizens are morally obligated to fulfill whatever tasks are necessary to sustain a good society. Failures in public safety are at least partially the result of citizens' shared assumption that the responsibility for public safety belongs entirely to the criminal justice system.

Questions About Community Justice

There are considerable obstacles to realizing a community justice ideal. The examples described in this chapter provide an intriguing glimpse of what might occur if community justice rather than traditional criminal justice were the dominant paradigm. But it must be stressed that these programs currently operate within the existing adversarial model, and in some ways they strain against that model in order to be responsive to the community. When a citizen advises a law enforcement official about priorities, it changes the accountability pattern of this function; when local residential preferences for social control help to determine allocation of time and other resources, requirements of practice become different from one area of a city to the next. Shifts such as these raise fundamental questions about the rationale and practicality of community justice ideals under traditional criminal law. Because the movement toward community justice has been haphazard, some of these questions have not surfaced very clearly. But any attempt to systematically embrace the community justice ideal will inevitably raise these issues to a new level of visibility and controversy.

What About Community Justice and Individual Rights?

If community justice takes the improvement of community life as its central aim, an important question is how much consensus exists about what constitutes improvement. We would expect nearly universal agreement that a reduction of crime is desirable, but we can also expect much disagreement over the price. To obtain a high level of security, some citizens might advocate that high walls be built to separate those who pose a risk from those who pose little. Some citizens might willingly sacrifice the rights of others as well as many of their own rights in order to ensure protection against crime—encouraging universal curfews, drug tests, and identification cards; the surveillance of public spaces, workplace computers, and private bank accounts; new and tougher punishments for a wider array of nonconforming behaviors; and new regulations on the manufacture and sale of goods that are implements or objects of crime (for example, firearms). Other citizens might reject such measures as intolerable signs of encroaching state tyranny; if the price of freedom is a high level of social disorder, then they would still prefer freedom.

We would argue that the Hobbesian exchange of freedom for security is a mischaracterization of the problem. First of all, the contest is not merely between the individual and state but also involves civil society, which occupies the middle ground between the two. Freedom is made possible not only by protection from state power but also by the cultivation of cultural conditions that enable and encourage the growth of competent individuals who can make positive contributions both to their own lives and to the general welfare. Second, we recognize that freedom is limited not only by the expansion of social order but also by movements toward disorder. City air may make men (and women) free, but it also keeps many behind bolted doors. Individuals need a substantial baseline of security in order to pursue their own happiness.

In a democratic community justice model, there may be variations in the way that different communities adjudicate between the two goals of social order and individual autonomy. For example, if localities are allowed to determine justice (and anticrime) priorities, then it follows that services such as policing and prosecution may operate with differences in resource allocation and even practical action, even though they operate under an identical criminal code. How far may these differences go before they are deemed to violate our belief in equality under the law? To what extent may a locality exert its unique vision of social control without infringing upon freedoms of "deviant" members who are in the minority? Will a neighborhood justice movement take on some characteristics of vigilantism; if it has not yet, what is to stop it from doing so in the future?

As citizens become more active in various aspects of the justice process, the state's role in presiding over that process can be undercut. The adversarial ideal assumes that the state accuses a citizen and brings evidence to bear in support of the accusation. The dispute is between the state and the accused. Inserting other citizens—neighbors and residents—into that arrangement muddies the water by creating a third party to the dispute. It is unclear precisely what that third party's role ought to be—it could be observational, participatory, advisory, or even advocative—but the presence of that party means that the state and its adversary can no longer be concerned only about each other. The concern for rights protections extends beyond those of the accused to the rights of victims and of community members who are indirectly affected.

Although it seems natural for the state and the accused to seek full vindication—a declaration of guilt or innocence—as an outcome of a contest, a third party's interest may be in alternative outcomes. For instance, the community may want assurance of future protection, some restoration of the victim, assurance that the accused's family will not suffer from punishments, and so forth. Creative resolutions of the dispute also reshape the contest itself, suggesting that it is less about blaming and more about restoring peace in the community.

We must be uneasy about the implications of any developments that undermine the protection of rights. Perhaps the finest contribution of Western civilization to modern civil life is the idea of the sanctity and dignity of the individual. This idea is given life in the form of legal rights by which citizens stand equal to one another as well as to the state. Any movement toward community justice taken at the expense of this priceless heritage would impose a cultural cost of profound dimensions. Community justice ideals *will* alter established practices of substantive and procedural criminal law. The test will be to devise ways of protecting precious civil liberties in the process.

What About Community Justice and Social Inequality?

Neighborhoods differ not only in their crime control priorities but also in their capacities, resources, and resilience in addressing crime problems.

The same inequality that characterizes America at the individual level plays out as a community dynamic. The justice system operates really as two different systems, one for people with financial resources and another for the poor. Is there any assurance that the same kind of inequality will not come to characterize community justice?

This concern is well founded: Research shows that poor communities, particularly those hit hard by crime, tend also to lack resources to regulate neighborhood problems and pursue social control (Bursik and Grasmick 1993a). These communities do not come together to solve problems, and they have low rates of citizen participation in official business. One of the lessons of community policing has been that in troubled neighborhoods, it is often difficult to get citizens to take responsible action in response to their crime problems (Rosenbaum 1988; Skogan 1990).

More prosperous localities have disproportionate political influence in many city and county governments. They tend to be better at organizing to influence anticrime priorities, to direct funding decisions, and to protect their residents from negative impacts of change. A community justice model that enables localities to pursue interests and preferences will inevitably create the possibility that more successful communities will strengthen their position at the expense of other localities. The community justice ideal, therefore, cannot treat all communities as of equal importance or as independent from one another. Communities exist within larger social and political systems and matrixes of local problems; and public policies to address them must be understood within this broader context.

Inequality breeds crime. It would be a dismal irony if community justice, advanced as a way of helping places deal more effectively with their crime problems, exacerbated the very dynamics that created those problems. If the problem of inequality is to be avoided, some local areas will likely require differential resource investment in order to take advantage of the promise of community justice.

What About Community Justice and the Increasing Costs of Criminal Justice?

We spend nearly $100 billion on official criminal justice in the United States every year (United States Bureau of Justice Statistics 1997a).[3] The cost of justice is increasing, and the tax burden it places on local areas interferes with the local capacity to fund schools, provide child health care, and maintain basic services. A community justice model calls for criminal justice organizations to augment current services. How will these be paid for?

---

[3]Another $52 billion is spent on private security annually (Cunningham et al. 1991).

The disparity between community resources and crime rates means that local revenues cannot be the basis for funding community justice. As indicated above, the very communities that suffer most from crime are least able to pay to combat it. Some mechanism for moving financial support of community justice from affluent communities to impoverished ones will be needed. This will obviously raise sensitive political issues—American taxpayers are leery of spending for services from which they do not directly benefit.

Moreover, some way of shifting costs *within* the existing justice budget will be needed. New money for new programs is scarce, and a proposal to greatly increase public funding of justice work will be met with skepticism. Instead, community justice needs to be based upon a shifting of resources within existing justice functions. Justice dollars must be reallocated to provide support for new activities in place of, or supplementing, previous functions. Community justice advocates seek greater collaboration between criminal justice agencies and other governmental and community social welfare agencies and services. Coordinated efforts will enhance effectiveness by combining the resources of different agencies using similar strategies to obtain different ends. For example, even though an agency's primary objective might be to increase employment within a neighborhood, its pursuit of this goal might also reduce criminal activity.

Will Community Justice Improve Community Life in America?

The principles outlined above and the examples drawn from today's justice practices are responses to changes in crime and community life. They evidence a public demand for a justice system that is more attuned to the need to improve the quality of community life in America. They also contain the seeds of safer communities and more responsible community members. The vision promoted by these changes is of an increasingly relevant, increasingly purposeful set of justice practices carried out in close cooperation with citizens affected by those practices.

This is of course an attractive vision. A justice apparatus that had as its aim the sustaining of community would indeed be of great value. But the potential perils are also important: Community justice must also protect individual rights and autonomy, reduce social inequalities, and be cost-effective. In the chapters that follow, we take up these important concerns. The first order of business is to gain an understanding of the ways in which neighborhood conditions influence rates of crime and disorder, and how crime and disorder and even many of our current criminal justice practices undermine the quality of community life. The next chapter explores in greater depth why the community matters, and how the current system of justice is failing to meet the needs of the community.

2

Crime, Community, and Criminal Justice

Crime—its presence, absence, and substantial impact on individuals and neighborhoods—stands at the heart of community life in America. It might be said that Americans have a preoccupation with crime. The topic dominates conversation, news, and political life throughout the country; and wherever Americans go abroad, the image of a society inundated by crime follows them.

And this image is not illusory: Over 42 million crimes were committed in the United States in 1994 alone (United States Bureau of Justice Statistics 1997b). The country leads the world in violent crime rates (Lynch 1995). It also leads the world in its use of incarceration as a cure-all for all crime, whether violent or nonviolent (Lynch 1995). The government at local, state, and federal levels spent a combined $94 billion on crime in 1992 (United States Bureau of Justice Statistics 1997a). Today, Americans take solace in the fact that in recent years, crime rates in the United States (especially the rate of violent crimes) have been declining (Rand et al. 1997). Yet we sense that this is a temporary reprieve, like a small bank error in our favor; we are relieved, but we remain troubled by the bottom line. There is too much crime in America.

In this chapter, the relationship between crime and community life is explored. It is important to recognize the complexity of this relationship. We often think about the ways in which crime alters community life; but we seldom consider the myriad conditions that precipitate crime, or how our common responses to crime might be further undermining community life.

There is little formal research on the relationship between external regulation of behavior and internal regulation in communities. Conceptually, the two forms of control are thought to operate within the same functional space. For example, it is thought that when the state fails to exert proper controls upon members, vigilantism will result, as individuals take the regulatory function upon themselves (Marx 1989; Weisburd 1988). It is also widely believed that informal control mechanisms that operate in wealthier communities not only reduce the amount of crime but also make the work of formal agents of control easier by augmenting them in informal ways. In wealthy neighborhoods, delinquent boys can be placed in boarding schools, put into counseling programs, or be disciplined through denial of goods or services that other boys will never be offered.

When agents of the state become the key problem solvers, they might be filling a void in community; but just as in interpersonal relationships, so in community functioning, once a function is being performed by one party it becomes unnecessary for another to take it on. It is plausible to think of the formal agents of the state as supporting the social control processes of community life, but it is perhaps just as accurate to think they take them over. Weak informal control systems are gradually replaced by the stronger formal social control processes: parents expect police or schools to control their children; neighbors expect police to prevent late night noise from people on their street; and citizens expect the courts to resolve disputes. In localities where formal social control systems become the main regulating mechanism, informal control systems may atrophy like dormant muscles, and citizens may come to see the formal system as existing to mediate all conflicts.

This chapter outlines a model in which formal social control—police, judges, and jails—is neither the only possible response to crime nor one that is best constituted to improve the quality of community life (e.g., reduce crime). We shall argue that this is so primarily because traditional formal social control tends to diminish the capacity for action in those communities hardest hit by crime. An important reason why formal social control has weakened the capacity for self-regulation within communities is the *form* of external coercion on those communities. When the state deals with crime in localities, it tends to do so by removing citizens from those localities, severing the ties between offenders and the community and exacerbating the problems of an already fragile social order. In recent years, this trend has become even stronger. In 1973, 60 percent of felons received community probation terms; by 1994, only 30 percent of felons were sentenced to probation (Clear 1994). We believe that this approach, in its extreme forms, is at best problematic and at worst self-defeating.

A full model of the relationship between crime and community (see Figure 2.1) shows a system in which changes in one element feed back into other elements (for an important discussion of a community-level systems model, see Bursik and Grasmick 1993a). The model in Figure 2.1 posits several relationships:

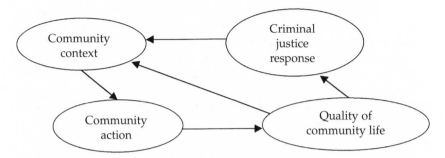

FIGURE 2.1   Systemic Model of Community Life and Criminal Justice

- The community context—the social characteristics of a community—strongly determines the ability of the community to engage in community action.
- Community action—collective action to benefit all members of the community—affects the quality of all aspects of community life, from safety to community spirit.
- Reductions in the quality of community life undermine the community context, creating a spiral of decline.
- Reductions in the quality of community life also engender a criminal justice response—generally, aggressive attempts to restore order, and the expansion of the prison system.
- Criminal justice responses that damage community capacity weaken rather than strengthen community context.

The figure represents a spiraling pattern of crime and community life in which a weak community context provides few resources for collective action and thus results in a poor quality of life. As community members respond to crime by withdrawing from community life, they decrease community resources for resisting crime. As external social control approaches become the standard for dealing with crime, the internal resources for opposing crime become irrelevant.

We may think of a community as a commons, and of the quality of community life as dependent on two principle factors. The first is the ecology of the community, the resource base upon which community members can draw when pursuing their own and common goals. The second is the responsiveness of community members and the larger society to the given context. Community resources are scarce, but renewable. The response may be withdrawal and abandonment, or coordinated collective action to replenish the resource base. If the former response is chosen, the community will experience a "tragedy of the commons" much like Garrett Hardin's (1968) well-known metaphor of a common grazing land.[1] The two underlying questions to be examined here are: What are the important "environmental" conditions that help sustain community life? What actions must be taken by community members and the larger society in order to sustain and improve community conditions? To further explicate the basic systemic model, we detail below what is meant by each factor in the model and how these factors are related.

Community Context

Community context is the landscape of community. As explained in Chapter 1, community justice takes a neighborhood-level view of crime and community. Although we can certainly speak of community without necessarily limiting it to particular geographic spaces, much of social life takes place in local areas. A conception of communities as neighborhoods is especially relevant to an understanding of crime and disorder, which induce fear, mistrust, and dissatisfaction with the quality of community life. Therefore, we define *community context* as a set of neighborhood conditions—structural and social conditions—that create the context for community social life. The community context is the set of neighborhood characteristics that determine the community's resource base: its social, physical, and human capital. Chief among these characteristics are stability, social ties, and institutional capacity.

Neighborhood stability refers to the frequency of population turnover. In a stable neighborhood, newcomers settle in for long periods of time. In unstable neighborhoods, there are constant waves of in-migration and out-migration. Just as constant turnover can threaten the profitability of a commercial organization, community instability erodes institutional memory, reduces cooperation, and limits loyalty. Skogan (1990) demonstrates a strong correlation between instability and social disorder, and many urban sociologists show the importance of neighborhood stability (Bursik 1986; Guest 1984; Sampson 1995).

Social ties are the relationships formed between community members. They can be weak or strong along several dimensions (Lyon 1987; Well-

---

[1] In his cautionary tale, Hardin described the practices of herdsmen who grazed their cattle on a common pastureland. For some time, the herdsmen successfully sustained the commons because the land was fertile and the herdsmen owned few cattle. However, the herdsmen began to give more attention to their own situation and less and less to the welfare of the commons. Gradually, they added cattle to their own stocks, reasoning that a few more cattle could do little damage to the shared resource. The aggregate result was overgrazing, which not only destroyed the commons but also undermined each herdsman's individual interest.

BOX 2.1   Community Context

- stability
- social ties
- institutional capacity

---

man and Leighton 1979). In a neighborhood with strong social ties, community members know one another well. Strong social ties are also characterized by families—even extended families—living within the local area; by neighbors who know one another by sight and by name, and who find most of their friends close by. Strong social ties are also multidimensional: One might be friends with the dentist; attend church with a child's teacher; or have gone to high school with a next door neighbor, who also happens to be the president of the local civic association. A neighborhood with weak social ties might result when residents live as relatively isolated individuals or have their primary interpersonal ties outside the neighborhood; in either case, the neighborhood experience will be one of anonymity.

Stability and social networks are obviously interrelated: Length of residence is an excellent predictor of both extensive and intensive social ties. Both factors have an effect on the commitment of residents to the neighborhood (Guest 1984). Committed residents invest in their community and are deeply concerned about protecting their investment. They attend community meetings and participate in local actions to protect property value, improve parkland, support schools, solve traffic problems, and reduce crime. Uncommitted residents will leave rather than fight to protect a threatened neighborhood; or if they stay, they will withdraw into obscurity, passively watching the community decline.

Probably the most important neighborhood characteristic is institutional capacity (Bellah et al. 1991). Every neighborhood contains a variety of social institutions: families, schools, and voluntary and formal community organizations. Neighborhoods are described as having a strong institutional capacity when their institutions have a high degree of integrity; for example, when most households contain two parents, or when schools have low dropout rates and high rates of parental involvement. Institutional capacity is also measured by organizational proliferation and participation—as evident, for example, in the number of churches or grassroots organizations per capita and the rates of active participation in them. Finally, institutional capacity is reflected in both internal and external linkages. Strong institutional capacity is marked by the existence of local coalitions and by their linkages to external brokers for community development.

American neighborhoods vary tremendously in their institutional capacity, and this variation goes a long way in explaining why some neighborhoods are attractive and safe while others induce fear and demoralization. In our systemic model, community context—in particular, the degree of stability and the strength of social ties and institutional capacity—can either facilitate or hinder community action.

Community Action

Social disorganization theory in criminology argues that disorganized communities are unable to advance collective agendas (Bursik 1988; Kornhauser 1978). The central point is not that extreme conflict or dissension over core values characterizes these communities but that they lack the capacity to realize important shared values about quality of life. Obviously, there are no advocates of violent crime, contaminated drinking water, or child abuse; and there are no rallies to end children's education, to reduce job opportunities, to dig more potholes, or to stop collecting the trash. Yet these communities suffer from lack of jobs, poor schools, environmental degradation, and high crime. Disorganization theorists view these outcomes as a problem of means, not ends. These communities, because of their instability, their weak social networks, and their weak institutional capacity, cannot engage in the kinds of community action necessary to provide collectively valued goods such as public safety.

We take a holistic view of communities as complex social entities existing over extended periods of time. Cooperative action on the part of community members to provide goods they all see as valuable is not simply a matter of community meetings and a grassroots campaign. Collective goods are provided in large part by the creation of a normative culture that reinforces the values and practices that support the general welfare of the community (Etzioni 1996b). Public safety, for example, is not achieved simply by securing additional police support. It is born of a commitment by the community to reinforce law-abiding behavior and cultivate in its young members values such as respect for others and nonviolent conflict resolution. Community action takes three forms: socialization, informal social control, and resource leveraging.

Socialization is an ongoing process of educating community members, particularly but not exclusively the young, and reinforcing compliance with accepted standards for behavioral conduct (Corsaro and Eder 1994). Compliance does not necessarily require stultifying conformity, for community members can be socialized to be self-directing (Kohn and Slomczynski 1990). But they must inevitably learn to successfully negotiate their way through the social world, and this requires some level of compliance with agreed-upon standards. Socialization is primarily the work

---

BOX 2.2   Community Action

- socialization
- informal social control
- resource leveraging

---

of families and schools; but recent thinking about policing has recognized the role that police officers can play as models for youth and generally as standard-bearers (Greene and McLaughlin 1993; Williams 1996). Recent evaluations have underscored the importance of interventions that enhance the socialization capacities of parents. For example, home visitation programs that assist parents in childrearing reduce the incidence of child abuse and of later delinquency (Sherman 1997b). School-based programs that focus on the communication and clarification of normative standards also reduce delinquency (Gottfredson 1997).

Informal social control is a community process of eliciting compliance to normative standards (Greenberg and Rohe 1986). Communities may engage in actions that motivate compliance for reasons having little to do with state-based coercion. A decision not to shoplift, for example, may be motivated by a concern for social approval rather than a fear of the legal repercussions (Braithwaite 1989). Community action may complement formal (state-based) social control. For example, a citizen patrol enhances local surveillance, potentially increasing the risk of offender apprehension by police. These complementary actions remain informal in that the police do not conduct the patrol and community members themselves are responsible for implementation. In essence, informal social control refers to myriad activities that encourage or enforce compliance with injunctive social norms. The primary function of socialization is the education and internalization of norms, whereas the purpose of informal control is enforcement. Socialization occurs when parents supervise the time and activities of teenagers; when inappropriate behavior (e.g., public urination) is reprimanded by bystanders; when "Take Back the Night" marches are organized; when neighbors voice concern about a household's late-night noise; when graffiti is quickly painted over; and in a thousand other small acts of surveillance and intervention.

Resource leveraging refers specifically to actions to bring extralocal resources to the community through fund-raising or political activism. It is particularly important because of a widespread tendency to assume that a community is, or should be, a closed system: If a community effectively articulates and enforces normative standards, all of its problems will be solved (Bennett, DiIulio, and Walters 1996). But communities are also influenced by external forces that profoundly influence the community context. Actions directed at leveraging external resources to improve the community context are the third major form of community action. Communities significantly vary in the extent to which they can successfully engage in this form of action, and as a result, some suffer significant disadvantage (Jargowsky 1997; Logan and Molotch 1987).

Quality of Community Life

Returning to the model in Figure 2.1, it is clear that the quality of community life is closely related to community context and community action. Weak social ties, instability, and institutional incapacity; faulty socialization, infrequent informal social control, and unsuccessful resource leveraging—all result in poor community outcomes (Elliott et al. 1996; Sampson 1995; Sampson and Lauritson 1994). The symptoms are witnessed in the neighborhood and in individual behaviors. At the neighborhood level we see physical and social disorder and serious crime, at the individual level, large numbers of people who are unable to make positive contributions to society and/or who lack a "sense of community."

At the neighborhood level, a poor quality of community life is vividly portrayed in various signs of physical disorder. These include dilapidated and abandoned commercial and residential buildings, graffiti and other signs of vandalism, abandoned cars, and litter. They also include the absence of signs of order—an empty lot where a community garden could be; boarded-up storefronts where markets or restaurants might be; and disconcerting proportions of some types of business (e.g., liquor stores and check-cashing vendors). Social disorder is no less noticeable. Its most visible signs include public drinking, street-corner congregations of youth, street harassment, and visible illegal drug markets (Lewis and Salem 1986; Skogan 1990). Social disorder is sometimes criminal (e.g., drug sales or prostitution) but more generally falls into gray areas that do not often generate police enforcement (e.g., aggressive panhandling, or groups of adolescents roving the neighborhood late at night). Of course, serious crime of any form is a strong signal of diminished quality of community life.

Less readily observable, but in the aggregate also meaningful to quality of life, is the status of individual competencies. Individual competencies are individual characteristics such as education and job skills, which reflect an individual's chances of being self-reliant and contributing wealth to the community. William J. Wilson (1987), for example, describes communities in terms of their pools of marriageable men. Communities with high numbers of unskilled and poorly educated young males who fail to thrive in the labor market provide few attractive marriage partners to young women. Such communities are likely to include a greater proportion of female-

---

BOX 2.3   Quality of Community Life

- physical disorder, social disorder, crime
- individual competencies
- sense of community

---

headed households. Though employability is primary, individual competencies might include any individual skills or qualities that contribute to the quality of the community (Bazemore and Maloney 1994; Selznick 1992). Thus, individual competencies are also indicated by the capacity of an individual to sustain deep relationships with others, to engage in moral decisionmaking, to exert self-control over antisocial impulses, to empathize with those in need, and to act in the service of others and the community.

A community's quality of life is objectively reflected in social order and individual competencies; but from the perspective of community members, quality of life is also subjective. If a true sense of community is lacking in the neighborhood where we live, we might feel that important qualities are missing from our lives. Research on this psychological "sense of community" has defined its central features (McMillan and Chavis 1986). A sense of community will be strong when individuals report feelings of (a) membership or belonging; (b) influence—that their membership matters to others, and that they are efficacious; (c) fulfillment—that their investment in the community is rewarded; and (d) emotional connection—that values and practices are shared in common and that bonds are more than instrumental. Community quality of life, then, is indicated both by objective community outcomes and by the subjective perceptions of its members.

The Feedback Loop

The quality of community life is not only an outcome of community context and community action. It also reciprocally influences them, sometimes generating a profound spiral of decline. The impact of pervasive crime on a community's quality of life has been well studied, and the implications of this work are that crime profoundly attacks a community's integrity. Three general arguments are made: Disorder weakens community action; street-level crime disrupts community context; and serious crime damages its victims.

Disorder Weakens Community Action.   The most well known statement of what is commonly called the "broken windows" hypothesis was written by Wilson and Kelling (1982; see also Kelling and Coles 1996; Skogan 1990), who argued that graffiti, abandoned cars, and other forms of personally created decay are evidence that a neighborhood is declining. Those who live in such a locality interpret such factors as indicators that rules do not matter and misbehavior will be tolerated. The result is a greater propensity toward vandalism and other petty criminality, and this in turn destabilizes community life and plants seeds of more serious offenses, especially among poorly supervised youth.

The "broken windows" thesis has been criticized as another form of "blaming the victim," because it seems to suggest that poor people permit criminality among themselves by tolerating petty disorder. In our view, however, the situation is more complex: Community members have some responsibility for exercising informal control; but their ability to do so is often weakened by external forces that help determine the community context. Whatever the merits of the "broken windows" hypothesis, the debate about crime and disorder became more important when New York City Chief of Police William Bratton claimed that large drops in crime beginning in 1994 were due to a policy of intolerance for disorderly street conduct, such as panhandling (Bratton 1995).

The link between disorder and informal control has received support from Skogan's (1990) studies of community crime patterns. He found that highly visible forms of neighborhood disorder—from pubic intoxication to abandoned buildings—create a climate that increases fear of crime and reduces informal control.

Street Crime Disrupts Community Context.   Crime has effects upon the community that are difficult to disentangle from the effects of the mere fear of crime, which may exceed the actual rates of victimization (Bursik and Grasmick 1993a). Nonetheless, the ways that residents and organizations respond to crime can be severely damaging to community conditions.

Crime reduces property values and neighborhood satisfaction (Taylor 1995). Residents afflicted by crime—particularly women and the elderly—tend to withdraw from community life (Miethe 1995). They are less willing to venture outside at night, and this inhibits the formation and maintenance of social clubs and other community activities. Businesses also will tend to close at night. The result is a more abandoned locality, offering fewer opportunities for building and maintaining social bonds among residents. Those who can afford to leave the neighborhood will do so, leaving behind an increasing concentration of the poor, the elderly, and those who are immobile for other reasons.

Many businesses that move away from inner cities attribute their decision to do so to crime rates. It has been estimated that between 1954 and

1982, Chicago lost almost 350,000 manufacturing jobs (Bursik and Gras-mick 1993a, p. 52). The loss of jobs deepens poverty, which in turn is associated with family breakup, school failure, and other social maladies. The removal of employment and business from neighborhoods also takes away a stabilizing influence and a source of mobilization for neighborhood improvement.

Serious Crime Damages Its Victims.   The previous points were that crime damages community by alienating people from the communities in which they live and corroding the preconditions for a satisfying quality of life. But we must not forget that crime affects more than community structure; it also has intensely personal consequences. Crime victims become less willing to take risks, and they become more likely to define ordinary community life as risky. Victims of serious crime feel estranged from their neighbors and their social system (Elias 1986).

Cost estimates of crime's consequences for victims are controversial; but a recent study by Miller, Cohen, and Wiersma (1996) estimates the intangible costs of crime, in the form of fear, pain, suffering, and decreased quality of life, at $345 billion per year (nearly three times the tangible costs).[2] The sum total of these effects—disorder, street crime, and serious crime—is severe damage to communities. Crime reduces residents' ability to participate in community life, and it makes their interest in community life distorted toward personal safety and away from other activities that might improve neighborhood life more generally. Businesses move out and jobs disappear; individuals become inactive residents, unable or unwilling to support organizational life at the community level. As a result, the community context is damaged, undermining the community's capacity to defend itself against crime.

Criminal Justice Response

Since 1973, the annual incarceration rate in the United States has grown from about 90 per 100,000 of the total population to more than 400 per 100,000; and the total prison population has increased from 200,000 to more than 1 million (United States Bureau of Justice Statistics 1995; Sentencing Project 1997). Though the accumulation of additional prisoners has been gradual, the net impact of this profound shift in the collective experience of incarceration is important to understand. Growth in imprisonment has disproportionately affected the poor and people of color.

---

[2]Tangible costs, which amount to $105 billion annually, include property damage and loss, medical and mental health care, police and fire services, victim services, and lost productivity.

Black males have a 28 percent chance of being incarcerated in their life-times, whereas white males have a 4 percent chance (Sentencing Project 1997). When controlling for age and social class, it has been estimated that a minimum of 10 percent of underclass African American males between the ages of 26 and 30 were incarcerated in 1986 (Lynch and Sabol 1992)—a number that has certainly grown with the prison population, which nearly doubled in the 1990s. These statistics represent a drastic loss of male membership in these communities. Given the drastic increase in the rate of imprisonment since 1973, African American communities have suffered war-level casualties of adult males of parenting age.

One way to understand the consequences of imprisonment is to view crime and punishment from the perspective of a systems model in which criminals are seen as embedded in various interpersonal, family, eco-nomic, and political institutions. Communities depend upon the effective functioning of these various institutions. Removing large numbers of young males from the community seriously disrupts the web of relations on which these institutions are based. The result is a community with damaged economic, political, and social structures. Under these circum-stances, communities have difficulty creating a safe and supportive envi-ronment that enables individuals to flourish.

The systems model portrays crime as a social event occurring within a patterned social context. Large numbers of individuals cannot be re-moved from communities without affecting the structural conditions that are conducive to crime in multiple ways. Communities might be able to sustain small losses in numbers of residents (whether due to mobility or incarceration) without significant fallout; but removing greater numbers of residents could well have an impact on larger social relations.

Our point here is that the prevalent criminal justice response to crimi-nal offenders—incarceration—is potentially counterproductive for the community even though it is aimed at increasing public safety. We do not suggest that imprisonment be rejected altogether, nor that the alternatives currently available are sufficient for a community justice ideal. Instead, we argue that a community justice approach that purposefully attends to public safety finds ways to support rather than undermine community institutions. To explain some of the reasoning behind our position, we outline below some of the undesirable community-level consequences of a criminal justice system that depends so heavily on imprisonment.

Family Consequences

Communities that contribute higher rates of members to incarceration ex-perience higher rates of family disruption, single-parent families, and births to young, single adults (Lynch and Sabol 1992). The close association between the removal of young males from underclass, racial minority communities suggests a plausible hypothesis that one is in part a product of another (or at least that they are mutually reinforcing phenomena). What are the implications of this pattern?

It is well established that children suffer when parents are removed from the home. What is less clear is the nature and extent of disruption that follows an incarceration. Studies of this problem have tended to focus on incarcerated mothers (Gabel 1992); but there also have been a few attempts to document the effects of incarcerating fathers (Brodsky 1975; Carlson and Carrera 1992; Fishman 1990; King 1993; Lowstein 1986). If the latter effects are potent, the ripple effects of a father's incarceration could be significant. John Hagan (1996) drew upon this literature as well as on the conventional theoretical perspectives of strain, socialization, and stigmatization to show the detrimental effects of overincarceration.

We might expect that the removal of a criminally active father from the home would improve the environment for the children. But this is not supported by the available data. One study of a jail intake sample among males finds preliminary evidence for the existence of substantial positive parenting prior to incarceration (Smith and Clear 1995). After the male's imprisonment, the effects of his incarceration on his family included relocation to more cramped quarters and new school districts; disruptions in family life and childrearing caused by the entrance and exit of transitory, unrelated males; reduced maternal parenting due to the need for supplementary employment; and similar events. All are potentially disruptive to the family and tend to decrease family cohesiveness—an important predictor of delinquency (Sampson 1987). In cases where offenders pose no risk of violence to their families and neighbors, why not develop strategies that hold offenders accountable for their crimes but also keep families together?

Economic Consequences

Family members earning money contribute to the welfare of their families, and this remains true even when a portion of those earnings are from criminal activities such as drug sales. Prior to incarceration, most prisoners are an economic resource to their neighborhoods and their immediate families. Mercer Sullivan (1989) describes how a work-age male in an impoverished neighborhood generates economic activity that translates into purchases at the local deli, child support, and so forth. This economic value is generated by a variety of endeavors, including off-the-books work, intermittent illicit drug trade, welfare, and part-time employment, and might be as much as $12,000 a year. After he is arrested and incarcerated, this young man's economic value is transformed and transferred. It is translated into penal capital—the demand for a salaried correctional employee to provide security. It is also transferred to the locality of the prison, where the penal system's employees reside and live. Thus, the value of a resident of Bedford-Stuyvesant, New York, who is arrested and convicted, is transformed from, say, $12,000 in his community to $30,000 in a sleepy upstate village. This type of transfer of wealth applies to as many as 70 percent of the state's 69,000 inmates (Clines 1992).

What happens to a community that experiences a steady increase in these transfers of wealth? Economic hardship is one of the strongest geographic predictors of crime rates. The socially embedded nature of crime and unemployment suggests that communities suffering deprivation experience greater criminal involvement among residents (Hagan 1993). Taylor and Covington (1988) have shown that violent crime is associated with a community's relative deprivation; and Block (1979) found a link between a community's crime rate and its ratio of wealthy to impoverished residents. These studies confirm that social processes damaging a community's economic viability may also tend to raise its crime rate. Therefore, it is reasonable to assume that a community experiencing economic loss as a result of incarceration will experience an increase in crime.

Imprisonment not only has an economic effect on the community that was home to the prisoner; it also affects the prisoner directly. Grogger (1995) demonstrated that merely being arrested has a short-term, negative impact on earnings, and Freeman (1992) has shown that conviction and imprisonment have a permanent impact on earning potential. Experience with the criminal justice system contributes to the very inequality in economic means that promotes street crime in the first place (Braithwaite 1979). Thus the criminal justice system leaves economic scars on its clients long after its formal involvement in their lives has ended.

Again, our point is not that we should indulge illicit economic activity because it contributes wealth to a community. It is that current criminal justice responses typically fail to account for community-level effects such as the transfer of wealth out of desperate areas. With this in mind, greater efforts should be made to bring wealth to high-crime areas, in part through strategies that develop individual competencies in convicted offenders.

Consequences for Law-Abiding Citizenship

Every minority child in an impoverished area can tell stories of racism in the criminal justice system, and the validation of these tales is apparent to the eye. One-third of African American males in their twenties are under some form of formal justice system control; in many cities, half of this group are subjects of the system (Mauer 1995). The overwhelming presence of criminal justice in these communities goes a long way to defining the meaning of the state for this segment of society. The state is most likely to be encountered as a coercive agent of control rather than a "fair" agent of justice; and when this is true, people are likely to view the system as illegitimate (Tyler 1990).

In communities with high rates of incarceration, beliefs about the state may be contentious. In Philadelphia, a small cadre of police (perhaps as few as ten) was found to have been planting evidence and falsifying testimony to achieve convictions in African American neighborhoods (New York Times 1996). As a result of this revelation, hundreds of convictions were overturned and dozens of wrongfully incarcerated offenders were released from prison, including a grandmother whose conviction was obtained through planted drugs as a way to teach her drug-dealing grandson "a lesson." In the several years preceding the event, this group of police officers had been responsible for nearly 2,000 convictions—all of which the authorities must now review for illegalities. One can imagine the collective impression of victims of the perhaps 1,000 false imprisonments, and the impressions of their children, siblings, spouses, and in-laws. The effect of a malfeasance of the law within these communities is geometric. This is one reason why it would surprise few of us to learn that many inner-city young people define the power of the state as a nemesis to be avoided rather than an ally to be cultivated. When conventional society is viewed as illegitimate, oppositional subcultures are likely to form that reject the values and practices of the larger society, and crime and delinquency therefore increase (Anderson 1990; Braithwaite 1989; Massey and Denton 1993).

Our determined overreliance on incarceration might actually reduce prison's effectiveness as a deterrent. Finckenauer's (1982) study of Rahway prison's "Scared Straight" program found that most first-time offenders who were deliberately subjected to harsh, accusatory taunting by lifers actually had *higher* subsequent rates of delinquency than a comparison group not exposed to the program. Finckenauer does not make much of this difference, except to conclude that scare tactics do not work. But his results are consistent with a belief that the brutalizing effects of prison experiences may not only fail to deter but may actually inure a person to fear of prison's consequences.

Stated another way, part of the deterrent power of the prison may be the mystery that surrounds it. Once experienced, prison, no matter how harsh, is transformed from an awful mystery to a real-life experience that can be suffered and survived. High recidivism rates throughout the years are consistent with the idea that prison experiences fail to deter. Fear of prison (especially among the middle-class citizens who have not experienced it) may be a real deterrent only when it is based in unfamiliarity with prisons.

In minority communities, prison is a part of life. A black ten-year-old boy is likely to have at least one and possible more ex-cons among his close relatives (father, uncles, brothers) and neighbors. The lesson is that prison is not awesome but survivable. Widespread use of prison might lead to a widespread reassurance that prison is "normal" as well as to increasing resentment against the system. Prison becomes an increasingly marginal deterrent.

Ways Out of the Cycle

The picture presented by these data is of a malignant cycle. Crime produces deterioration in communities' capacity for self-regulation; this leads to an increased presence of external forces (the justice system officials of the state) to supplement the community's damaged control mechanisms; and this, in turn, further damages self-regulation. The downward spiral continues as communities' internal resources become so depleted and their integrity so fragmented that residents are unable to contribute to the general welfare. Operating at the level of survival, many law-abiding citizens become willing to sacrifice key civil liberties in the pursuit of a tolerable minimum of security (Rosenbaum 1993). With the loss of liberty, quality of life further deteriorates; a cycle of destruction is established.

The problem involves two interacting systems. The first is the crime-community system: Weak self-regulation allows disorder of various kinds to spill over into the community—everything from noisy streets to the public conduct of criminal enterprise. The lack of resources (jobs and organization) to strengthen self-regulation further stimulates disruptive behaviors that tend to reinforce their own existence. At the same time, the crime-control system further depletes the resources communities use for self-regulation, removing offending citizens at high rates. Because disruption levels are already very high in these communities, a large number of citizens qualify for removal, and strong formal control systems have little regard for the contribution these citizens make (or could make) to community self-regulation. Some observers argue that the high incarceration rates for drug offenders, for example, destabilized local drug markets enough that drug trade became more territorial, markets more volatile, and drug work more violent in protection of (or absorption of) market share (Blumstein 1995). In addition, ethnographies of street gangs have confirmed the valuable resource some gang members are to their families and neighbors.

Intervening in this interlocked system is problematic. The failure to support communities with external resources leaves many communities only marginally capable of taking action. Yet aggressive formal social control of these same localities, particularly through unidimensional policies of incarceration, further undermines the community context: Released offenders return to their communities with fewer legitimate bonds intact and diminished human capital to contribute to community well-being.

Toward Supportive Formal Social Control

A key distinction in this predicament may be that the criminal justice system tends to act as a *force upon* local communities rather than a *resource to* those communities. In localities with so few resources to begin with, the justice system can seem an alien contingency to be coped with rather than a service center to be exploited. If criminal justice agencies could be reconfigured to operate as supports for community action rather than as drains upon it, the dynamics would change considerably. We believe this ought to be the aim of the criminal justice system in a community justice model.

In this scenario, the task of criminal justice agencies is not to attack crime directly but to strengthen community resources (by supporting community action) that counteract crime and disorder. Instead of further weakening the informal social control functions of the community, this approach would act directly upon a community's capacity to exercise the natural sources of social control existing inside it. We are not suggesting that police should be dismissed but that their mission be reoriented toward partnership with the community rather than insurgency into enemy territory.

Improving the quality of the relationship between the criminal justice system and local residents and institutions is critical to the overall strength of communities, and there are abundant examples of this. When it comes to policing, for example, the distinction between viewing police as an occupying army versus police as a local service agency is well established in the literature (Goldstein 1976). In the former case, law enforcement seems to act as a net drain on community resources, with an antagonistic relationship to local citizenry. Police tend to define citizens as "the problem" and hold locals in very low regard, and this mutual dislike characterizes interaction among the parties. The opposite often happens when police place themselves in service to the community; the antagonistic pattern dissipates, and police see citizens in a sympathetic light. Citizens, in turn, view police as a source of local harmony.

The priorities of police would no longer be only to identify and control offenders but also to strengthen the relationships that improve community conditions and promote community action. People then would begin to act upon their own problems: They may meet to discuss problems and set priorities for action; form groups to counteract problems of crime and disorder; and cooperate with law enforcement authorities in crime prevention.

In many communities, a favorable community context reduces the magnitude and complications of our current criminal justice response (Clear and Rose, 1996). Stable communities with strong social networks and institutions lose relatively low numbers of offenders to external coercive controls, and the losses have minimal impact upon informal social control systems. This is not the case in communities suffering from depleted capacities for self-regulation—precisely those communities afflicted by high rates of crime. An exclusive focus on removing residents as a crime-prevention strategy disrupts the meager internal controls that exist without supplying replacements. Moreover, temporarily removed offenders—because they are alienated from extant social networks—return to these same neighborhoods less capable of participating in community action.

The need for criminal justice system support varies from locality to locality. Communities that effectively self-regulate will use formal social controls to augment already strong capacities for community action. Other communities, lacking such capacities, will be at odds with criminal justice agencies. In such communities, the system must not only provide protection for individual citizens but must also increase the strength of (or even help create) indigenous social control capacities, and thereby improve the community context.

Toward a Focus on Quality of Community Life

In this chapter we have argued that the criminal justice system in the United States has failed to take seriously the nature and promise of community life. Instead, it has focused almost obsessively on the removal and punishment of offenders. We concur that holding offenders accountable for their crimes is vital in the achievement of justice; but we do not agree that accountability is a sufficient condition for achieving justice, or that incarceration is the only means available for making offenders accountable. A community-oriented approach would try to identify ways of repairing the damage done by the offenses to victims and to the community as a whole. It would also be responsive to the criminogenic conditions of a community, proactively enhancing a community's capacity to ensure public safety.

The quality of community life is a function of community context: primarily of its stability, social ties, and institutional capacity. These in turn enable community action to provide valued collective goods, especially public safety. A favorable community context engenders effective action in three vital spheres: socialization in conventional values and practices, enforcement of normative standards through informal social control, and social action to leverage external resources for community development.

Rebuilding a sense of community is perhaps the most elusive and ambitious agenda for a community justice model. In large part, it requires a renewed confidence in the justice system. To renew citizens' confidence, a profound shift must take place in the way we define justice. A wave of support is growing for an improved community focus in criminal justice policy, and we argue that it has strong theoretical support. The time appears ripe for implementing the ideals of community justice.

A long tradition of locally operated justice functions—jails, sheriffs, municipal courts, and so on—suggests falsely that community justice is a return to earlier organizational models and not a very profound change. But the current talk about what is wrong with criminal justice is not merely a jurisdictional complaint. People feel alienated from the logic of justice. Some of the recent community justice experiments—neighborhood justice centers, community policing, restorative justice, and community-oriented policing—challenge us to think about what justice *means* at the local level of practice. Does the quality of basic justice require a different substantive experience for citizens in different communities? Is community justice merely a locally tailored plan for law enforcement, or does it connote a deeper commitment to residents, to helping them regain greater control of their quality of life? Embracing the idea of "community safety" shifts our attention from "what is to be done about people" to "what is to be done about the places in which people live and work."

This is a profoundly different view of justice than the traditional view, and it leads to questions about the philosophical foundations of Western justice. For example, it raises questions about the adversarial model in which rights (such as the right to live in a community) reside in individuals and can be taken away from individuals. The community justice model is not contradictory to individual rights, but it gives higher priority to what might be understood as a social value—the way in which people live and the circumstances that affect their lives.

Moreover, the protection of rights as entitlements of individuals has been a cornerstone of the way we understand the relationship between the individual and the state. Individual rights have been a resource used to advance the important civil rights of groups. It would be unwise to propose an abatement of individual rights for this and many other reasons. Rather, we recognize that both ideas—individual rights and community quality of life—are meant to empower individuals and the groups in which they live. This goal can be achieved in the realm of justice only if a local justice strategy can be devised that belongs to the people who live under it as much as it belongs to the state that operates it.

To some degree the community model rejects (or at least devalues) the adversarial idea of the individual versus the state. In place of this idea, it proposes a community ideal emphasizing the obligations of citizens to one another. As a springboard to any advancement of community justice, there is a need for creative thought about the conceptual and philosophical underpinnings of neighborhood-based justice. In the next chapter, we develop a set of ideals of community life that takes seriously the problem of balancing individual rights and collective goods.

A community justice model built around an ideal of community safety and community self-regulation is incompatible with the idea of removing citizens and placing them in a prison. What is a community if it is not the people who live there? How can safety be valued as a thing for some persons in the community but not for those who have been removed? Is public safety a realistic outcome when offenders' removal is a temporary phenomenon eventuating in a return of those individuals in even more blighted shape? These questions reach fundamentally to the problem of what we should do about persons who have committed wrongful acts; what we should do about the needs and concerns of victims; and how we can work with victims, offenders, and their neighbors to increase the level of safety for all. These questions are taken up in detail in Chapter 4, where we consider a community justice response to criminal incidents. We develop three basic principles of community justice: (1) justice entails the affirmation of community norms; (2) justice requires the restoration of victims and of the community; and (3) justice occurs when the safety of community members is assured.

Community justice cannot simply mean a response to individual criminal incidents. It must also attend to the precursors of crime, from the community context and the community's capacity for action, to the counterproductive approaches of the traditional justice system. To what extent must community justice approaches address social inequalities? To what extent should offenders be treated as community members and incarceration be avoided in favor of community corrections? How much can we expect law-abiding behavior and even prosocial community action from citizens without coercion from the state for their obedience and participation? In Chapter 5, we develop four principles of community justice that address the community conditions that foster criminality. We argue that community justice strives for (1) equality, particularly in the reduction of concentrated poverty and residential segregation; (2) inclusion of offenders in community life; (3) mutuality, or the promotion of incentives that bring individual interests into line with collective interests; and (4) stewardship by the community, particularly in promoting its long-term welfare.

This book would not be complete without addressing a number of practical issues about implementing community justice. In Chapter 6, we raise a number of questions about community justice in practice. For example, what aspects of community are particularly relevant to justice programs—geographic boundaries, functional interdependencies, shared identities? Another question asks whether or not legal concerns such as equality before the law can be reconciled with community variation in approaches to justice. To what degree does the criminal law require flexibility in order to be responsive to localities? A related question asks how communities and representatives of the justice system can be held accountable to higher standards when they are given greater autonomy and authority to fulfill a community agenda.

At the practical level, there are other questions needing analysis: How do justice agencies interact and coordinate their efforts under this approach? What new responsibilities, practices, and perspectives are needed? Are current corporate structures of justice adequate for the community model? If not, how might these agencies be reshaped? How might they be funded? What formal roles can community members fulfill? How can they be mobilized, and how effectively can they represent other community members?

In Chapter 7, we describe how community justice initiatives might be evaluated in terms of their component parts. We illustrate the implementation of the seven principles of community justice described in Chapters 4 and 5 with a set of existing programs showing what we mean by the core principles of community justice.

3

A Positive View
of Community Life

Who is the client of a community justice system? What is meant by the term *community*—who is being served? To answer these questions is not as easy as it might seem, but the very core of what is valuable about community justice is revealed in the exercise. In our usage, the "community" served by community justice is not simply some group of people. We think of community justice as a strategy of community life, interested not just in people, but also the way they live and seek to live: their very possibilities. In this chapter, we consider what is at stake in promoting what we have referred to as "the community justice ideal." We begin by considering the nature of modern community life, especially why so many of us seem troubled about it. We then provide a critical assessment of the role of adversarial justice in community life—or rather, its lack of a role. Finally, we define a set of aspirations that express our most cherished view of community life, and we suggest some ways that the justice system might promote those aspirations.

The aim of this chapter is to address two questions. First, we consider the meaning of the community, and we touch on the implications of criminal justice for that meaning. Second, we articulate the essentials of what might be called "rich" community life. It is these essentials, we suggest, that a community justice ideal would treat as core objectives. This discussion is a preamble to the discussions in Chapters 4 and 5, in which we propose a set of principles that should undergird community justice programs—the principles of the community justice ideal.

What Is Community?

There are many meanings to *community*. We use the word colloquially to refer to occupational groups (the community of scholars), ethnic affiliations (the Asian community), and even voluntary associations (the Methodist community). We also use the term to refer to local neighborhoods, as in "the Haight-Ashbury community." More than four decades ago, Hillery (1955) noted that sociologists had proffered more than ninety definitions of community with little commonality between them. No wonder the term seems vague, and no wonder we often confuse ourselves when we use it. To fully understand what is meant by *community justice*, we must gain a deeper appreciation for the meaning and significance of *community*.

That the meaning of the word seems vague should not stop us from talking about community life. The lack of a single, clear definition of the concept of "community" does not mean that it is devoid of content but that it is so important to us that summary references to it fail to capture its complexity and range. Community life carries deep symbolism and meaning for Americans' culture and identity. We think of community as the place from which we hail and the safe haven to which we owe our self-knowledge. In this sense, *community* is an entity—a geographic area or a group—to which we belong. But we also think of community as a quality of social existence: an indication of solidarity, shared practices and traditions, and emotional connectedness. This kind of community cannot be located on any map.

Community is an entirely practical concept, not merely an ephemeral term of art. We all, most of our lives, obtain our daily experience in the various communities to which we devote our attention. We live each day, driving from here to there, inside the spatial context of community. We derive our self-concept from embracing and challenging the rituals and practices sanctioned by our communities, and we profoundly depend upon those with whom we live, work, and play for our survival and our fulfillment. For each of us, community is the complex interlocking of human relationships upon which we rely to live daily life. In modern societies, these are diverse, multiple, and individual, but they are no less substantial for their variety.

Most of us live in multiple communities. We encounter them at work, in our residence, and where our children spend their days. Some are dense and meaningful to us; others are shallow, and we feel indifferent toward them. Yet the basis for all of them, as Fukuyama (1995) argues, is some form of trust: a confidence in our belonging and a faith that others will cooperate with us in pursuit of common ends. We are deeply troubled when this trust is diminished, when we believe that community is disintegrating. The modern citizen is forced to interact with many communities over time; and summoning trust in them—especially on the basis of limited knowledge—can be daunting even under the best of circumstances. By far the most central of these communities are those where we live, work, and relax. When we begin to think that these communities are unsafe, unreliable, or foreign, it is a serious loss indeed.

Community justice is not simply a proposal for citizen participation in the criminal justice system. It is an approach that assumes crime is a warning signal about the quality of community life. The response is at once about building community, preventing crime, and finding justice.

Convergent and Divergent Experiences of Community

Two broad themes underlie the experience of community life. First, where one lives and works has a great deal to do with how (and how well) one lives. There is variation across communities, particularly in the distribution of advantage and opportunity. Second, it seems that across most communities in the United States today there is a sense of loss. Even in the wealthiest suburbs, individuals feel anonymous, as if they were disconnected from their communities (Baumgartner 1988; Nisbet 1953).

Themes of Divergence

Disposable wealth largely determines housing location, which, in turn, defines much about one's lifestyle. In cities, especially, location is directly tied to wealth, and this has enormous implications for crime control: The poorer neighborhoods are almost always those with higher crime. Thus, wealth is also access—to safety as well as to everyday amenities.

There is every indication that the distance between the rich and the poor has grown in recent decades. The spending power of the middle class has been stagnant or in decline for two decades; and the percentage of wealth in the hands of a small minority is increasing at the same rate at which it is declining in the hands of the poorest (Fischer et al. 1996). A two-decade-long trend toward economic equalization in the 1950s and 1960s has been followed by nearly three decades of increasing disparity in wealth. If money buys location, the capacity to do so is slipping out of the hands of many Americans.

This pattern has fueled a belief that the "American dream" is no longer viable. The belief that one's children would live an improved life has been discredited by the soaring costs of higher education and the instability of work. The past quarter century has seen the solidification of an urban underclass that has no reasonable chance of leaving destitution behind, and knows it (Wilson 1987; 1996).

Community life in America increasingly means differentiated, disparate ways of living, aligned not only on the basis of traditional demographic identifications of region and density (Northeast/South; urban/rural) but also on economic opportunity, racial segregation, class reproduction, and family structure. Increasing costs of higher education close doorways to opportunity for many Americans, and class reproduction confines many to lives of entrenched impoverishment. Increasingly rigid lines of social class isolate neighborhoods of disadvantage from mainstream economic and social life. The result is that *where* a person lives has more and more influence on *how* that person lives.

Themes of Convergence

Despite the diversity in American community life, some changes are occurring that apply to nearly every locality, regardless of demographic characteristics. These are convergent themes, for they redefine a community life grown more unequal with a consistent overlay of forces affecting those communities.

Perhaps the most apparent change is that community social life has become less abundant. Robert Putnam (1995) has argued that fewer people join local social organizations, participate in community affairs, and donate time and/or money to charitable causes; less time is spent in social contact with others, and more time is spent at work and in transit between work and home. These patterns have affected family life, as well, making families less stable and supportive (Hochschild 1997; Popenoe 1988). Parents devote less time to child care. Children spend more time alone or with their peers than with family members. More marriages end in divorce. More children are born to young, single parents, and more children grow up in impoverished circumstances. These are all patterns that reduce the quality of family life and leave families more vulnerable to child criminality.

Political life also has become more polarized and less characterized by relations of trust. Partly because of the fragmentation of opportunity, a fragmentation of interest groups has diluted the power of traditional political parties. There has been a struggle for a new coalition of voting interests, but none has emerged. Disenchantment with organized politics has grown, and the result has been a declining belief in the viability of political institutions (Barber 1984). The percentage of eligible voters casting ballots in elections is low, often a minority of the electorate. These are all signals that citizens see political life as less and less relevant to their interests. The natural result is a decline in responsible citizenship.

Many Americans therefore believe that the quality of community life has declined, and they have evidence to support this belief in a number of objective measures (Etzioni 1993). The perception of declining community life has destabilized relations among citizens within communities and has reduced the social yield of community ties. Most important, it has led many citizens to search for ideas and processes that "recover" community.

Contemporary Selves, Contemporary Society

Building community: It seems a platitude that no one could protest. Our vague acknowledgment that community is "good" and that we should therefore seek more of it leaves us with an equally vague agenda for action. The importance of the community in community justice requires that we develop a clear vision of community that is relevant to the often conflicting goals of contemporary Americans. We certainly cannot abide a vision of community grounded in nostalgia.

In thinking about community, there is tension along two dimensions. First, the idea of community tugs against the experience of modern social life. Must we therefore move away from the city, relinquishing its amenities in order to recover the practices and conventions of an earlier time? We assume that American society is powerfully influenced by the conditions of modernity. Modernity, to use Blau's (1977) formulation, is a context of heterogeneity and inequality; of cosmopolitanism, rationalization, bureaucracy, and mass society. There is no turning back the clock to a small-town America. Even if it were possible to do so, the prejudice and insularity that often accompany the nostalgic vision of small-town life offer no solution to the social alienation and crime that plague our communities.

Second, there is tension between the desire for more independence and a sense of belonging. We assume that individuals in society are neither fully free nor fully constrained. They are "social selves." Individuals have great potential for self-determination, moral autonomy, and free-riding, but are nevertheless highly socialized and deeply influenced by the values, beliefs, practices, and opportunities handed to them by their communities. A relevant conception of community must consider the context of modernity and of social selves.

Modernity

Modern social life is complicated by the explicit intrusion into private life of large-scale social forces. Benjamin Barber (1995) has described modernity as "McWorld," while George Ritzer (1993) describes the "McDonaldization" of society. These metaphors invoke themes that have been central to sociological analysis since Durkheim's identification of the division of labor and Weber's analysis of the rational/legal order: the dissociation of the individual from the community; a transition from the religious to the secular; and a market order in which social relations are increasingly seen as fleeting, contractual, and instrumental. For Philip Selznick (1992, p. 4), the distinguishing characteristic of modernity is "the steady weakening of traditional social bonds and the concomitant creation of new unities based on more rational, more impersonal, more fragmented forms of thought and action."

The context for understanding community life is modernity. We live in a society of weak social ties. This is not to say that our ties are few. Rather, the average person in his or her lifetime will have more contacts with a greater variety of people than did previous generations. But these contacts are short and are guided primarily by the expedient exchange of cash for goods and services. Individuals feel anonymous and lost in the shuffle, hustle, and bustle.

Modernity, ironically, has created more independence and more interdependence. With occupational differentiation and specialization, individuals have more freedom to choose careers that suit their sensibilities. With greater affluence, we are free to quit jobs we do not like, leave bad marriages, ignore authoritative parents, or come out of the closet. The liberties of modern life are cherished, and no vision of contemporary community can dismiss the powerful desire for autonomy and self-determination. Of course, this is not to say that such freedoms do not often have adverse consequences (divorce, for example, throws many women into poverty), but only that modernity gives us these choices. This independence arises from a distinct "separation of spheres" of social life. We do not work where we live, parents are not involved in their children's schools, and extended families live far apart. Independence seems to mean less commitment—or at least, less unified, overlapping commitments.

At the same time, the complexity of social systems creates greater interdependencies. As the provision of collective goods occurs on ever larger scales, self-sufficiency becomes an empty abstraction. We rarely barter, for our skills are generally too limited to exchange with the great variety of others upon whom we depend. The most educated among us, college professors, can only teach 10 or 20 courses in their field of specialization out of the 800 or 1,000 courses offered at a major university. We cannot individually produce our own food and water supplies; we cannot construct for ourselves the apartments or houses in which we live; we cannot build our own cars, boats, and planes, or our own schools and hospitals; and we cannot defend ourselves against foreign invasion. We are desperately dependent upon one another to collectively provide such goods. As Alan Wolfe (1989, p. 3) put it, "To be modern is to face the consequences of decisions made by complete strangers while making decisions that will affect the lives of people one will never know." Anonymity and interdependence converge in modern society.

The puzzle of modernity is to find community in a mass society. In Louis Wirth's (1938) well-known formulation, the condition of modernity, exemplified by the urban form, is best understood in the context of large populations, high levels of density, and great heterogeneity—from occupational differentiation to multiculturalism to social inequality. The prospect of community is deeply challenged by the unconstrained fragmentation and faceless anonymity of modernity. It seems that just as large-scale social forces, global economic markets, and even mass politics with its electronic town halls, Madison Avenue campaigns, and poll-driven platforms increase the pace and profits of daily life, they also increase superficial, ephemeral human contacts.

The Social Self

Improving community life is partly an ongoing process of resisting the atomizing forces of modernity. But it also involves the creation of meaningful self-identities. Self-identity is derived from the experience of social life. The concept of personal autonomy is, in a sense, a fiction, because no one is completely independent of others—not even for the understanding of oneself as a distinct individual. George H. Mead (1956, p. 226) once wrote, "One has to be a member of a community in order to be a self."

Sociologists tend to view individuals as partially but not completely determined by society. We use the term *social self* to reflect both the latitude individuals have in creating their own histories and the social constraints that limit, organize, and direct the individual life course. This moderate view is particularly important because it frames our attributions of responsibility for individual conduct. Is a criminal offender, for example, exclusively responsible for an offense, or does society share culpability because it fosters the conditions that precipitate crime? Community, we assume, plays a large role in individual self-definition; if nothing else, it frames the possibilities. A search for community, then, entails some consideration of who we are as individuals and who we want to be.

The social self is constructed from the various roles performed by individuals in society and by their membership in various social groups. Answers given to Kuhn and McPartland's (1954) Who Am I/Twenty Statements Test are telling in this regard. Generally, when individuals provide open-ended responses to the question "Who am I?" many of their responses reflect social roles: daughter, teacher, activist, friend (Triandis et al. 1990). Moreover, these roles are accompanied by social expectations that help define proper performance: Friends do not betray, daughters care for their parents, and activists mobilize support for a cause. The realized, social self is no island but rather a set of particular relations, obligations, and potentialities.

There are four important aspects to the idea of a social self. First, individuals are *situated in time and place;* that is, in the context of specific social relationships. The experience of daily life is a social experience. Studies of human development demonstrate the necessity of human connection (Stern 1985). The need for emotional attachments to others is a basic human motivation. Infants who are separated from their mothers and not given tender care but who otherwise have their basic needs fulfilled suffer from depression and fail to thrive (Anderson et al., in press). We live in a world of relationships, and the more important of these have a strong affective component. These relations are not random but are fostered by proximity and framed by their endurance. We have deep investments in our relationships and do not sacrifice them lightly. Thus, we are often quite willing to share, negotiate, reciprocate, and cooperate rather than withdraw, avoid, or antagonize. Our close relations make us cognizant of others' needs and of the social requirements that enable these relationships to last over time.

A second aspect of the social self is the necessity of *socialization*. Though some may argue that cooperation is a genetic endowment (Axelrod 1984; Caporael et al. 1989), myriad social processes transform a self-regarding, dependent infant into an other-regarding, independent/interdependent adult. These processes involve the transmission of language, values, beliefs, traditions, norms, and practices that ensure a cooperative sensibility. Of course, socialization is neither automatic nor complete. On this subject, Amitai Etzioni (1996b, p. 97) noted:

> The fact that cultures have a normative starting point does not mean that individuals do not play a role in sorting out values; "all" that cultures provide individuals is a foundation. Individuals may rebel against their culture, form new cultural elements, or fashion them out of traditional elements combined with new ones; however, the background against which these individuals rebel, and which partially defines the direction and content of their rebellion, is their society's set of values.

Cultures reproduce themselves through socialization, which is a vital means of maintaining social order. Individuals may make their own choices, but they do so within the context of received wisdom. We do not assume, however, that order is best found in cultural reproduction or best understood as the imposition of cultural standards upon a resistant but mutable soul. Instead, we assume individuals are a product of socialization and negotiation—a product of an *interaction order* (Wrong 1994). This is a third aspect of the social self.

The central idea is that daily life is a series of social encounters, and we enter these encounters with predictions or expectations about how they will proceed. When we place an order at lunch, we predict with great confidence that the waiter will respond in a particular way; not pulling a gun, not bursting into tears, not sitting on our lap. Our expectations become routinized as implicitly understood social norms. Social norms and their implicit understanding provide social stability. At the same time, the interaction order is context-specific and creative in its formation. Sometimes waiters do strange things; sometimes we ourselves do the unexpected. Since the ritual encounters of daily life are predictable but not predetermined, there is room for novelty, innovation, and rebellion. Thus, the interaction order is also a source of social change.

A fourth aspect of the social self is that individuals are *moral agents.* Certainly, much behavior is instrumental and self-interested. However, it is not possible to realize common ends (at least not in the long run) either through the aggregation of self-interested action or through the coercive repression of self-interest in the service of society. Much of our behavior is voluntary and other-directed, often at the expense of immediate self-gain (Piliavin and Charng 1990). We assume that human interaction is normative as well as instrumental.

Individual and collective aspirations are constructed in concrete, social contexts by moral, situated agents. In short, individuals are guided by a "grounded morality." Individuals treat each other well and cooperate in collective endeavors sometimes because of threat, sometimes because of self-interest, but primarily because they learn through practice that they are the beneficiaries of social progress and that society can progress when individuals are willing to contribute to collective ends. The expression of moral agency is undertaken in "moral dialogues" (Etzioni 1996b) and by the use of "moral language" (Bellah et al. 1985). This is necessary because of the "problem of order" (Wrong 1994): Humans are perpetually confronted with the need to cooperate because of material scarcity. Without cooperation, we would find ourselves in a Hobbesian state of violent competition. Instead, we make use of our sociability and engage in moral discourse that defines common ends and common means.

Given the social self, the modern community serves a vital purpose. The contemporary community may be understood as the sphere of social life that protects and nourishes the liberties and goods provided by modernity and the sphere that cultivates meaningful social connections over and above those conditioned by the market. It fosters self-identity, sometimes even an identity based on rebellion. Almost paradoxically, it is in the context of community that individuality is manifest. Indeed, we draw heavily upon our surroundings for an understanding of ourselves. Modernity can be a blessing and a curse. We can shed identities that conflict with deeper intuitions about ourselves, but in the absence of strong community, we continually risk substitution with prepackaged, emotionally limiting alternatives presented to us through the media of mass society. Community provides more than free agents; it cultivates morally competent, emotionally engaged selves able to pursue their own interests and those we share in common.

Modern Justice and the Social Self

If a major purpose of community is providing collective goods (goods that could not be produced by individuals working alone), and one of these goods is the security and freedom to pursue one's selfhood, then we can never escape the tension between the requirements of ensuring social order and the press to free oneself from conventional expectations. The criminal justice process is, today, the main structure to which we look for social order, for the security of our neighborhoods. The modern criminal justice process is an adversarial bureaucracy housed in a tradition of liberal political theory. It is adversarial in that it pits the accused citizen against an accusing state; it is bureaucratic by virtue of its internal specialization and external isolation. Liberal, adversarial justice seeks to respect freedom by providing citizens certain rights, while it pursues security by procedures of accusation and sanction.

Liberalism, it is said, provides a just procedural framework for the preservation of liberties and the diminution of social inequalities (Rawls 1971). This procedural framework is especially necessary because of the inherent imbalance of power between the state and the individual. Were the state to exercise full control, the machinery of social control would quickly overwhelm the fragile ecology of autonomous self-development. Liberalism fosters the preconditions for self-realization through the protection of constitutional rights. Liberalism itself is predicated on a doctrine of individualism that upholds "a belief in the inherent dignity and, indeed, sacredness of the human person . . . [and] a belief that the individual has a primary reality whereas society is a second-order, derived or artificial construct" (Bellah et al. 1985, p. 334). Thus, liberalism offsets the power of the state by prioritizing the individual, emphasizing rights protection and individual autonomy.

Community justice cannot be based upon a rejection of liberalism—a reversal of priorities in which the individual ought to be "sacrificed at the altar of the public good." Instead, liberalism—as it respects the rights of citizens for self-determination—is foundational. The doctrine is an ethical minimum upon which a richer understanding of the reciprocal obligations between self and society can be articulated.

Our critique of liberalism is that in its emphasis on autonomy, it embraces an adversarial model of justice. This model assumes that free individuals pursue their own interests, often clashing with the interests of others and of the collectivity. Such conflicts must be mediated through rational discourse and a freedom to reach agreements of mutual advantage. Although we share liberalism's concern for the protection of rights, we believe a community justice model must treat self-development not as an autonomous or competitive process in which the claims of one are only achieved at the expense of another, but as a process embedded within a system of community relationships. Let us elaborate.

As we have argued, the citizen of the modern state faces the threat of alienation, a kind of fragmentation of the social self. A bureaucratic, adversarial system of justice is not a remedy to this problem, nor was it designed to be. The idea of individual rights was invented to neutralize the awesome power of the sovereign and to provide citizens with tools for sustaining their individual interests in the face of enormous community pressures for conformity to norms. Modern citizens experience less pressure toward conformity, have expanded personal choices, and face an impersonal state instead of a personal sovereign. Traditional liberal versions of the criminal law protect important personal rights; but adversarial bureaucracy does little to connect citizens to their communities, nor does it promote the expression of the self as a member of the community. It is ironic that a most common result of the bureaucratic adversarial process is the separation of the citizen-offender from the community. We need to redefine the liberal idea of rights within a stronger conceptualization of community.

Carol Gilligan's (1982) insightful critique of a liberal justice model sharply draws the distinction between this model and a community justice model. In her account, two sixth-graders, Jake and Amy, puzzled over a moral dilemma. Both offered sophisticated but quite different resolutions. In the dilemma, it was asked whether a man named Heinz should steal (because he could not afford it) a drug to save the life of his wife. Jake believed he should, for in a contest of rights, life took precedence over property. Even though it was a crime, the act was legitimated by the purpose. Amy, however, was more ambivalent about the theft. Instead, she viewed the problem not as a conflict of interests (Heinz's interest in saving his wife versus the pharmacist's economic interest) but as a breakdown in community relationships. If the bonds were stronger between Heinz and the pharmacist, the relationship would not be based simply on the prospect of economic transaction but also on the moral obligations of community members to assist one another in times of need. This view of community connections does not diminish the dignity or sacredness of individuals. Instead it provides a richer context for self-development than the adversarial model.

The modern community is vacuous without additional moral claims beyond those provided by liberalism. In short, community justice is guided by several moral and social ideals that extend the framework of liberalism. Community justice seeks to incorporate critical community ideals into the justice process. The aim is not a justice that enables the separation of the community and the offender but a justice that seeks to advance the interests of community life. Three community ideals stand out: strengthening social ties; reconciling order and autonomy; and promoting the common good through voluntary cooperation.

Strengthening Social Ties

The challenge for contemporary community is to preserve the achievements of modernity while actively responding to its liabilities. Support of community need not involve rejection of reason, science, rights, or individual autonomy. Individuals can look to community for the transmission of wisdom; for a sense of belonging; for exchange relations based on reciprocity, commitment, and cooperation; for collective responsiveness to individual needs; and ultimately, for self-definition and realization. Support of community likewise implies no denial of the functional interdependence of individuals. Instead, it implies a recognition of the exchange relations that result in use and misuse of power; the systemic coordination of the market; and the rationalization associated with bureaucracy. It acknowledges individuals' strong motivation to strategically enhance their own social and economic outcomes. Interdependence and the need for exchange are the basis of society. Nevertheless, community life is more than instrumental. The goal is not, as rational choice theorists would have it, to identify mechanisms of cooperation and coordination that are congruent with immediate self-interest (e.g., Hechter 1987; Yamagishi 1994) but to cultivate voluntary cooperation based on shared goals and a concern both for oneself and for other members of the community. In Selznick's words: "As we move to association, and from association to community, mutuality reaches beyond exchange to create more enduring bonds of interdependence, caring, and commitment. There is a transition, we may say, from reciprocity to solidarity, and from there to fellowship" (Selznick 1992, p. 362).

The community ideal stresses the importance of intimate, supportive relationships. Without doubt, modernity requires innumerable contacts based purely on exchange, and these will lack emotional ties or extended concern; but this fact only heightens the need for conscious efforts to counteract the broad tendency. Efforts to build community are fueled by the hope that more relationships can be founded on the basis of trust and honest communication; that there can be greater recognition of members' intrinsic worth and depth as well as of their need for personal development, security, and sense of belonging; and that obligations can be seen in the context of an ongoing, long-term commitment rather than as an immediate quid pro quo.

Reconciling Order and Autonomy

Protecting individual rights while promoting the common good is tricky business. Some would say that the two tendencies conflict and must be "balanced" against each other; too much of either is a bad thing.[1] We believe that order and autonomy can coexist but that they operate on different (albeit intersecting) planes: One can have autonomy in a well-ordered environment. Order and autonomy interact in a particular way—autonomy is made feasible by a foundation of order. When order and autonomy are seen as incompatible, the stage is set for authoritarian controls. Yet everyone would agree that order and autonomy coexist in a state of tension and do sometimes conflict. How are they to be reconciled?

Liberalism's weakness is its inability to attend to the collective consequences of autonomous individual action. The maximization of individual self-interest is felt each time a father refuses to pay child-support, a commuter chooses to drive alone instead of using mass transit, a corporate actor illegally dumps hazardous waste, a voter fails to support a school levy, a taxpayer knowingly takes a few too many deductions, and a neighbor ignores the call to join a crime-watch campaign. The experience of repeated failures to provide collective goods may cause community members to choose authoritarian approaches in order to obtain these goods. Indeed, free-rider behavior may be the greatest threat to liberalism, for its pervasiveness undermines the credibility and effectiveness of a free society. Community justice is a response to our modern experience with liberalism, which has led us to the discovery that autonomy can threaten community quality of life.

The community ideal, however, is not to promote the common good such that individual rights are dismissed. Order is not valued over individual autonomy. Instead the two must be reconciled. Autonomy is supported not by liberty alone but by investment into the institutions that protect autonomy and foster self-development. Alternatively, order is empty without its sincere legitimation by community members. If order undermines personal autonomy, then its value is dubious.

Thus we would urge the following formulation of the relationship between order and autonomy in a community: Expressions of autonomy that eradicate order cannot be permitted; likewise, requirements of order that deny the value of autonomy cannot be tolerated. When there are conflicts between the two, we would not adopt a compromise position giving temporary priority, or redress, to one or the other according to the particular set of circumstances; rather, we would attempt to find a "third

---

[1]"This line of argument suggests that it is as wrong to make a fetish of solidarity as it is to glorify unconditional independence. Each in its own way corrodes community. The first, in reaching for total integration, turns community into a parody of itself. The second offers an ethos too thin to sustain more than a minimal moral order. A genuinely communitarian doctrine—one rooted in the experience of common life—resists both extremes. It seeks theories and strategies that promise stable accommodation and conjoint fulfillment of all the values entailed by the ideal community" (Selznick 1992, p. 370).

way"—a solution that recognizes the collective needs of social order even as it acknowledges our shared interest in each person's fullest autonomy.[2] We would make creative problem solving our goal instead of "balance." If we attempt instead to solve the conflict between order and autonomy by asserting one over the other, our solution to the problem will only create more problems.

Individuals need the freedom to develop their own understandings and their own moral commitments. This occurs only as individuals become creative, empathetic, reasoning, and assertive social actors. Ordinary social life is built upon day-to-day challenges. As individuals confront personal obstacles, they must select from among an array of responses that have consequences for themselves and for others. To choose effectively—in a way that provides benefits—individuals must be more than obedient automatons or reckless egoists; they must be sensitive persons of integrity and forethought. However, such a project in human development cannot take place if the individual is persistently threatened by either a coercive social conformity or a dangerously chaotic and unpredictable social environment where concern for survival rules the day. Thus, community life must be measured both by its ability "to pull in members' commitments, energies, time, and resources for what the community as a collectivity endorses as its notion of the common good" (Etzioni 1996a, p. 5) and by the "contribution it makes to the flourishing of unique and responsible persons" (Selznick 1992, p. 363).

Voluntary Cooperation

A community approach is clearly distinguishable from an economic approach that relies on market mechanisms to provide for the common good and from an authoritarian approach that relies on the coercive power of the state to ensure individual compliance with collective agendas (Sullivan and Karp 1997). In criminal justice, the contrasting approaches are particularly distinct. For authoritarians, reducing crime means ratcheting up coercive deterrence: more surveillance, more arrests, more convictions, more sentences. Reducing crime by the market approach is guided by the equation of self-interest with collective interests. This would include policy initiatives that make obedience to the law more attractive, either by defining deviance down (e.g., by legalizing so-called victimless crimes) or by increasing incentives to play by the rules. The latter might range from superficial, temporary measures—such as gun buy-back programs—to more significant, long-lasting

---

[2]In such a proposal, the devil is in the details, we know. In the next chapter, we illustrate what is possible in our descriptions of a "third way" to approach community justice.

steps—such as economic investment in disadvantaged communities. In contrast, a community-oriented approach recognizes that obedience to the law is motivated by much more than economic self-interest or fear of sanctions. Laws are followed largely because they have moral stature: Citizens believe in the validity of the laws and in the legitimacy of legislation and law-enforcement generally. Community justice differs from other approaches also in that it is predicated on the possibility of moral self-transcendence.

The community ideal rejects a choice between the lesser of two evils: either a social order based on the desperate need for security in the face of hostile social motivations or one based on the benign (and groundless) assumption that the aggregate pursuit of self-interest will effectively provide for the general welfare. The community ideal instead is based on the belief that community members will voluntarily contribute to the common good without fear of sanctions and in spite of the free-rider temptation. Such voluntarism is grounded in the capacity of individuals to develop and exercise moral competence, in the same sense that Rawls (1971) has thought moral sentiment a human virtue.

Social order is fragile and complex. It cannot be understood purely in market terms, authoritarian terms, or even normative terms (Wrong 1994).[3] We acknowledge the essential realities of market and state, egoism and coercion. Cooperation, however, is a moral endeavor to be cultivated in the face of economic rationality and in the absence of authoritarian control. Reliance on the market is too likely to result in excessive individualism, disposing "each member of the community to sever himself from the mass" (Tocqueville 1945, p. 104). This outcome, based on the desire for autonomy, is likely to backfire as market failures cause increased competition for scarce goods, more mistrust and withdrawal from cooperative endeavors, and more crime and deviance. Where the market fails, the community provides an alternative to state coercion.

The community ideal emphasizes a moral order that is dependent not on rational actors or fearful conformists but on committed agents capable of understanding the consequences of their actions for others and trusting that others will also see the benefits of collective action. These agents are

---

[3]"Hobbes's solution was coercive, Locke's stressed mutual self-interest, and the Rousseau of *The Social Contract* gave primacy to normative consensus. Precisely because there is no justification for assuming that one solution precludes or subsumes the others, but that on the contrary all three may operate conjointly in concrete human societies, it is important not to identify the problem of order with any of its proposed solutions. If the characteristic error of sociologists, most notably of Durkheim and Parsons, has been to overemphasize consensus on norms and values as the solution, the Machiavellian-Hobbesian tradition in political thought has tended to exaggerate the role of force, and economists, including Marx, have notoriously overstressed economic interest" (Wrong 1994, p. 9).

not driven to cooperative coalitions solely because of mutual advantage. Mancur Olson (1965) compellingly argued that such coalitions cannot be sustained because rational actors would rather leave the hard work of coalition building to others. Nor would they be driven to coalitions on the basis of individual claims to entitlements denied coincidentally to other potential coalition members. Such "rights talk" only extends the rational actor model to a higher unit of analysis without solving the essential problem of manifesting a collective will to provide for the common good (Glendon 1991). Such coalitions become surrogates for their individual members' private interests, failing to take into account the consequences of their subgroup's claims for the whole of society.

Voluntary cooperation means above all the cultivation of socially astute, "emotionally intelligent" community members who are as deeply concerned with the life of community as they are with their own lives. Community concern is a moral ideal grounded in the experiences and attachments of individuals to one another over time. In the words of Alan Wolfe:

> Cognizance of space and time is at the heart of moral maturity. When we sacrifice for the sake of future generations or take into consideration the viewpoints of spatially situated others, we consider our obligations to our moral selves to be superior to any monetary or political advantage that might come from taking an easier option. (Wolfe 1989, p. 217)

Families, friends, neighbors, and co-organizers of communal endeavors are valued as members of one's community, and therefore the necessity of cooperation with them is experienced as self-evident or natural rather than as dreaded or imposed. The ideal is a community of individuals who are free to choose and who choose wisely: sometimes taking care of themselves as need be, sometimes taking care of others, always considering the collective consequences of their choices.

Taken together, strengthening social ties, balancing order and autonomy, and cultivating voluntary cooperation are primary ideals of a community model. They serve as philosophical benchmarks against which policy initiatives and programs can be evaluated. In our view, the criminal justice system often conflicts with these ideals. Where the ties between the community, victims, and offenders are weakest, the adversarial model severs and isolates. When criminal justice becomes "crime control" and "crime fighting," aggressive and sometimes brutal tactics shatter a normative order based on institutional legitimacy and individual dignity. If community members are not offered the responsibilities incumbent upon citizens in a democracy to consider and support the general welfare, then their pursuits will be increasingly narrow and self-interested; the spirit of voluntarism will dissipate. Where there is no voluntarism, we are left with the choice of disorder or coercion.

Community Mechanisms

Three basic community ideals and the mechanisms by which they can be realized are summarized in Box 3.1. First, community institutions play a central role in socializing individuals into the norms of the community and in protecting individuals from both alienation and domination. Second, socialization and informal social control cultivate individuals' conformity to moral standards through intrapsychic nudges to transcend the individual self and through interpersonal influences. Third, democratic participation provides a vital form of social engagement that ensures that individuals will have a voice and that they will remain loyal to their community, as they define it.

In Chapter 4 we describe the principles of a democratic community justice approach that relies heavily on the three mechanisms described below. Here we explore each of these mechanisms in turn, in order to lay a firm groundwork for the approaches we advocate in succeeding chapters.

Community Institutions

Institutions are the basic building blocks of community. Community institutions are partially captured by the concept of civil society: the myriad social systems that exist between the market and the state. They include families, schools, churches, civic associations, nonprofit organizations, and other mediating entities that give individuals a concrete experience of cohesive social life. But in an important way, the institutional framework is more broadly conceived than as an organizational typology or as contrasted with the market and the state. Institutions function as normative constructs and as conceptual frameworks that orient individuals to their place in the larger social order. In this sense, institutions are inclusive of economic and political processes and systems. The conceptual framework does more than provide concrete social experience; it offers a sense of place and direction—in short, a sense of community.

Institutions are vital to individuals because they are an opportunity structure. Families and schools are crucial to children's development; and neighborhoods and their local organizations create social networks that provide guidance, employment, recreation, and spiritual development. Institutions not only provide opportunity but also frame aspirations and expectations. Bad cops, corrupt politicians, abusive parents, and indifferent teachers are striking because they stand in defiance to the cultural standards that are so closely associated with these institutional roles.

Institutions form individuals by making possible or impossible certain ways of behaving and relating to others. They shape character by assigning re-

---

BOX 3.1   Community Ideals and Mechanisms

Community ideals include

- strengthening social ties
- reconciling order and autonomy
- voluntary cooperation

Community mechanisms include

- community institutions
- socialization and informal social control
- civic participation

---

sponsibility, demanding accountability, and providing the standards in terms of which each person recognizes the excellence of his or her achievements. Each individual's possibilities depend on the opportunities opened up within the institutional contexts to which that person has access. (Bellah et al. 1991, p. 40)

Thus, institutions have both instrumental and normative components.

Modernity tends to widen the gap between individual and society; community institutions serve to fill it. Perhaps most important is their vital function of orienting isolated individuals toward collective agendas. Parents plan for their children's higher education; teachers shape character and teach the art of cooperation; neighborhood groups form a citizen patrol; and political organizations lobby for services to crime victims, drug addicts, or offenders on parole. Whereas individuals have a tendency to drift toward autonomous endeavor, community institutions remind us of the needs of the collectivity.

Socialization and Informal Social Control

A democratic society depends on processes of socialization (and resocialization) of individuals into the values of the community in order to minimize selfish disregard of others and to avoid coercive measures to maintain order and conformity. Normative influence is a powerful tool because it can effectively regulate social behavior and because it does so by cultivating reasoned understandings of common purposes and voluntary commitments to fulfill these ends. And because there is a difference between knowing what is best for the community and doing what is best, a good society is one that fosters a web of controls based primarily on members' legitimation of the forms of control and the values that underlie them.

Socialization is a process of transmitting normative standards—for example, not stealing and not raping, supporting your children and paying taxes—so that members of the community internalize these standards and external supervision is not necessary for compliance. Internalization refers to individuals' motivation to comply with a moral injunction because they agree with the rightness of its intent. Regardless of other forces that might motivate them not to comply, their internal conviction of the moral rectitude of the injunction (their conscience) will not permit them to disobey. A person who has fully internalized the social norm will refrain from stealing simply because he or she believes it is wrong to do so, not because the action is seen as strategically disadvantageous or because of a fear of getting caught. However, although internalized values may account for much self-transcendent behavior (Schwartz 1992), conscience cannot be relied upon completely. It must continuously be supplemented by normative pressure to conform. Etzioni (1996b, pp. 120, 124, italics added) describes this normative pressure as a moral voice.

> The moral voice is a peculiar form of motivation: *It encourages people to adhere to values to which they subscribe.* . . . The moral voice is often ignored by casual observers (and, to some extent, by social scientists) because it is informal, subtle, and highly incorporated into daily life. It often works through frowns, gentle snide comments (and some that are not so gentle), praise, censure, and approbation.

The emphasis on the pressure to conform to values *already endorsed* is essential for distinguishing the moral voice from coercion. The moral voice appeals to internalized values that might not withstand internal and external counterpressures for transgression.

The foundation for socialization and informal control is the deep emotional and material interdependence of community members on one another. By engaging in ongoing relationships, we come to depend on and expect others to behave in regular and predictable ways. Normative order is grounded in long-term relations and the practical experience of conduct. Dennis Wrong (1994, pp. 43–44) argues that our expressed expectations of others' conduct

> may be regarded less as threats than as efforts at what Parsons called the "activation of commitments," that is, as moral appeals or exhortations. . . . The crucial point is that the stated expectation is not a mere prediction of occurrences that are seen as bound to take place in any event but an intentional effort to *make happen* or bring about certain behavior by other persons, as a result of influencing their minds and wills. . . . I have chosen to stress a certain ambiguity in the use of the term "expectation," not primarily in order to call

attention to power relations among persons, but rather to bring out the much more general circumstance that awareness of the expectations of others in itself may provide those expectations with a normative aura, may serve to endow them with an imperative character that constrains the Actor who is conscious of them to fulfill or conform to them. . . . The rule of expectations in this broad sense is basic to the achievement of social order.

In this account, the moral voice is a communication of expectations to conform to a set of socially constructed behavioral norms. The "normative aura" and "moral exhortation" reflect the way in which values are internalized through a type of socialization that is not based on coercion or threat. Granted, on some level, it is difficult to distinguish coercive and noncoercive elements. Indeed, the power of informal control is not simply found in reawakening or making salient an internalized value. There is also a threat of status loss (Karp 1998b). To the extent that individuals are dependent upon others, it is a concrete risk to violate a social norm—stigmatization and exclusion are real costs and help explain why the moral voice is influential. When informal social control is activated for those who reject the moral injunction in principle—for example, when anti-abortion protesters personally target women seeking abortion services—then it is clearly coercive. The point is that informal control primarily operates as a mechanism for maintaining moral and social order by reaffirming accepted values of the community. It depends upon a motivation to conform that is based neither in egoism or fearful conformity. Instead it is based on processes of socialization and moral development grounded in day-to-day relationships, emotional attachments, and moral concern for the welfare of others.

Civic Participation

Community institutions, socialization, and informal social control orient individuals toward the needs of the community. They also provide the means for cultivating social responsibility and for holding individuals accountable. A third mechanism for achieving community ideals is particularly necessary for guaranteeing that the needs of the community are reconciled with individuals' need for autonomy. In an interdependent community, individuals cannot justify a pursuit of their own interests without regard to collective consequences, because autonomous action, particularly in the aggregate, has direct effects on the lives of others. Thus the autonomy of one necessarily impinges on the autonomy of others. The only recourse toward reconciling the conflicting needs for autonomy and for order is through the democratic participation of individuals who are free to assert their needs, concerns, and desires in a forum that encourages reflection of the consequences of various practices for the community.

Civic participation is not merely an ideal but an instrument for articulating, amending, and endorsing communal values and priorities. Democracy is predicated upon "the idea of a self-governing community of citizens who are united less by homogeneous interests than by civil education and who are capable of common purpose and mutual action by virtue of their civic attitudes and participatory institutions rather than their altruism or their good nature" (Barber 1984, p. 117). The mechanism is a vibrant, robust local governance process in which citizens determine local priorities, establish the future allocation of resources, and plan for the development of the communities in which they live. It is not abdication of responsibility through elected representation; rather, it is the fulfillment of civic responsibility to participate in the continual process of citizenship.

Communities and their shared values are not static entities. They are created and recreated in the processes of members' sharing their values and testing one another's views by disagreement—a process that leads to the continual transformation of views and ideas. Civic participation is a safe forum for civil discourse, a forum that challenges participants to advance their conceptions of the good (Gutmann and Thompson 1996). Citizens participate not merely by voting but also by attending, considering, and speaking. The main purpose of civic participation is to disseminate information and ideas, based on the assumption that people are capable of self-reflection and intelligent adjudication of their individual and collective interests if they are supplied with complete information.

The Adversarial Model and Community Ideals

The status quo in the criminal justice system militates against the ideals of community life. In numerous ways it weakens rather than strengthens community ties, poorly adjudicates conflicts between rights and order, and undermines voluntarism. The adversarial bureaucracy bases itself on a subtle tautology. It claims that the very existence of the law provides sufficient reason for citizens voluntarily to obey it. When citizens fail to do so, the common assumption today seems to be that because voluntary means have failed, greater coercion is required. In a community justice perspective, however, obedience to the law is perceived as deriving from a complex set of social and personal factors. In turn, the violation of the law, far from calling for an immediate response of coercion, requires us to consider which social and personal factors are working toward the commission of the crime. It seems facile to assume that the law, even backed by the threat of coercion, is a sufficient instrument to guarantee public safety or quality of community life. Indeed, it seems obvious to us that the competence of the current model of social control must be questioned because of the pervasiveness of crime.

In the previous chapter, we argued that overreliance on incarceration has community-level consequences. Strategies of temporary removal backfire when offenders return from prison with fewer legitimate social ties and an expanded network of criminal ties. Family disruption, a leading cause of delinquency, is fueled by our inability to reintegrate offenders. With our attention on punishment as the sole criterion of justice, we have also failed crime victims. Justice for them is not merely retribution but restitution, restoration, and healing. And these latter three goods are rarely supplied by the criminal justice system. Victims' ties to the community are weakened by the criminal incident. Not only do many victims experience increased fear and respond by withdrawing from community life, but they also often experience "secondary victimization" in which others fail to offer support and even blame them for their misfortune. Therefore, the first priority of a community justice model must be to identify strategies that will strengthen the ties between community members. This entails a shift in orientation: Crime must be understood foremost as a community event rather than as an act against the state.

We do not underestimate the importance of this statement. Crime and justice have been seen as the domain of prosecutors and judges, and punishment, as the domain of wardens. But this approach concentrates the profoundly important safety interests of the community in the hands of people who have no particular interest in community life other than that dictated by their circumscribed function as agents of formal social control. To make crime a community problem (or rather, a problem of community) instead of a state problem is to place the citizenry at center stage. The community then will be transformed from a vague idea that may or may not be in the minds of officials to a crucial participant in the endeavor.

We recognize that this formulation of the problem shifts the meaning of rights and of autonomy. When rights and order are viewed as antagonistic, the criminal justice system responds to the needs of each in contradictory and inconsistent ways. We debate the relative importance of rights and order when our desire to hold offenders accountable is offset by the need to try cases consistently and fairly; but such procedural fairness can cause a case to be dismissed on "technicalities," although ample evidence exists that a defendant was guilty. The debate occurs when we discover the vast majority of tenants in a public housing complex seek—even demand—gun sweeps by police but such procedures are disallowed by the courts. It is debated when reports surface on the use of unscientific "profiling" by police, typically by race, subjecting many innocent citizens to an arbitrary and often hostile police authority. We see this public debate also in controversies over the legitimacy of arresting people for standing together on a street corner; giving sixth- or seventh-graders drug tests; seizing the property of suspected (not convicted) drug dealers or evicting them from their residences; and using anonymous tips as evidence in courts.

We have a tendency to take these problems on a case-by-case basis without developing a broader understanding of rights and order, an understanding that a person's dignity is eroded by crime and by excessive use of state power. A community approach is not a compromise between authoritarian order and a rights-oriented disorder. It is an argument that order is found through community action and social integration, and that rights are protected by nurturing the conditions in which individuals can develop their own identities and interests as well as their own capacities for voluntaristic commitment.

The criminal justice system is built on the professional administration of justice, providing few avenues for citizen participation and usurping community-level opportunities for the exercise of informal social control. Lawyers speak for their clients; the true stakeholders are excluded from the process. Defendants are expected to deny culpability, victims are expected to be tough and not to forgive, community residents are expected to be the "eyes and ears" of the police but not to resolve their own conflicts. A community justice model reverses these expectations, vastly increasing the roles and responsibilities of victims, offenders, and other members of the community in the pursuit of public safety and justice.

Conclusion

Community in contemporary society is sometimes thought to be a lost cause, a useless nostalgia for an era long gone and best forgotten. Sometimes it is thought to be alive and well, continuously and spontaneously re-created despite the structural and doctrinal metaforces that undermine it. And sometimes it is thought to exist in completely new forms as a result of modern advances in communications and transportation. In this view, community is a reference not only to place but to myriad social ties that can be sustained over great distances. Thus community is sometimes thought of as lost, saved, or liberated (Wellman and Leighton 1979). A call for community justice is not predicated on a wish to resurrect the community ideal of a bygone era or to focus special law-enforcement efforts on a particular locale or group of people. It is aimed at identifying and revalidating the unique contributions of community to all of social life, including the creation and maintenance of justice.

Those who adopt a community perspective aspire to a community life that is rich enough to accommodate both the interests of individuals in their self-determination and the demands of a social existence in which individuals must cooperate with others to ensure social order, institutional vitality, and the production of collective goods. The formation of community, the provision of collective goods, the protection of rights, the innovations of social change, and the accountability to social norms all involve moral decisions, for they require considerations of collective consequences. Grounded in this perspective, in the next two chapters we develop principles of community justice that address the dual concerns of crime prevention and the achievement of justice for offenders, victims, and communities. Following these principles will enable us to strengthen community institutions, enhance socialization and informal social control, and identify new mechanisms for citizen participation in the criminal justice system.

4

Principles of
a Democratic
Community Justice

Criminal justice is confronted by two paradoxes. First, as discussed in Chapter 2, both crime and crime fighting carry the potential to damage community life. The second paradox, discussed in Chapter 3, is that conflicts exist between the tradition of individual rights upheld in the criminal law and the pursuit of community life in postindustrial society.

These paradoxes pose a challenge for criminal justice policy. Aggressive attempts to police communities using external enforcement resources may result in temporary alleviation of criminal events by removing the most criminally active citizens. However, when practiced to the extreme, this strategy disregards and damages the very resources the community needs in order to sustain its life. By the same token, an individual rights strategy for understanding citizenship inevitably intensifies the conflicting interests between the citizen and the community in which the citizen lives.

We see evidence of these two paradoxes in today's crime and justice. Communities beset by crime call out for more effective criminal justice, at the same time as many members of those communities harbor a deep distrust of the aims and benefits of coercive government action. Meanwhile, the "rights" of criminals are increasingly seen as destructive of ordinary community life, even though in objective terms the exercise of civil rights is rarely a good explanation of specific criminal events and is a poor predictor of broad offending trends.

In this chapter, we propose an alternative approach to criminal justice based on the ideal of social justice as defined by community life. We call this model *community justice*. The community justice model begins with a reconsideration of the social meaning of criminal events. Based on that reconsideration, new responsibilities and interests of the participants in criminal events can be defined. Finally, a broader aim of community justice can be described, based on the new vision of the social significance of criminal behavior. This alternative holds the promise of finding a way out of the bitter cycle of twenty years of increasing criminal justice in the absence of social justice.

This chapter does not provide a detailed description of a new system of justice. We do discuss some pragmatic aspects of such a system in Chapter 6 and profile particular programs in Chapter 7. Yet the reader should bear in mind that the approach advocated here calls for flexibility in application from one locality to the next, and thus a detailed description with uniform meaning will not be possible. The purpose here is to outline and justify the conceptual elements of a community justice response to criminal incidents. In the next chapter, we will develop principles of community justice for crime prevention, particularly in neighborhoods with high crime rates.

Crime: The Shattering of Community

In practical terms, crime is simply a violation of written penal law. But another way of viewing a criminal event is to see how it symbolizes the social and moral relationships of the various parties to it. In this discussion, we borrow liberally from an analysis by Jeffrie Murphy and Jeanne Hampton (1988). Their discussion draws heavily on Kant and Durkheim, recognizing that at the same time that all laws have multiple justifications, a frequent justification is that a given law exists to promote fair and legitimate social relations among those living under the law. Laws define the formal boundaries of social relations and are based in the moral content of social relations (see also Cragg 1992; Hart 1963).

When an offender violates the law, the act represents a symbolic claim that the offender has no obligation to observe fairness in social relations. The offender claims, instead, the right to use others' observance of the law to unfair social advantage. Others exist for the offender's personal pleasure; therefore, the offender has the right to abuse others' rights to property or person and to disregard their prerogatives. In short, offenders are making a social claim that they have no communal obligations, and they are forcing other community members to associate with them at their own peril. That claim is imprinted upon the person of the victim and made public by the existence of third-party onlookers.

Crime victims suffer losses that are both real and abstract. The real losses involve damage to property or self that results from crime. The abstract loss is less tangible, if no less painful: a certain loss of status as a community member who may expect to be protected by the fairness and legitimacy of commonly applicable law. Having been badly used by the offender, the victim suffers from a kind of public, moral ambiguity. Are victims worth the same consideration as any other community member or do they deserve less protection of their rights to fairness and legitimacy?

Onlookers are related to the criminal event by association or observation. They might have witnessed the crime, or they might be tied to the victim or offender by acquaintance, friendship, or kinship. Onlookers might also be connected to the event less directly, by virtue of their stake in the neighborhood. The onlooker is the citizen who faces a criminal event as a moral challenge. An associate—a fellow citizen—has claimed the "right" to injure other community members. The person on the perimeter of this event must take a stand. Shall this claim by one fellow citizen to exploit another be allowed to stand? The actions of the onlooking community member symbolize the fairness upon which the law is based.

Seen in this light, the criminal act is both a practical and a symbolic denial of community. It breaks trust between citizens and sets up a predicament in which community members must determine how to contradict the moral message of the crime: that the offender is above the law and the victim beneath its reach. In this sense, the criminal incident invokes the moral agency of the social self. This is a profoundly social view of crime. It exposes the way in which crime is not merely a challenge to *safety* in the community; it is a challenge to the very essence of community life. Yet the *response* to crime is also a challenge to community life. If a crime serves to question the rules under which social interaction progresses, what community members do about these instances defines the relationship between any community and all potential offenders within it. In this sense, to the extent that community life relies upon a shared sense of fairness and interdependence, a criminal event shatters the foundation of community. A crime is a social act that is acutely moral in content. The crime challenges the moral basis of community life, in which all members may expect to live under stated, accepted behavioral limits. How the members of a community respond to this moral challenge will define what it means to be one of the community's members and will contain instruction for members as they choose future action.

This view of crime and responses to crime reveals why the bureaucratic response of the state as community proprietor is so dissatisfying. By taking the role of final arbiter, the state unintentionally denies the victim's need to be affirmed and isolates community members from the conflict between the offender and the victim. The state may do so with the claim of representing the community's interest or the victim's claim, but this representation is abstract and attenuated by politics and bureaucracy. Institutions of the state act, instead, to affirm the state's hierarchical place in authority over disputes, and thus these disputes are transformed from social events in community life to legal events in political life.

A community justice approach to the law not only de-emphasizes the bureaucratic state as dispenser of coercive criminal justice but also revises the adversarial view of criminal accusation. The state would have the crime problem defined as one between those who break the law and those who enforce the law. The victims' movement alters that formulation to one in which the dispute is between accused and accuser, with one or the other to emerge as winner. Neither formulation has much room for community interests. Yet the onlookers are closely tied to offenders and victims alike; they are people who have pasts and futures that correspond to the needs and experiences of both parties.

The link between the onlookers' interests and those of the victim or offender in a criminal dispute has several dimensions. The most basic is that the onlooker might someday be an offender or a victim in a criminal event and therefore has a deep-seated interest in the management of such disputes. The onlooker will also be obliged to live with the victim and (ordinarily) the offender after the dispute is resolved. Onlookers also take cues from the dispute's resolution—not only in assessing their own safety in the community but also in understanding the nature of social discourse and cooperation. The process is a mechanism for norm formation that dictates onlookers' expectations about one another's behavior.

The void in contemporary criminal law is that there is no room for the community to become a responsible player in responding to the crime. Because the adversarial model posits a contest, the model shifts only slightly when victims come into the picture, becoming a contest between the rights of one community member against those of another. The community is left to assume that its values, interests, and solutions will be reflected in the resolution of the contest between whichever parties are allowed at the table. If public opinion about crime is any indicator that the community is well served, then the public has its doubts.

This discussion of the communal relevance of criminal incidents and their response can be summarized as follows:

- A crime symbolizes a claim by one citizen that he or she may use, to selfish advantage, the person or property of another in violation of accepted legal prescriptions for conduct.
- Criminal events challenge community life by shattering the shared moral structure that supports community members' interdependence; thus citizens dispute the claim implicit in an offender's conduct.
- The parties to a criminal event include victim, offender, onlookers, and the state; each has an interest in the management and outcome of the criminal dispute.

- In U.S. jurisprudence, the state has usurped the role of the on-looker, and has robbed the community of its place in the criminal dispute.

This analysis suggests that however important, the proving of guilt or innocence is but an interim outcome for community justice. The larger outcome is a restoration of the social foundation for interpersonal conduct. The crime has shattered the community's confidence in members' rights and duties; justice is made possible when steps are taken to help members recover their confidence.

Recovering Community

The ideal of community justice is that the community recover from the physical and symbolic damage of crime. This ideal includes recovery for everyone affected by the crime. Recovery begins with the recognition that the criminal act that tears the fabric of community is at the same time both a product of community and an impediment to be overcome, if community is to be reclaimed.

Crime is a product of community for reasons that should be obvious but too often are forgotten. Criminal behavior is deeply rooted in social processes occurring at two levels, both of which are community-based. First, criminal behavior is housed in community structures such as inequality, neighborhood stability, wealth, and opportunity. These social forces are ever-present correlates of criminality, and the ubiquity of their influence on crime reminds us that the character of a locality's quality of life is interconnected with its level of criminality.

Second, crime is a product of an individual's experiences and choices as bounded by social contexts. Children who are raised abusively, who struggle in schools and family circles, and who act out psychological stresses will more frequently grow up as offenders (Widom 1994). Communities that provide ameliorative supports for children who have these experiences will reduce the predominance of the crime that results from them. There is certainly an interplay between structural contexts and moral decision making. Some neighborhoods are destined to produce oppositional subcultures that reject values of respect for others and conventional pathways to success.

That the existence of crime is an impediment for communities to overcome is axiomatic to literature on community. What would a process look like that successfully overcomes the impediment of crime? The answer lies in a recognition that the community justice ideal is far more than the blaming and sanctioning process suggested by a model of adversaries. Instead, a justice model in which community is restored envisions a problem-solving process in which the parties to the criminal dispute have certain tasks derived from their relationship to the criminal event and its claims upon the disputants.[1] These tasks are outlined below.

The Tasks of Parties to Criminal Incidents

We have described crime as a challenge to (and a breaking of) the cohesion of community life. Responding to that challenge (repairing the breakage) is the responsibility of all parties to the criminal dispute. Understanding their roles in resolving the dispute is the first step in defining the ideal of community justice. We begin by redefining the purposes of the criminal justice process as fact finding, problem solving, and sanctioning. Each of the parties to a criminal event has specific responsibilities in establishing facts and determining sanctions. Each party's role connotes a set of tasks that must be performed.

These tasks can be roughly classified by three overarching principles of a democratic community justice process.[2] First, since a criminal incident violates the normative and legal standards of the community, it is important to reaffirm the relevance and importance of these standards to the community. Second, the criminal incident causes measurable harm to victims and the community; justice requires their restoration. Third, the criminal incident is a warning sign of possible future transgression by the offender or others. A just response must address the need for public safety. Table 4.1 summarizes the tasks of the key parties: offenders, victims, onlookers, and community institutions. After describing these tasks below, we turn to the role of the criminal justice system, which serves as a support to the key parties.

The Tasks of the Offender

The offender's conduct has been a moral and social offense against the community. The behavior raises questions about the offender's willingness to live within the community according to its prescribed conduct rules, and about the symbolic claim that one citizen may use others in the community unfairly. Both stand as a challenge to continuing community

---

[1]We realize that in taking this view we adopt a "responsibilities" framework to augment the typical "rights" approach in today's criminal justice. To speak of crime as a problem requiring solutions, and to see solutions as suggesting a set of necessary tasks, is to house our argument squarely within the communitarian tradition.

[2]In Chapter 5, we introduce four more community justice principles that specifically address community responses to criminogenic conditions.

TABLE 4.1   The Tasks of Parties to Criminal Incidents

	Offender	Victim / Onlooker	Community institutions
Norm affirmation	Admit responsibility	Specify harm of offense	Articulate local standards
Restoration	Repair harm	Determine require-ments for restoration	Provide restorative opportunities for victims and offenders
Public safety	Demonstrate commitment to obey laws	Identify conditions reducing fear and resentment	Safely reintegrate offenders; insulate victims

life and place the offender at odds with the community. The criminal incident in effect suspends the offender's status in the community until a just response to the crime is achieved. A suspected offender, of course, may be innocent, and is entitled to seek the clearance of his or her name. In addition, the offender may be guilty of the offense, but may protest the legitimacy of the normative standard. In this case, the offender must demonstrate that the transgression does no harm to community life. Where guilt is established and the transgression's harm is manifest, the offender's task is to strive for readmission into the community. This involves three separable steps. First, the offender must take responsibility for the offense. This happens when the offender admits the behavior and that it was wrong to have done it. The admission is an acknowledgment of the conventional moral order. It is a reassurance that the offender does not, in principle or understanding, reject the community's normative standards. Second, the offender must take responsibility for undoing the effects of the offense on the victim and on the community. The effects on the victim include tangible costs that may be reimbursed through financial or labor restitution. There are also less tangible victim effects, such as loss of trust. Responsibility for these effects can be taken through symbolic acts of restitution to the victim and the community, such as the performance of community service (Adler 1991; Bazemore and Maloney 1994; Morris and Tonry 1990).

The community has lost confidence in the offender's behavior and has little reason to think the offender may be relied upon to be a citizen of fair living. Thus, the offender's third task is one of assurance; by maintaining community-affirmative behavior, the offender will give community members a reason to believe the claim that crimes will not again occur. Affirmative acts will include involvement in activities that reduce the likelihood of future offending, such as participation in a residential drug program, or adherence to a set of limits on behavior (e.g., a curfew). They also include activities that increase the likelihood of success in conventional living, such as entry into educational or job training programs. These steps will be taken to assure the victim and the community that the risk of new crimes is minimal. This assurance process is both symbolic and practical. It symbolizes the joint recognition of the break between citizen and community that occurs in a crime, and it symbolizes the tasks needed to reestablish connection and membership. In John Braithwaite's (1989) terms, this is a process of reintegrative shaming, for it addresses directly the offenders' suspended status in the community and their reintegration into the moral order and social milieu. At a practical level, the dual legal functions of sanctioning and risk management are enhanced by offenders' actions of remorse, repair, and reform.

This may seem a Pollyannaish view of what an offender must do to make the amends necessary to restore community. Many people looking at this list would wonder what brand of offenders we might be thinking about in describing these tasks. Yet when the Vermont Department of Corrections commissioned a series of focus groups to obtain a better understanding of what "ordinary citizens" as consumers of corrections want to get from punishing offenders, they heard the following list of priorities (Gorczyk 1996):

- For the offender to take responsibility for the crime.
- For the offender to make restitution to the victim.
- For the offender to contribute something back to the community as a symbol of remorse.
- For the offender to take steps to insure that the crime won't happen again.
- For the offender to learn something from the experience.

The Tasks of the Victim and Onlookers

The victim plays a key role in repairing community, but naturally has less burdensome tasks than the offender. The victim's tasks are related to the end aim of a sanctioning process designed to recover community: a full capacity to function as a member of the community. Onlookers, secondarily affected by the offense, share the same tasks as the victim but to a much lesser degree. A return to full sharing in community life can be impeded in any (or all) of several ways. The victim may be disabled physically, emotionally, or both. The victim may feel guilty about the offense, or may wonder what he or she did to warrant being victimized. The victim may harbor deep malice toward the offender because of the crime and its effects. All of these are common and understandable responses to victimization (Zehr 1990).

To overcome these obstacles, the victim first must be able to state the scope of losses, tangible and intangible, that have resulted from the crime. This is vital to the affirmation of norms, for it both vindicates the victim's suffering and clearly establishes that the offender's act was morally wrong. Then the victim must determine the types of resources, financial and otherwise, that would be necessary to restore, as much as is possible, the losses suffered. Finally, the victim must lay out the conditions under which any fear of and/or resentment toward the offender may be diminished.

These are, for most victims, enormously difficult objectives. They may also be so complex that a simple statement is impossible. Thus, the victim is not required to achieve these ends but instead is obliged to participate in a process in which these aims are addressed. That we suggest victims have a responsibility in the community justice process is indicative of the voluntary and moral commitments we believe undergird the democratic community. Whether that process will be successful is dependent not just upon the strengths of the victim but also upon the responses of the offender and of the community to the process.

The Tasks of Community Institutions

It is the community's laws that have been violated, and the community's life that has been disturbed. When confronted by criminality in its midst, the community must play a role in the recovery of community life, a role too often neglected or misunderstood. Community activity in responding to crime is central, in part because the victim who hopes to be restored is a member of the community but also because the offender (and the offender's conduct) also emanated from the community. Thus, the community is the context for the criminal events within it, and it must be a presence in the reply to those events. By *community*, we mean the myriad institutions of which social life is comprised—from family and friendship networks to voluntary organizations and social welfare agencies.

First, the community is obligated to clarify local normative standards, expressing to the offender in particular what is and is not acceptable behavior. Certainly there is room here both for moral education and for democratic discourse about the legitimacy of a given standard. Most important, however, is the collective process that reminds all parties of the significance of the standards in the face of a concrete manifestation of harm wrought by transgression. Representatives of local institutions such as schools or churches play a particularly important role as standard-bearers of their institutions, lending depth, tradition, and credibility to the communication of community norms.

The community has a responsibility to the victim. This responsibility involves recognition of the importance of losses resulting from victimization, and a commitment to provide supports necessary for the victim to achieve the optimal recovery. This responsibility may include a willingness upon the part of the community to accept as normal the anger, frustration, withdrawal, and alienation that often accompany victimization experiences, and not only to provide financial supports that help restore the victim.

The community also has a responsibility to the offender. This responsibility includes providing two opportunities; one for the offender to perform reparative tasks for the victim and the community, and the other for the offender to obtain the assistance, supervision, and supports—including treatment and intervention programs—necessary to live in the community crime-free. The first responsibility sets the stage for the offender to make amends for the offense; the second allows both the offender and the community to have confidence in the future behavior of the offender.

Thus the obligations of the community are to its members—to provide the possibility of recovery and restoration for victims and offenders alike. The community is responsible for building and maintaining the supports necessary for victims and offenders to carry out their tasks, so that both may resume their places as community members.

The Role of the Justice System

Figure 4.1 shows the reciprocal nature of the tasks of victims, offenders, and communities. In each case, the responsibilities of one party are matched by duties of the other, so that the parties exist in a closely coupled pattern of obligations and mutual tasks. This figure illustrates why an adversarial model fails to achieve the end aim of improved community life: It makes contestants out of those whose roles are interdependent.

The tasks of victims and offenders are complicated and formidable. They will not be able to carry them out without assistance. It is the responsibility of the justice system at the local, state, and federal levels to assist these parties in performing their tasks. From this perspective, the state is not the principal defender of law and order but merely a consultant and manager to the community, which bears ultimate responsibility for the justice process. System officials are responsible for designing and managing a process that makes feasible the accomplishment of victims', offenders', and communities' tasks.

The responsibility of the justice system will require extraordinary sensitivity to the diversity of offenders, victims, and communities. Similar criminal events may need to be handled differently; the emphasis will be on communication and problem solving, on working out options and ex-

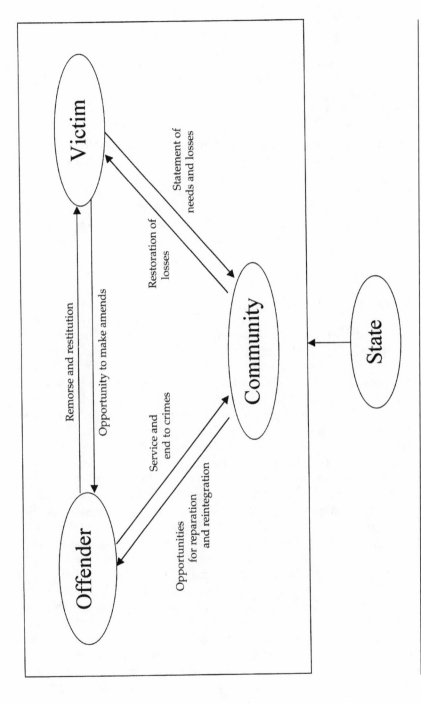

FIGURE 4.1   Core Responsibilities of Parties to the Sanctioning Process

ploring them. Thus the system will need flexible and evolving models, and a degree of patience to allow the parties to mature within the reclamation process. At the same time, the justice system is responsible for ensuring fair treatment to both offenders and victims. Offenders cannot be denied due process; victims cannot be excluded or ignored. More detail on how flexibility and equal treatment under the law may be reconciled is provided in Chapter 6.

The difficulty of a community justice ideal is obvious from this simple statement of principles. A major problem arises in the case of nonperformance of tasks by one or more of the parties. This will certainly occur at least occasionally, and especially given the contrary style of the adversarial model. It is the task of justice system officials to manage a process designed maximally to promote community, and so they will be called upon when parties fail in their tasks. The officials face different dilemmas, depending on which party to crime is failing.

When the Offender Fails

Offenders' tasks are complex and numerous, and offenders might fail for several reasons. Different reasons lead to differing responses by justice officials. The most basic challenge to community justice occurs when offenders deny responsibility for their transgressions—by refusing to admit guilt or by denying the harmful consequences of their acts. Such denials might be truthful: Offenders who deny guilt must then be vindicated by trial in a court of law. Or if offenders make a persuasive case that their transgressions caused no harm, then the community might be challenged to reevaluate its normative standards. But it is also fairly common for those accused of crimes to proclaim their innocence when they are guilty, in defiance or in personal protest: "They can't prove I did it." Whatever their feelings about the quality of the system's case against them, most defendants (more than 80 percent) eventually elect to plead guilty. The guilty plea is typically a product of bargaining in which the defendant trades an admission of guilt (which is tantamount to a conviction) for a lesser penalty.

There can be no escaping the fact that an offender who protests innocence loses status in the community after a conviction, whereas one who owns up to the wrong and proceeds to make amends has a better chance of recouping lost status (Braithwaite 1989). One can easily imagine a recalcitrant offender feeling resentment and even outrage, faced with a conviction with which he does not agree. Nonetheless, the struggle faced by community justice is to find a way to allow individuals who have unsuccessfully asserted their innocence to be able to return to full community.

Whether or not the offender takes steps of responsibility for the offense, the system must be concerned about his or her risk to the community.

Risk management programs are more effective when the offender is motivated to stay out of trouble; but regardless of motivation, the community must be assured that the offender will refrain from committing new crimes. Treatment and other risk reduction programs may have to be imposed coercively rather than developed in joint interaction with the offender, but designing and implementing these programs will be essential when offenders resist fulfilling their responsibilities as community members. When the offender fails, there will still be a need to provide ameliorative interventions such as victim-offender mediation or cognitive skills programs that may lead to a realization of responsibility for offending and of its consequences. There will also be a need for an effective risk assessment and risk management program that is sufficiently rigorous to stimulate community confidence in its effects. But these initiatives need to be taken in a way that does not thwart the ultimate aim of recovery to the community.

When the Victim Fails

Victims will fail when they are unable or unwilling to entertain the offender's eventual full return to community life. They also fail when they cannot overcome the losses they have suffered due to the crime. The inability to overcome losses is often the reason for victims' unwillingness to accept an offender's reintegration in the community. When confronted with victim failure, justice officials must be patient. It may take time and trial and error to achieve the goal of victim restoration; and it certainly cannot be done if the actions of justice officials deny the validity of the deep and often complex feelings that can result from victimization. Instead, these feelings and reactions must be acknowledged as valid and worked with carefully.

The process begins with supportive counseling in which the victim is encouraged to confront the losses by articulating them. Justice officials then begin to identify ways in which the tangible losses may be restored. This may eventually open up the discussion of symbolic harm resulting from being a victim, the kind far more difficult to alleviate; and in the uncovering of such harm, a process may occur in which the victim begins to overcome the hurt.

In the end, the victim must be seen as having a special status in the community recovery process. Until the victim returns to a sense of full citizenship, the shattering of community cannot fully be overcome. When a victim is reticent to receive the assurances of the offender or any restitution, then one can reasonably conclude that the offender has not yet performed the necessary social and moral gestures in a way that suffices. In this sense, the victim's ability to be restored controls the recovery process for the community. But it also must be said that the victim's finding a way to allow the offender to make amends is not simply a choice that may be made or not; rather, it is a type of obligation. The victim has a duty to enable the offender to return, just as the offender has an equivalent obligation to find terms under which victims may be allowed to feel that way.

When the Community Fails

Most community failure will result from one of two reasons: lack of resources (especially institutional capacity) or closedness to the process. The response of justice officials to the first problem is community development activity. The response to the second is insistence upon community involvement in justice processes.

Community development will be necessary in several instances. When the types of treatment intervention programs needed by offenders are not available or when the concrete supports needed by victims are lacking, they must be developed. Their development will require the allocation of resources—in many cases, even the production of resources—to meet these needs. To achieve this goal is a complicated matter, and we give it separate attention in Chapter 5.

The requirement that communities involve themselves in their crime problems is a different matter. There is a long list of reasons, from traditional reluctance to be involved to fear of consequences of involvement. Each community will possess a different array of reasons why involvement may not be easy to achieve. These reasons must be overcome on a community-by-community basis. In Chapter 6, we address ways to overcome the resistance and to locate resources for community justice programming. Here it is sufficient to recognize that such problems will occur and will need to be addressed.

Finally, we return to the role of the state. Our critique began with recognition that the state has expropriated the crime problem from its rightful owners—the people who are affected by it (see Christie 1977). But in the discussion of a community justice model, the term "justice officials" frequently arose, indicating that a role exists for the state under this ideal. Below we outline the basic relationship of the state to the community justice ideal. Various professional specialists will be needed in community justice to work with victims, offenders, and their communities in solving crime problems and recovering an acceptable quality of community life. These professionals will engage in a number of tasks; but their most important tasks will be those they perform with regard to the main participants in crime events. The role will differ with each category of participant, but generally it is to oversee a process that promotes recovery.

The Justice System and the Offender

Justice officials will work with offenders on two parallel fronts. The first involves confronting the implications of criminality; the second provides for the development of effective risk management strategies.

Taking Responsibility for the Offense

Offenders typically rationalize their offenses by using one or more "neutralization" strategies that depersonalize the victim or deny the impact or immorality of the offense (Sykes and Matza 1957). The aim of community justice is to have the offender affirm his connection to the community by taking personal responsibility for having wronged another. This requires breaking through the rationalizations, and one responsibility of the system is to foster experiences that promote such realizations.

This can be done from a variety of vantage points. One of the more successful techniques involves victim-offender dialogues, in which victims have the opportunity to confront offenders with the personal consequences of their offenses (Umbreit and Coates 1993). In these meetings, victims are provided a forum to express their losses directly to someone who has been responsible for such an injury (often victims choose not to confront their specific offender but to speak to someone who has committed a similar offense with regard to somebody else). After they have had the opportunity to think and talk about the confrontation, offenders are given the chance to express their penitence for the crime and offer ways to compensate for the losses. Studies show that these types of sessions often result in a greater sense of justice on the part of both the offender and the victim (Quinn 1996; Umbreit 1994).

In cases where offenders or victims are unwilling (or unable) to engage in such interaction, justice professionals might use other methods of confronting the offender with the impact of his conduct. Group-based programs that focus on cognitive skill development for offenders generally have an element that considers the offense and its implications (Andrews and Bonta 1994). A short-term realization by the offender that criminality is self-destructive is a first step in finding ways to reduce criminal conduct in the long term.

These are two examples of the initial responsibility of justice officials to offenders, which is aimed at helping the offender discover the need for an attachment to the community and seeing how the criminal behavior damages that attachment. It is certain that numerous other approaches could be developed to address this aim; the point here is to emphasize the significance of this component of community justice.

Managing Risk and Promising Safety

The second set of responsibilities borne by the justice system involves the design and oversight of a credible risk management program for the offender. Risk management programs are important for two reasons. First, the high rate of repeat offending among identified offenders is well established, and a program of risk management is essential to provide for safer communities. Second, community members—victims and their neighbors—deserve a reason to be reassured that the return of a given offender to the locality does not present a serious risk to others.

An effective risk management program is divided into risk assessment and risk intervention. Much is known about risk factors, and current research is adding to that knowledge rapidly. A good risk assessment strategy will take into account current and developing knowledge about effective intervention (Andrews and Bonta 1996). Figure 4.2 displays a schematic for such a risk assessment program.

The model in Figure 4.2 proposes two general arenas of risk assessment, the problem set and the opportunity set. The problem set involves factors that the offender brings to the day-to-day world and that have an impact on the probability of reoffending. The opportunity set is based on implications drawn from the rapidly developing field of situational crime prevention (Clarke 1995), showing that situational characteristics promote (or defy) criminal events. By including the opportunity set in risk assessment and intervention planning, we formally incorporate the community as a factor in the risk management program.

Most risk assessment begins and ends with systemic factors within the offender's problem set. That is to say, we know that the variables of age, sex, intelligence, personality, and prior experience all combine to predict new offending (Andrews and Bonta 1994). These risk factors are "historical"—that is, they are not generally subject to change. It is less typical (though not unknown) for risk assessments to take into account situational factors, which might vary over time: employment, living situation, lifestyle, and support system (as well as occasional events that might create or reduce risk-related stressors in life). These changeable aspects of the offender's situation have well-known, broad relationships to risk, so targeting them to reduce risk may be an appropriate strategy—for example, helping an offender obtain good employment or support for coping with marital stress or for parenting a newborn child (Sampson and Laub 1993).

The opportunity set includes situational components of risk, and borrows from routine activities theory (Cohen and Felson 1979), which states that crimes occur when four components correspond in space and time: The presence of a motivated offender and a suitable target is combined with the absence of an effective guardian (a person who provides surveil-

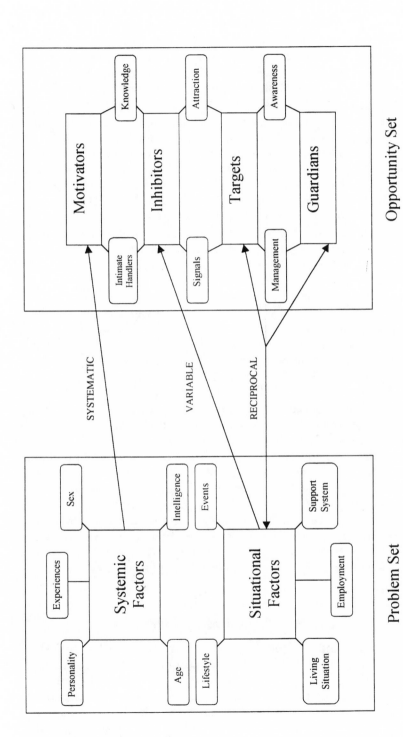

FIGURE 4.2   Risk Assessment for Intervention

lance or supervision in a criminogenic situation) or an intimate handler (a loved one who reinforces crime-free living). Each of these elements may be a target of an intervention program. For example, developing techniques for controlling temptation, such as anger management or relaxation methods, may reduce the offender's motivation level. The presence of intimate handlers may also act on motivation levels by strengthening inhibitors. Targets may be "hardened" in traditional ways by locks or streetlights; but when targets are individual community members, they may be hardened by informing them about the signals of reoffending (Pithers 1987) or by providing potential guardians more access to knowledge of the offender and of possible targets (Felson 1996). The opportunity set shows just how important the community is to crime prevention, even when the prevention focuses on the offender. Moreover, it opens up a new array of potential crime prevention activities designed as risk management interventions run by justice system officials working with offenders and the people with whom they live.

Under the model, systemic factors such as age and personality have a reliable, systematic impact on an offender's motivation for criminality. Situational factors have a variable impact on motivation and on inhibitors—as criminogenic situations occur, motivation increases or inhibitors decrease. Most importantly, situational factors have a reciprocal relationship with targets and guardians. The former can strengthen the latter, but the former may also be augmented by planned changes in the latter. This suggests that community members' participation in crime prevention, with offenders being "recovered" to community, can be a central contribution to overall community safety.

Our assessment model highlights the range of intervention programs different communities might develop under guidance from crime prevention specialists. There might be target-hardening programs for families of offenders that improve their capacities as intimate handlers and capable guardians. There could be job programs to alter situational factors, and individual treatment programs targeting crime motivators and inhibitors. There could also be a wide range of community-based crime prevention strategies focused on targets and guardians, discussed in more detail later in this chapter.

Risk and Community Justice

Every time an offender is convicted, the community is asked to take a risk. A prison term risks the eventual return of an offender who is ill equipped to comply with the law. A community penalty risks a similar outcome, only sooner. Even an extreme penalty such as capital punishment risks the loss of a potential community asset, and inflicts damage on community values. No community can develop a risk-free crime policy. In the end, when it comes to crime, communities are forced to choose between this and that risk situation.

A community justice ideal does not ask the community to embrace all risks, no matter how problematic. Our concern for risk assessment and intervention is proposed precisely to put into context the community's risk paradox. If a reasonable risk management plan can be established, then the community is free to choose it. Should no reasonable risk management plan emerge, the community may be wise to postpone its risk until after a prison sentence has been served. In rare cases, even that risk may prove too extreme for a community to tolerate.

Our risk management proposal is meant to take seriously the community's desire for public safety, but to place it in a broader context where restoration of the community is a valued outcome. If perfect public safety is out of reach, then an imperfect community justice may be a preferable choice. A risk-free community is not attainable, but a rational, controlled-risk approach can be implemented. Such a system, once in place, will provide the community with more than a reasonable risk management regime; it will enable the community to become involved in controlling its own risks, something not possible when the offender is removed and sent to prison.

The Justice System and the Victim

In present-day victims' services, a main interest of the state in providing services to victims is to guarantee their cooperation in the prosecution of the defendant and to help make a case for harsh punishment. After the criminal case has been prosecuted, the disappearance of the state reinforces a message that the interest of the state in the victim's losses was only to the extent that the painfulness of the losses helped the state build a case against the offender. Under the ideal of community justice, the justice system has a broader interest in the victim's suffering, over and above the offender's liability for it. The state seeks to see the victim restored to community life, reinforced as a fully functioning community member and supported so as to recover, insofar as is possible, citizenship.

Justice officials interested in crime prevention might well begin their work with the victim. Studies show that those who have been victimized once have a higher probability of future victimization. Programs that focus on the prevention of repeat victimization have shown significant promise of reducing crime and reducing the suffering of victims (Farrell 1995; Hope 1991). Repeat victimization prevention programs focus on an analysis of the circumstances of the crime, and help the victim learn the techniques of crime prevention. The first aim of community justice efforts with victims should be crime prevention—helping them to feel that they can avoid repeat victimization.

The second responsibility of justice officials is to obtain a full accounting of the various losses the victim has suffered. Already, probation offices and prosecutors' staffs develop "victim impact" statements for the court; but these generally are designed to tell the story of the losses caused by the crime. There is not ordinarily a reparative focus to these statements (except insofar as they address restitution). Justice officials will need to help the victim think about the kinds of *responses* from the offender and the state that could begin to overcome the impact of those losses and allow the victim to be made whole. In cases of serious crime, this may involve counseling services as well as tangible financial supports. A complete victim impact statement also serves as a starting point for offenders' own restitution plans.

The most challenging aspect of the justice officials' role with victims will be to help them define the circumstances under which they would accept their victimizers as comembers of the community. There are three general issues here. First, with the offender taking responsibility for the offense, the moral attack the offense contains is somewhat alleviated, and the victim can feel that the offender recognizes and vindicates the victim's right to live free of crime. Second, with a plan for restitution and restoration of the losses, the victim may feel that the practical injury of the crime is also going to be alleviated. But the final task is to establish a sense of return to safety; the offender's assessment of risk and intervention plan, and the victim's acknowledgment of the soundness of that plan, accomplish this.

Justice officials administer a process in which a crime's losses are accounted for and (to the degree possible) ameliorated, the offender publicly states the wrongfulness of the criminal behavior, and the offender devises a plan of action that will give cocitizens confidence he or she is serious about refraining from crime in the future. Given this process, it is reasonable to expect the victim to consider the offender's return to social standing as a fully participating citizen.

Processes such as this are under way around the world. They go under various titles: restorative justice, victim-offender mediation, family group conferencing, reintegrative shaming, and so on (see Galaway and Hudson 1996; Van Ness and Strong 1997; Zehr 1990). Common to these processes is the priority given to the following aims:

- Develop a plan to state the victim's losses.
- Provide a forum for the victim to confront the offender and to explain the significance of the offense.
- Allow the offender to experience personally the impact of the offense on a cocitizen.

- Allow the offender to declare publicly regret for the offense and commitment to live differently.
- Assist the offender in carrying out his or her promise to the victim and the community for making amends.

These processes are based upon recognition that the offender, victim, and community are deeply interdependent when it comes to community safety. In order to fully promote a vision of safety, each party must recognize how the crime challenges the safe relationships among them; must commit to specific means for repairing the damage; and must agree to a recovered, harmonious set of community relationships based upon a belief in mutual commitment to safety from crime. From a restoration of community safety, a sense of community justice will emerge.

The Justice System and the Community

Although examples of all of the community justice activities described above now exist, they are often operated without much attention to community involvement beyond the specific offender and victim. To try to advance community justice without a commitment to increasing community influence on the justice processes would be a mistake. The final responsibility of professional justice officials at the community level is to activate and energize community responsibility for addressing crime problems, not only after specific criminal events but universally in community life.

Three general types of local organizing activity in community contexts occur: development, planning, and social action (Duffee 1997). Community justice approaches will involve all three, but the emphasis will be on development, in which local residents organize themselves into decision-making structures that identify and attack local problems.

Community justice is a special form of community development in which the criminal justice system assists local residents in organizing to confront crime problems. There is a tension between the formal, bureaucratic operatives providing the impetus for social organization and the informal organizational resources and networks that sustain community action. The greater the influence or control by formal agencies, the less the penetration of the community into crime prevention and criminal justice. Therefore, the involvement of justice officials in the community is a paradox. In order to empower the community, local residents must be in charge of action on crime; in order to empower local residents, justice officials often must initiate the organizational activity. This is one of the lessons of community policing. On the one hand, city executives such as police are often distrustful of local leaders as potential adversaries in political contexts (Moynihan 1969). On the other, local residents may be hesitant for various reasons to devote much time to crime-related problems, especially if those problems are defined as the responsibility of the police.

The paradox is resolved when the justice system becomes a support to the community rather than an outside and sometimes hostile power. In a civil society, the line between community and state is blurred, as government agencies become truly representatives of and advocates for community members. As we noted in Chapter 2, the quality of community life is often a function of social forces beyond community control. The justice system may serve as a conduit for the acquisition of extralocal resources to help combat the negative consequences of these forces. Community justice cannot be understood solely as a model for internal community action but must also be seen to address the larger social context within which communities struggle for success. We therefore devote the next chapter to outlining a community justice response to criminogenic conditions in a community.

The Community Justice Process

We conclude this chapter with a summary definition or general model of the community justice process. The aim of this process is the recovery of community in the face of crime. By *recovery* we mean responsiveness to the needs and concerns of crime victims; reintegration of the offender into the community as a full-fledged and contributing member; and restoration of community confidence in both parties' participation in community life.

When a victim reports a crime, the community justice agency would begin its work by helping the victim come to grips with the losses. There would be a series of meetings with the victim in which the identification of losses would begin, and the victim would be prepared to deal with the offender. If a comprehensive listing of losses includes substantial emotional turmoil, counseling sessions would be offered immediately, to commence as soon as the victim is ready. If the victim has concerns about how the justice response is being handled, he or she would be able to meet with the functional citizen board on community justice. A volunteer counselor—a local resident—would be assigned to maintain contact regarding the offense and would be present at any official meetings, should the victim desire assistance.

Once somebody has been apprehended for the crime, a parallel process would begin with that citizen. The opening conversation would be about responsibility. If the defendant was willing to admit responsibility, then the process would begin to develop a statement of responsibility and a proposal for restitution to the victim and the community. At the same time, a community crime prevention specialist would work with the offender to conduct a risk assessment and a proposal for risk management interventions. The defendant would be assigned a lawyer and a volunteer community counselor, who would be present at all official functions, should the defendant wish. If the defendant asserts that he or she is not guilty, all processes would stop, and a trial would commence. Only after a conviction would the reintegrative process be reactivated.

After the victim and offender have established their initial statements, they would be moved toward a meeting to discuss face to face the crime and the consequences. Following the family group conference model (Braithwaite and Mugford 1994; Hudson et al. 1996), the meeting will pull together supporters of both the victim and the offender: family members, friends, mentors, and role models. Only if the victim is willing will the meeting take place; if the victim does not want to confront the offender, the victim board will stand in. Community volunteers will coach the victim and the offender, separately, on what they can expect from the process. Multiple meetings will occur, if necessary, to reach a conclusion. The aim is to obtain a statement of responsibility from the offender and to negotiate restitution, community service, and risk management commitments that the victim can accept. Once all parties have agreed to the statements, the offender begins to fulfill the agreement, and the victim continues any restorative activity still to be done. Crime prevention professionals monitor the continuation of the agreement.

This model takes explicit account of the mechanisms of community we described in Chapter 3. It begins by building a place in the justice process for the participation of citizens and the institutions that enrich their lives. To give both victims and offenders a participatory role in re-establishing a just circumstance in response to the criminal event is to invite a kind of civic participation that is obviously missing from adversarial bureaucracy. When claims of multiple citizenry can be voiced at the same table, civic participation becomes meaningful instead of the empty gesture it so often is today. Just as significantly, the living entity of the community can also actively participate through its role in the sanctioning process.

The aim of all of this process is, explicitly, to strengthen informal social controls. This could occur through many different channels. To the extent that family members are involved in the process, their ability to shape the commitments and behavior of the offender are strengthened and given a direction. Victims, by voicing their concerns and leading authorities toward actions that are not simply punitive but are also protective, can emerge from the justice process with a deepened sense of their capacity to work toward their own safety. Institutions, the source of parochial social control, are steered toward an active role in community safety and offender resocialization. This is, we recognize, an ambitious and potent agenda in comparison with that of today's justice system.

In this chapter we have identified three central principles of a community justice ideal. They are the affirmation of community norms of conduct; the restoration of those affected by the crime—victims, offenders, and their neighbors—to a renewed sense of community; and the establishment of a basis for improved public safety. These three principles apply to the actors who would engage in the crime-related processes of democratic community justice. Next we will broaden our discussion to confront questions about quality of life that are not tied to specific criminal events. In our view, community justice, to be egalitarian, must attend to these broader quality-of-life issues. In the next chapter, we explain how and why this is so.

5

Principles of Egalitarian Community Justice

In the previous chapter, we considered the moral obligations of various community members when confronted with a crime. The focus, therefore, was necessarily reactive—the tasks of offenders, victims, onlookers, and justice officials in solving an immediate problem according to a community justice ideal. The significant difference between this ideal and traditional approaches is in the broadened scope of obligations under the former. Although offenders bear the greatest burden in demonstrating a commitment to reparation and normative conformity, all members of the community, by virtue of their interdependence, become implicated in the pursuit of justice.

This chapter extends the community justice model by considering the social obligations of a community for the prevention of crime. This model assumes that crime patterns are not random, that they can be predicted with some accuracy, and that steps can be taken before crime occurs to reduce its likelihood. Community justice is not achieved by responding to particular criminal incidents as they occur. The shift from traditional to community justice requires a change in purpose from a narrowly conceived agenda of crime control to a broadly determined mission of enhancing the quality of community life. Naturally, crime, fear of crime, and disorder figure prominently in the quality of life, and these remain of the utmost concern. It is our belief that a community justice approach to criminal incidents is a viable and significant contribution to both justice and prevention, for it has a great chance of redirecting the life course of offenders and inspiring community action in the service of socialization and informal social control. However, the reactive approach falls short when it comes to addressing the structural and situational antecedents to crime. Community justice, therefore, must also respond to criminogenic community conditions—the conditions that facilitate criminal events.

In the previous chapter, our concern for a just response to criminal incidents necessarily directed our attention toward the personal responsibilities of the key parties to a criminal incident. By emphasizing the tasks incumbent upon these individuals, we do not mean to diminish the responsibility of the community and the larger society as collective actors charged with the task of cultivating an environment conducive to the individual pursuit of happiness. When individuals suffer from social injustices, we cannot expect them to comply perfectly with normative standards or to willingly contribute to civic life as necessary to sustain a democratic society.

Four Principles of Egalitarian Justice

To escape the perennial debate between conservatives who argue that crime is ultimately a matter of personal responsibility and liberals who place the blame on social conditions, we must recognize the symbiotic relationship between individual and collective obligations. In an important recent article, Philip Selznick (1996, p. 14) wrote:

> Personal responsibility is most likely to flourish when there is genuine opportunity to participate in social life. These conditions require substantial investment by the community and its institutions. At the same time, how much the community invests, and what kind of investment it makes, will depend on the prevalence of a sense of personal responsibility for the common good.

To ensure the opportunity to participate, Selznick argued, a community must adhere to four basic principles of justice. These principles speak directly to the concern for improving the quality of community life and are summarized as equality, inclusion, mutuality, and stewardship. We extend his work by linking each principle directly to criminogenic community conditions.

In Chapter 2, we argued that the quality of community life is signaled by three factors in particular: the subjective "sense of community" felt by its members; the objective ability of community members to be instrumentally and morally competent; and the structural capacity of the community to improve collective outcomes by providing for the general welfare—for example, by ensuring public safety. Below, we draw on Selznick's conceptualization to assert principles of egalitarian community justice and their relevance to the key indicators of the quality of community life: sense of community, individual competencies, and collective outcomes (see Table 5.1).

Equality is the principle of justice that makes fairness a priority over social subordination. This principle is directed at the problem of social inequality, which gives rise to numerous social problems—high proportions of single parent households, teenage pregnancy, high dropout rates, joblessness, drug abuse, disorder, and crime. The principle of equality as-

TABLE 5.1   Principles of Egalitarian Community Justice

	Equality	*Inclusion*	*Mutuality*	*Stewardship*
Criminogenic condition	Social inequality	Social disintegration	Free-rider opportunity structure	Social/moral disorder
Moral concern	Fairness *over* Social subordination	Participation *over* Ostracism	Cooperation *over* Defection	Self-transcendence *over* Egoism
Sense of community	Fulfillment of needs	Membership	Influence	Emotional connection
Individual competencies	Mastery *over* Skills deficit	Sociability *over* Prejudice	Social identification *over* Isolation	Self-control/ empathy *over* Indifference
Collective outcomes	Distributive justice *over* Concentration of poverty	Social integration *over* Oppositional culture formation	Social coordination *over* Collective failure	Moral order *over* Excessive individualism

sumes that in a good society all communities are capable of providing the basics for individual and collective human existence. Here the moral objective is to treat each community and each individual with dignity and respect, avoiding the temptation to treat some with preference over others.

Community members experience a sense of community when they feel they are being treated fairly. At minimum, a community must be able to meet the basic needs of its members.[1] The equality principle also speaks to individual competencies by emphasizing the development of skills to overcome any individual shortcomings that result from social inequality. Lastly, it directly relates to collective outcomes by providing support for distributive justice aimed at eliminating pronounced inequalities— particularly concentrations of poverty—that plague our inner cities.

[1]McMillan and Chavis's (1986) psychological model of the sense of community has four dimensions, each corresponding closely to Selznick's four principles. A sense of community will be strong when individuals report feelings of (a) membership or belonging; (b) influence—that their membership matters to others, and that they are efficacious; (c) fulfillment—that their investment in the community is rewarded; and (d) emotional connection—that values and practices are shared in common and that bonds are more than instrumental. See Table 5.1 for the correspondence of these dimensions with Selznick's principles.

The second principle of justice is inclusion. Here we are particularly concerned with the means of integrating individuals into the activities of collective life. The point of tension is the community's response to marginal individuals. Are they stigmatized and excluded, weakening the community's internal cohesion? Or does the community seek to retain its members by developing the ability to enlist the positive participation of deviants? Communities are criminogenic when many of their members live on the margins of conventional social life.

In this regard, a sense of community is manifest by the quality of membership in the community. Individuals at the margins must gain a sense of belonging, a personal investment or stake in membership. Competency development is particularly important, paradoxically, for those who are well integrated; they need to overcome the temptation to exclude deviants from their midst. Inclusion is concerned with the capacity of individuals to relate to unknown others without prejudice or discrimination. The inclusion principle seeks to avoid the dissipation of collective life through fragmentation into subgroups, particularly oppositional subcultures, which occurs when the avenues of social integration and opportunity are closed.

Mutuality is the third principle of egalitarian community justice. This principle prioritizes the cooperation of community members in search of the common good over the unrestrained pursuit of self-interest by autonomous social actors. Mutuality is a recognition that collective goods cannot be provided by solitary individuals; they can be produced only through the coordinated efforts of a collective action. Criminogenic communities are unable to advance collective agendas, and their weak infrastructure provides numerous opportunities for individual withdrawal from collective responsibilities—and worse, for individual exploitation of criminal opportunities.

The interdependence of individuals upon one another raises the stakes of cooperation at the same time that it tragically diffuses the individual's sense of responsibility for cooperation. The sense of community relevant to mutuality is members' experience of influence. That is, in order to be motivated to contribute, community members must feel that their contributions matter. The presence of free riders—individuals who do not contribute—makes the provision of collective goods neither certain nor straightforward. Individual self-interest dictates that although collective goods are desirable to all, individuals who feel that their contribution makes no difference will decide to let others work to provide collective goods. The search for mutuality requires individual competency in linking one's own interests with those of the collectivity: in identifying with the community. Mutuality ultimately is manifested at the collective level by the social coordination of individual action to reduce free riding and the failure to provide collective goods.

The final principle of egalitarian justice is stewardship. Traditionally, stewardship has been viewed as a response to anomie—that is, to the experience of "normlessness," or moral disorder (Merton 1938). The classical concern for the cultural or normative environment has gained heightened attention recently as criminologists are finding links between social disorder and crime (see Kelling and Coles 1996; Skogan 1990; and for a contrasting view, Taylor 1997). The moral objective of stewardship is community members' transcendence of egoistic preoccupation and their demonstrable concern for the common good. Where stewardship is fulfilled, the burden of mutual social coordination is lessened.

Stewardship is also relevant in the formation of individual character—another dimension of competency—particularly in one's capacity for self-control and empathy for others. Thus, a sense of community is experienced through emotional connectedness or a feeling of closeness and concern for the welfare of other members of the community. Stewardship is the strongest moral claim of egalitarian community justice because its aspiration is the achievement of a "good society," (Bellah et al. 1991) or moral order, not just an efficient or equitable society for essentially separate individuals. Moral order is not necessarily synonymous with moral domination, stultifying conformity, or nostalgic traditionalism. Rather, it reflects the capacity of the community to advance collectively desired goods. In essence, stewardship is a claim consistent with communitarian ideals; in contrast, equality, inclusion, and mutuality—although they are not at all antithetical to communitarianism—are the foundations of liberalism.

The four principles are not orthogonal dimensions: Each principle builds upon the foundation of the previous one, heightening the moral expectations of the community. Equality is a necessary minimum; but fair treatment of community members might be achieved by cycling "problematic" community members out of the community so they no longer need to be treated with the same standard. Inclusion raises the stakes on the meaning of fair treatment. Mutuality places an additional moral demand on a community that may otherwise embrace inclusion and equality: It proscribes free riding as the means to maximize individual interests. Stewardship aspires to the loftiest of community goals: the capacity of individuals to look beyond their own needs and act in the service of others and the collectivity. Rawls (1971) referred to it as a high virtue. Below, we expand on these principles further and explain their special relevance to a model of community justice. In this vision, community justice is much more than the absence of crime, just as we think of peace as much more than the absence of war.

Equality

The first principle for an egalitarian model, naturally, is equality. By this we do not mean perfect equality of outcomes, for the inevitability of variation in talent, effort, and tastes prevents this as both a practicality and an ideal. What is meant by equality is, most of all, fair treatment (Rawls 1971). According to conventional morality, this may conform to a variety of just distributional outcomes (Deutsch 1975). In some instances, perfect equality is legitimate—as in the guarantee that all citizens have an equal right to a jury of their peers. Often, equity is appropriate, such as when one offender is paroled because of a demonstrated effort to conform to normative standards, but another is not, due to a lack of such effort. Even need is an appropriate measure in an egalitarian model: We see fairness in progressive tax structures, in committing health care resources to the sick before the healthy, in concentrating preservation efforts on endangered species, and in dedicating extra police resources to areas where the crime rate is high.

Fair treatment is grounded in a repudiation of social subordination (Selznick 1996). This idea, in turn, springs from the Western liberal tradition that embraces the concept of individual moral worth: "the ultimate moral principle of the supreme and intrinsic value, or dignity, of the individual human being" (Lukes 1973, p. 45). Thus, to give preferential treatment to some, or to intentionally disadvantage others, is to negate the moral foundations of the egalitarian ideal.

The pursuit of equality as a guiding principle is justified when it increases the sense of community among individuals. In David W. McMillan and David M. Chavis's (1986) psychological model, individuals may experience a sense of community along four dimensions. One dimension is characterized by the fulfillment of needs. Community satisfaction is high in communities that satisfy the basic needs of their members (Sagy et al. 1996). The equality principle commits a community to treating all of its members with dignity and respect. It cannot look away from the indignities of poverty or the disrespect of blocked opportunity. Where individuals do not feel the sting of prejudice and discrimination, they may feel a sense of community.

Just as the sense of community speaks to the subjective experience of community life, so individual competencies refer to the objective capacities of individuals that enable them to be successful members of the community. These capacities are a result of individual factors such as intelligence or drive as well as of environmental factors such as educational or occupational opportunity: The tone deaf are unlikely to become concert pianists, as are the musically adept who have no access to a piano. The egalitarian ideal is to maximize the opportunity for individuals to explore and select a life course best suited to their talents and inclinations. This explicitly means that a community justice approach would work to develop in individuals the skills necessary to succeed in conventional life, and to develop in communities the capacity to provide for their members' basic needs.

Poverty and Segregation

Most important for community justice is the correlation of neighborhood disadvantage and criminality. Although there is much debate about the exact causal relationship between poverty and crime (Tittle et al. 1978), it is undisputed that the poorest communities in the United States also suffer from the highest crime rates (Braithwaite 1979; Sampson 1995). A community justice approach must respond to the social inequalities that undermine the quality of community life.

Communities are variously affected by macrolevel forces that impact their vulnerability to crime. Robert J. Sampson and William Julius Wilson (1995, p. 38) argue that "macrosocial patterns of residential inequality give rise to the social isolation and ecological concentration of the truly disadvantaged, which in turn leads to structural barriers and cultural adaptations that undermine social organization and hence the control of crime." Social inequality poses a special problem for community justice. Is it important to address the structural correlates of crime? Can communities successfully address social inequalities?

When William J. Wilson (1987) introduced the concept of concentrated poverty, he argued that high levels of crime in communities are not associated with overall poverty levels but with how poverty is distributed geographically. The impact of poverty on an individual living among people who are equally poor is different from that on an individual living among people who are much better off. Concentrated poverty areas have the highest levels of joblessness, single-parent households, welfare dependency, and crime. In these areas, criminal opportunities abound (e.g., convenience stores and open-air drug markets); young males are often unemployed, truant, or unsupervised; and local institutions that facilitate social control are weak or relatively sparse (e.g., voluntary organizations, churches, schools, locally owned businesses, and municipal services).

Socially disorganized areas are defined by their inability to exert social controls and fulfill collective objectives (Bursik 1988). Individuals—even the poor or the unemployed—living in an area where poverty is not concentrated are confronted with a very different normative environment; an environment that challenges them to adopt standards of behavior consistent with a working, law-abiding existence. This normative contrast is closely related to important structural differences: Economic and social opportunities exist for these people as a consequence of local networks that are absent from areas of concentrated poverty.

Perhaps the most important structural factors are urban change and segregation. Urban change refers to the loss of blue-collar jobs in major cities from the 1970s to the 1990s, which has severely limited the employment opportunities of less-educated, urban workers. Segregation refers to the creation and maintenance of minority urban ghettos and provides one explanation for the disproportionate association of street crime with blacks—particularly with young, urban males. In essence, there is no other racial or ethnic group that has been as affected by both urban change and segregation. In the words of Douglas S. Massey and Nancy A. Denton (1993, p. 114), "Blacks remain the most spatially isolated population in U.S. history." Sampson and Wilson (1995, p. 42) noted, "The 'worst' urban contexts in which whites reside are considerably better than the average context of black communities."

American cities in recent decades have been transformed from places of production and distribution of goods to centers of administration, finance, and information (Kasarda 1989). As a result, blue-collar jobs, which once constituted the primary occupational category in the central city, have declined, and education-intensive, white-collar jobs have increased. Blue-collar jobs had been a traditional avenue of employment for urban blacks because they were relatively well paid, stable, and did not require high levels of education. Although educational levels among blacks have risen over time, the changes have not offset the impact of urban industrial change. The largest proportion of urban blacks is employed in low-education jobs, whereas high-education jobs have demonstrated the highest growth in the city. As a result of these changes, many blacks are jobless, and many others are marginally employed in service industries that do not provide the income or stability of their previous blue-collar jobs.

Historically, segregation has been a policy and practice of discrimination. When the inequalities associated with segregation practices could no longer be discounted, its official support receded. Yet blacks remain the most highly segregated group in America (Massey and Denton 1993). Although surveys demonstrate that many whites prefer not to live near blacks, blacks tend to prefer integration (Farley et al. 1978), suggesting that blacks are not explicitly choosing to self-segregate. Policies that located public housing in black neighborhoods not only increased the concentration of poverty but also helped maintain residential segregation. Widespread housing discrimination (Massey and Denton 1993) and suburban employment discrimination (Wilson 1996) prevent many blacks from moving away from urban ghettos. Nevertheless, many blacks do manage to escape ghetto life. Unfortunately, these tend to be the better educated and professionally employed. Thus, middle-class black outmigration further concentrates poverty and increases the social isolation of ghetto residents (Jargowsky 1997; Wilson 1987).

Poverty concentration and racial segregation have burdened inner-city communities with extremely high crime rates. Robert Crutchfield (1997) has shown how concentrations of poverty in neighborhoods makes these locations particularly vulnerable to fluctuations in the labor market and the economy, with the result that they experience greater levels of criminality. Communities have pursued various strategies to directly confront segregation and the concentration of poverty, usually by attempting to improve the economic conditions of the segregated ghetto through education, school-to-work programs, job training, Empowerment Zones/Enterprise Communities, community development corporations, civil enforcement of housing laws, "seed" components of "Weed and Seed" programs, and various other comprehensive community development programs (Connell et al. 1995). Various strategies also attempt to deconcentrate poverty and desegregate through relocation of public housing and by voucher programs, school busing and magnet school programs, redesign of public transit systems to facilitate travel to suburban work locations, and enforcement of fair housing laws. Some evidence demonstrates the effectiveness of such relocation for success in the labor market and in educational attainment (Jargowsky 1997). However beneficial, programmatic attempts to relocate low-income blacks into non–poverty areas usually meet great resistance. Moreover, although the relocated individuals might be helped, these approaches may further undermine the high-poverty neighborhood by luring competent members away.

What is obvious from this analysis is the disjunction between white suburbs and black urban ghettos. David Rusk (1995) argues that little will change unless cities are reorganized into metropolitan governments facilitating the linkage between these distant worlds. Michael Buerger (1994) creatively suggests the formation of sister neighborhoods in which economically distant communities join forces at the local level. Community justice is not likely to succeed unless these broader structural issues are addressed. Rarely do communities organize with the express purpose of deconcentrating poverty. This would require intercommunity efforts in the face of political challenges to their implementation. It would force community advocates to expand their horizons beyond geographically narrow conceptions of community in order to foster greater interdependence between urban and suburban areas. A community justice approach must recognize that individual communities are parts of larger systems, deeply affected by public policies and economic forces well beyond community control. This interdependence of communities means that community justice must advocate distributive justice across the metropolitan landscape. In the near term, this may require that community justice resources be disproportionately allocated to ameliorate entrenched patterns of social inequality.

Inclusion

The second principle of egalitarian community justice is the unending effort to reduce the marginalization of community members and subgroups.

Each member of the community is to be given the opportunity to participate in community life, to have a voice in community affairs. In the ideal,
community members should desire inclusion, and participation would be
encouraged. Segregation and the concentration of poverty relegate entire
communities to the margins of national society. Thus, the pursuit of equality by reducing prejudice and discrimination is an important complement
to the ideal of inclusion. At the community level we make choices about the
treatment of deviants—those who do not conform to the common standards and practices of the community. We experience a persisting tension
between the virtue of tolerance for heterogeneous practices and the desire
for uniformity of behavior and predictability of social interaction.

The principle of inclusion asserts that all members of the community
have a place in the community in spite of their attitudes or behaviors that
may challenge the community code. Instead of isolating deviants, our goal
is to encourage their greater participation, for two important reasons. First,
by enhancing connections we increase the communication of normative
standards and the opportunities for formal and informal social control. Second, the greater participation of deviant members also means that their
voices can be heard, and their concerns and interests articulated, opening
the way to social change. The possibility of social change exists only when
the conventional community considers and tolerates—or perhaps even endorses and gradually embraces—nonconforming practices. This point is especially important for the perpetuation of a universalist ideal that maintains respect and tolerance for the diversity of human life.

The quality of community life is partly reflected in the sense of community experienced by its members. In this context, the important dimension
of community satisfaction is membership. Individuals feel a sense of
community when they feel a sense of belonging, when they identify with
the collectivity (McMillan and Chavis 1986). Where this sense of membership is diminished we find either alienation, as if one were alone in the
company of strangers, or worse, outright rejection and ostracism. Clearly,
such reactions are antithetical to vibrant community life. Community life
may also be measured in its capacity to develop individual competencies—in this case, individual competence in forming and sustaining
meaningful relationships with other members of the community. The
principle of inclusion flags prejudice and discrimination as contrary to
the functioning of communities and the precursors to intergroup conflict
and social inequality.

Shame, Stigma, and Exclusion

In Chapter 2 we explained that the quality of community life largely depends on a community's capacity to engage in three forms of collective
action: socialization, informal social control, and external resource lever-

aging. The leveraging of resources is a mechanism for reducing social inequality. Socialization and informal control are mechanisms for cultivating participation in conventional community life. They are the means of defining and enforcing community standards of behavior.

A central feature of socialization and informal control is shame (Braithwaite 1989; Karp 1998b; Scheff 1996). Individuals desire membership in the community and fear any disapproval that places their social status at risk. To avoid shame, individuals conform. However, shaming may stigmatize the deviant when the community not only expresses disapproval of the act but also of the person. Stigmatization can lead to shunning. Ostracized, the individual's opportunities for successful conventional existence are reduced and the deviant seeks the company and approval of other outcasts. Subcultures form that reject the dominant moral order and reward nonconformity and delinquency (Wilkins 1964). According to Braithwaite (1989, p. 55):

> Reintegrative shaming means that expressions of community disapproval, which may range from mild rebuke to degradation ceremonies, are followed by gestures of reacceptance into the community of law-abiding citizens. These gestures of reacceptance will vary from a simple smile expressing forgiveness and love to quite formal ceremonies to decertify the offender as deviant. Disintegrative shaming (stigmatization), in contrast, divides the community by creating a class of outcasts.

Braithwaite (1989; Braithwaite and Mugford 1994) argues that stigmatization and exclusion are the most significant risks of shaming. Such a process is very likely to lead to oppositional culture formation. It works like this: A person shoplifts from a store. Others label this person a thief. This label does more than merely describe the act; it says something about the person's character. The label is likely to stick when those who label—say, the storekeeper, the cop, or the judge—are viewed as servants of the public good rather than as individuals seeking to malign the character of the offender. As a result, the offender comes to be seen as deviant, and others distance themselves socially ("Don't hang around with him") or formally, as when the offender is expelled from school or sentenced to prison. Shunned by conventional society, the deviant seeks the company of deviant others and rejects the standards of conventional morality. Shaming in this light is counterproductive because oppositional cultural formation systematizes criminality.

Sociologists have long observed subcultural formations that reject the dominant normative standards. In their classic studies of Chicago, Clifford R. Shaw and Henry D. McKay wrote:

> In the areas of low rates of delinquents there is more or less uniformity, consistency, and universality of conventional values and attitudes with respect

to child care, conformity to law, and related matters; whereas in the high-rate areas, systems of competing and conflicting moral values have developed. Even though in the latter situation conventional traditions and institutions are dominant, delinquency has developed as a powerful competing way of life. (1942, p. 164)

Oscar Lewis (1968) argued that in order to cope with high rates of poverty and few economic opportunities, many ghetto communities had developed a "culture of poverty" in which adherence to mainstream values such as the work ethic was diminished because the intended rewards of such adherence were not forthcoming (see also Merton 1957). More recently, Elijah Anderson (1990) has described the emergence of an oppositional culture in which marginalized youth have not only diminished their adherence to mainstream values but actively reject them, replacing them with a system of gang values supportive of crime.

A telling example of oppositional cultural formation is Anderson's analysis of the relationship between "old heads" and young boys.

An old head was a man of stable means who was strongly committed to family life, to church, and most important, to passing on his philosophy, developed through his own rewarding experience with work, to young boys he found worthy. He personified the work ethic and equated it with value and high standards of morality. . . . But as meaningful employment has become increasingly scarce, drugs more accessible, and crime a way of life for many young black men, this institution has undergone stress and significant change. (Anderson 1990, p. 69)

In essence, the moral lessons of old heads have fallen on deaf ears primarily because the young men do not believe that their efforts to lead a conventional life will yield the desired outcomes. For them, particularly given the social isolation of the ghetto, opportunities for legitimate success are few compared with the allure of illegal opportunities and the escapes to be found in alcohol and drugs.

Social relationships continue despite weakened social institutions. A community does not relinquish its moral order to a vacuum. Rather, new standards and new leaders who model and enforce these standards immediately replace it. Anderson argues that as old heads disappear, individuals who reject their predecessors' moral message fill their role. Anderson's portrayal is an ethnography of a ghetto community unable to maintain informal control. It is a description of community whose conventional mores are being supplanted by those of the street. Though most residents still identify with and try to uphold conventional values, they fail, in large part because their claims are predicated on avenues of success closed to many members of the community.

What is unique about shame as a form of informal social control is that it is indicative of the bond between the various members of the community. Where there is no bond, there is no shame. The stronger the bond, the more easily a person is shamed. But there is an irony here. Effective shaming depends upon the stake a person has in the community. If a person cares nothing about the opinion any person holds of him or her, shame is a useless tool. But such a person is extremely rare in society and is classified by a psychiatric disorder. More common is the person who cares little about the opinion of those who hold mainstream values. Instead, he or she cares about the opinion of other members of an oppositional subculture. Shaming remains quite effective, but only within the subgroup boundaries. The trick is to increase the stake of the norm violator in the larger community.

From the perspective of control theory (Hirschi 1969), crime is committed most by those who have the greatest freedom and the smallest stake in the community: young, unemployed, unmarried, urban, nonwhite males. The larger community must offer a compelling reason to embrace mainstream values and behaviors. Thus, where shame fails, it is an indication of the offender's low stake, and the proper recourse is not stigmatization but integration. The appropriate focus may be individualistic at first; but once it is determined that the offender is not subject to shaming because of a marginal status in the larger community, then efforts need to be directed toward inclusion. Preventive measures are warranted in such places as underclass ghettos, where large numbers of individuals are disenfranchised.

It is not easy for a justice process to increase the sense of inclusion, to strengthen the bonds to the community, when it has as its objective removing the offender from the community. Nor is the desired outcome likely when community members, family members, and the victim are excluded from the justice process. In our view, by committing a crime, the offender calls forth reasonable questions about his or her degree of commitment to membership in the community. Without a process in which those questions can be addressed together with the community, we can expect little from the justice process other than a further deterioration of the basis by which an offender would feel shame. The question facing the community justice approach is how to create and strengthen the bonds that restrain criminality. A "balanced" approach that emphasizes restorative, community-based sanctions, offender competency development, and community protection is a model for achieving inclusion (Bazemore and Maloney 1994; Bazemore and Umbreit 1994).

Mutuality

Mutuality, the third principle of egalitarian community justice, underpins the coordinated efforts of individuals who share interests in common, such as personal safety. Mutuality is an instrumental principle based on the fact that the pursuit of individual interests is often enhanced through cooperative endeavor, or at least cannot be undertaken without reference to the impact of such pursuits on others. In Selznick's words (1996, p. 18): "Mutuality arises from all the ways people are knit together by interdependence, reciprocity, and self-interest. . . . Mutuality also invokes the distinctive moralities of negotiation, contract, and association, especially trust, good faith, and reliance. It thereby creates the moral infrastructure of cooperation."

The problem addressed by the mutuality principle is straightforward. How can individuals organize themselves so as to minimize or adjudicate conflicts of interest and to maximize efficient, coordinated joint pursuits of common interests? For rational choice theorists, "one of the most fundamental theoretical issues . . . is whether or not cooperation is possible among egoists" (Yamagishi 1994, p. 317). That is, we must ask how it is possible to gain cooperation between people who are less concerned about the general welfare and more concerned about bettering their own lives. What are the mechanisms that moderate negative aggregate consequences of individually self-interested action and what are the mechanisms that engender economies of scale in producing collective goods? More specifically for our purposes, the mutuality principle speaks to the problem of galvanizing support for crime prevention efforts and identifying strategies that reduce the incentives for first-order noncooperation or free riding (engaging in criminal activity) and for second-order noncooperation (failing to prevent others from engaging in criminal activity or free riding).

Mutuality is a principle that recognizes the powerful effects of the self-interest motive and seeks forms of social organization that either capitalize on it or directly keep it in check through sanctioning noncooperation. Capitalizing on the self-interest motive is a market approach because it involves rewarding cooperative behavior. Sanctioning tends to be state based, because it involves a regulatory imposition of costs (Karp and Gaulding 1995). When the state is democratic, the sanctioning approach is characterized as "mutual coercion, mutually agreed-upon," to use Garrett Hardin's (1968) classic phrase. The assumption of self-interest, for sociologists such as Michael Hechter (1987) or James Coleman (1990), is an overarching principle for all human motivation and the root condition that should guide all explanations of social behavior. We do not agree with this view, but we nevertheless concur that much is to be gained by identifying the mechanisms that facilitate cooperation among self-interested actors. Such a perspective underlies some recent prominent explanations of criminal behavior (Cornish and Clarke 1986; Wilson and Herrnstein 1985).

The Prisoner's Dilemma

The mutuality principle has its intellectual origins in the experimental gaming literature, which has evolved primarily around the "prisoner's dilemma game" (Pruitt and Kimmel 1977). The game is a metaphor for a variety of social situations that demand cooperation to produce the best collective outcome, even though for any individual faced with the dilemma the best choice is noncooperation or "defection." This is the dilemma in its original formulation:

> Two suspects are taken into custody and separated. The district attorney is certain that they are guilty of a specific crime, but he does not have adequate evidence to convict them at a trial. He points out to each prisoner that each has two alternatives: to confess to the crime the police are sure they have done, or not to confess. If they both do not confess, then the district attorney states he will book them on some very minor trumped-up charge such as petty larceny and illegal possession of a weapon, and they will both receive minor punishments; if they both confess they will be prosecuted, but he will recommend less than the most severe sentence; but if one confesses and the other does not, then the confessor will receive lenient treatment for turning state's evidence whereas the latter will get "the book" slapped at him (Luce and Raiffa, 1957, p. 95).

The "game," of course, is to place oneself in the position of one of the prisoners and to make the choice of confessing or not confessing in a way that will produce the best outcome for oneself. The dilemma is captured in Table 5.2, where the columns represent the choice for Prisoner A and the rows represent the choice for Prisoner B. The problem with the decision is that one's own outcome is determined not only by one's own choice but also by the decision of the other. Should we assume the other prisoner will hold his or her tongue, securing the best possible joint outcome, or would we expect the other to confess in an attempt to secure the best individual outcome?

The prisoner's dilemma is not really about prisoners. It is about the possibility of cooperation in any situation where there is a conflict of interests. The "game" is figuring out a way to elicit cooperation when the rational pursuit of self-interest militates against it. Mutuality is a justice principle that seeks resolution to the dilemma by disclosing the nature of mutual interdependence and the incentive structure of cooperation.

Two variations of the prisoner's dilemma are especially relevant to community justice. The first is called the "iterated prisoner's dilemma." The lesson it teaches is that long-term relationships in a community counteract the motivation to defect because they supply opportunities for rewarding cooperation and punishing defection. The second is the "N-person prisoner's dilemma." Its lesson is the importance of individual efficacy in linking individuals to communities.

The iterated dilemma requires that the game be played repeatedly. Thus, the short-term gain of player A defecting when B cooperates is off-

TABLE 5.2   The Prisoner's Dilemma

		Prisoner A	
		Not to confess	*To confess*
Prisoner B	*Not to confess*	Good for A Good for B	Great for A Terrible for B
	To confess	Terrible for A Great for B	Bad for A Bad for B

set by B's memory of A's behavior and the ability to return the favor in the next round. Robert Axelrod's (1984) well-known conclusion regarding the iterated dilemma is that although defection can yield short-term benefits, cooperation is the only way to achieve the greatest gains in the long run. The principal lesson is the necessity to cultivate long-term relationships because it is here that individuals have the most incentive to cooperate. The mutuality principle thus builds upon the principle of inclusion by identifying the strategic value of integrating noncooperators.

The original, or one-shot, prisoner's dilemma is the incentive structure of short-term relationships, whereas the iterated game mirrors the incentives of long-term relationships. In a one-shot game, defection is the preferable choice of self-interested actors because it prevents the chance of being exploited and receiving the worst outcome, and offers the chance of gaining the best possible outcome by exploiting the other. This is why communities suffer when they are characterized by anonymity, instability, and instrumentality of relations. In the iterated dilemma, cooperation is the preferable choice because defection by one can be reciprocated by the other in the next round. A tit-for-tat relationship can bring about cooperation even among egoists. Mutuality is a principle that advocates enmeshing possible "defectors" (offenders) in long-term, interdependent relationships, where they can obtain the benefits of cooperation but are reciprocally subject to the costs of defection.

Mutual monitoring and sanctioning is well and good for the dyadic relationships of the iterated prisoner's dilemma, but the second variant of the experimental game calls attention to a substantial problem. Tit-for-tat works when one's influence on the others' outcome is direct and measurable. What happens, however, when the game is played with more than two players, as in the "N-person" prisoner's dilemma?

In the iterated game, one player's influence is quite high, directly affecting the other's outcomes. But in the N-person game, where the game is played with more than two players, one individual's influence declines proportionately with the number of players in the game. McMillan and

Chavis (1986) argue that influence is an important dimension of community satisfaction. Individuals feel a sense of community when they appreciate the relevance of their place in the collectivity—when they feel that they matter. This is especially true in terms of their own efficacy in influencing communal outcomes.

Imagine a call for collective action such as the organization of a neighborhood citizen patrol. Each resident may desire the enhanced security that a patrol might provide. However, residents quickly realize that with so large a pool of residents to draw from, their own participation would make little difference in the campaign. The campaign is not going to succeed or fail on the basis of their contribution, just as an election outcome is not swayed by the vote of one citizen. This "diffusion of responsibility" (Fleishman 1980) partly explains the difficulty in mounting community crime prevention campaigns (Rosenbaum 1988).

Studies of the N-person's dilemma point to two solutions to the problem of insufficient individual influence. The first is subjective and relies on our desire for group belonging (Caporael et al. 1989; Dawes et al. 1988; 1990). Without actually providing new incentives for cooperation, individuals are more likely to cooperate when they feel a strong sense of group identification than when they do not (Brewer and Kramer 1986; Kramer and Brewer 1986). Thus, group identity is often sufficient to overcome the sense of inefficacy that motivates noncooperation. A community approach cultivates the feeling of belonging by clarifying membership and making visible the reality of community. In other words, an important marker of individual competency is the capacity for social identification to overcome the isolation commonly felt in modern, mass society.

Studies also point to the need for strategies that increase the objective efficacy of individuals (Kerr 1989; 1993; Klandermans 1984). For a community justice approach, this means direct links must be shown between effort and outcomes, such as selective incentives for participation in collective action (free caps for joining a citizen patrol) or concrete rewards for actions that help integrate individuals into conventional life (e.g., guaranteed employment for at-risk students who maintain a certain high school grade-point average). The principle of mutuality posits that individuals have a stake in community life; but a contemporary ethos of individualism obscures this stake, and coherent strategies need to be developed that make it manifest. Thus mutuality builds upon inclusion by framing the individual's stake in community life in the context of disclosing and fostering social interdependencies.

The concern for efficacy applies not only to individuals living within communities but also to the relationship between communities. We have said that egalitarian community justice will require investments of resources in communities that are hard hit by crime. Those who live elsewhere may wonder why it is in their interest to do so. Indeed, for a well-off community to keep its own resources close to home might seem to pay off, especially in the short run. But policies that fail to strengthen the resources of high-crime communities inevitably affect the quality of life in every community: Just ask New Yorkers on the Upper West Side if crime in the Bronx worries them. Mutuality in this context supports strategies that disclose the interdependencies between communities so that each recognizes its stake in preserving the whole. In this sense, mutuality complements the principle of equality.

Stewardship

Stewardship is the final principle of egalitarian community justice. Stewardship might make the strongest claim of all these principles on members of the community. It asks not simply that citizens treat each other fairly (equality); that citizens take their own and others' membership in the community seriously (inclusion); and that citizens coordinate their own interests with those of the collectivity (mutuality). Stewardship also asks that citizens step into the shoes of others, show concern for the welfare of the community, and even be willing to sacrifice some of their own desires in the pursuit of the common good. Thus, stewardship is a principle that emphasizes moral development, pressing individuals to think of themselves as members of a community, with duties as well as rights.

Stewardship is a principle that demands attention to the cultural and structural conditions that facilitate collective regard. Stewardship demands that we preserve the environment for future generations and that corporations consider the welfare of their employees—even of the neighborhoods surrounding their plants—in addition to the corporate "bottom line" (Selznick 1996). Thus, stewardship calls for a cognizance of the needs of those whom we do not know personally or intimately and for the needs of the whole community. Stewardship directs our attention to the effects of crime on the community as well as to the social conditions that promote crime; it redirects our focus from incidents in isolation to a responsiveness to general patterns and trends.

The stewardship principle is less necessary in an authoritarian society, where coercive obedience to the law is the model for eliciting cooperation. In a market-based society, the principle of mutuality calls for an incentive-based approach designed to align individual and collective interests. Where possible, this should be encouraged. Stewardship implies, however, that a democracy needs much more. Indeed, it is a view that individuals, even for their own development, must do more than pursue their own interests. In part, they must be able to delay gratification of immediate interests for the sake of their future selves (Gottfredson and Hirschi 1990); but they must also be able to sympathize with the needs of others (Wilson 1993).

Recent research on values indicates an inevitable tension between self-enhancement values, such as valuing the attainment of social status or wealth, and self-transcendence values, such as concern for the welfare of others and of society (Schwartz 1992). The latter are often seen as indicators of moral development (Kohlberg 1968). Clearly, it is necessary for the functioning of a democracy to elicit the attention of its citizens to public affairs (Barber 1984; Fishkin 1992). Otherwise, the abdication of responsibility will lead to uneven distributions of power, and the needs and concerns of those outside the democratic process will go unmet. Thus, the democratic process serves as a means for ensuring equality and inclusion as well as a mechanism of drawing individual attention to collective problems and ideals.

Even Adam Smith (1966) once argued that sympathy for others is a prerequisite for a good society. It is necessary for people to feel emotionally connected to others in order for them to think and act for others' welfare (Sen 1978). McMillan and Chavis's "sense of community" construct includes a dimension of emotional connectedness. They argue that community satisfaction is partly predicated on the positive feelings community members hold toward one another and on the emotional investment they have in their relations. It is in this context of emotional bonds that individuals develop the capacity to "take the role of the other" (Mead 1956) and to consider the collective consequences of particular courses of action.

Moral Order

Stewardship is a principle of justice that draws attention to the need for sympathy in a society that is otherwise self-regarding. In essence, it tries to establish moral order amid the temptation to disregard others in the narrow pursuit of one's own interests. The problem involves more than mere coordination of individual interests; because—though it is laudable when successful—such coordination is not likely to be sufficient to the scale of the problem. Wrong (1994, p. 36) succinctly captures the inherent conflict:

> The problem of order arises out of the dual circumstance that human beings have limited (though not nonexistent) capacities for sympathy with their fellows and that they inhabit an environment that fails to provide them with sufficient resources to satisfy fully the needs of all of them. The problem of order is therefore a genuinely transhistorical problem rooted in inescapable conflict between the interests and desires of individuals and the requirements of society: to wit, the pacification of violent strife among men and the secure establishment of cooperative social relations making possible the pursuit of collective goals.

Stewardship is a principled response to excessive individualism, which in its extreme creates the Hobbesian war of all against all. In contemporary terms, developing stewardship in individuals is equivalent to moral and civic education; it is the creation of normative standards that demand more from individuals than selfishness or indifference toward communal needs. To use James Q. Wilson's (1993) phrase, it is the creation of a "moral sense" based on sympathy, fairness, self-control, and duty. A community justice approach, therefore, tries to cultivate voluntarism in community members and prioritizes service to victims and the community as an appropriate sanction to criminal offenders. However, community service is not simply punishment, and such an equation undermines its moral purpose and expressive significance as a sanction (Kahan 1996). Instead, its use as a sanction must be understood both as instrumental for restoration and as symbolic of the offender's commitment to conventional reintegration.

Stewardship as a principle of justice requires a democratic process of examining local standards of behavior and adjudicating between the tolerance for nonconformity and the setting and enforcement of limits. The current concern with disorder stems from a hypothesized link between the normative milieu and criminal behavior (Kelling and Coles 1996; Wilson and Kelling 1982). Disorder itself is primarily a concern because of the cues it provides about the vulnerability of a neighborhood to more serious crime. Presumably, it causes law-abiding residents to withdraw from community life and emboldens offenders, who perceive that their own actions will go unnoticed or unchallenged.

A community justice approach to maintaining order does not necessarily advocate more aggressive enforcement by police, or "defining deviance up." The approach begins with a community's careful consideration of normative standards and the consequences of nonconformity. Where harmful effects are clearly established, strategies for increasing informal social control are to be developed, typically in partnership with justice officials. This is a common theme in community justice approaches to policing (Kelling and Coles 1996), prosecution (Boland, 1998), and community courts (Rottman 1996).

Stewardship requires thoughtful consideration of the aggregate consequences of individual action—in effect, balancing individual freedoms against the common good. Without stewardship, a positive tolerance for diversity quickly degenerates into an inability to advance collective agendas and an incapacity to combat threats to public safety.

Conclusion

The principles of egalitarian community justice orient justice practices toward three crucial arenas in community life. First, they emphasize the subjective sense of community by attending to the fulfillment of needs, membership, influence, and emotional connection. Community justice seeks to enhance community members' personal experience of community life. Thus it is always concerned with questions of neighborhood satisfaction and perceptions of institutional responsiveness and fairness. Second, the principles speak to the development of individual competencies that empower community members to seek and fulfill their own and collective ends. In particular, these competencies include mastery of skills, sociability in relating to diverse others, identification with community, and social concern. Finally, the egalitarian principles are directed toward the achievement of common goals that underlie a just and capable community: distributive justice, social integration, social coordination, and moral order.

A community justice ideal can promote egalitarian concepts of community in various ways. A direct illustration is provided by the way offenders can improve stewardship by working on community-directed reclamation projects instead of occupying a prison cell. Imagine, as we have envisioned in our introduction to this manuscript, the benefits of several dozen workers who are providing free labor that renovates dilapidated local housing, serves the needs of the elderly, or provides assistance to residents with special needs. There is a double victory to such an arrangement: The improved local stewardship is obvious; but even more important is the trajectory of offender reintegration.

We also specifically design community justice as an inclusive ideal. Offenders are members of their communities, as are the victims of their crimes. If we are to think of them all as responsible members of a collective aspiration, then we must include them each in the designation of responses to the criminal incidents. The previous chapter makes our intentions in this regard explicit.

But in arguing for equality, inclusion, mutuality, and stewardship, we do not refer merely to the relations of individuals who live within communities; we refer as well to the relations of communities within a polity. As the idea of modernity makes clear, we live in a social reality of interconnectedness. The quality of life in one locality matters to other localities.

Our view of community justice begins with a proposal to treat communities as having equal value; and this requires that we focus first on those communities with the least basis for confronting their own crime problems. In the next chapter, we will propose an investment in the community justice infrastructure of these communities. Although we strongly believe that there are sufficient public funds to support this work—and we will indicate where those funds ought to come from—in the end, we recognize that wealthy communities will need to invest in the poorest communities, or very little will be possible. In a sense, we argue along the lines of Dworkin (1984) that justice requires an equal playing field and that until there is an equal capacity for action, there will be no true equality of responsibility for action. Such cooperation between communities requires a clear disclosure of their interdependence and a commitment to the principles of equality and mutuality.

The ideal of community justice—that community-based efforts and a supportive criminal justice system enhance community life—is reflected in egalitarian principles that set a philosophical standard for criminal justice practice. It is not enough to punish an offender by locking him or her up, if the result is social disintegration or an exacerbation of current social inequalities. Nor is it expedient to lubricate social coordination by rewarding self-interested behavior, if this undermines the moral development of citizens. Each principle must be advanced without violating another. This is the true challenge of community justice.

6

Realizing
Community Justice

The case for community justice is a call for a fundamental rethinking of the purpose and practice of justice. The shift toward community would open up the justice system to include a deeper involvement of victims and other citizens, and it would set its sights upon improving the quality of community life. The isolation of the justice professions would be replaced by a more interdependent relationship with community life. Undoubtedly, a common pursuit of the ideal of community justice would precipitate changes in almost every aspect of today's justice traditions.

This chapter identifies a number of issues that system workers, citizens, and elected officials must reconcile in a move toward a community justice ideal. It must be emphasized that this discussion is *not* meant to serve as a blueprint for change. Everything we have said about community justice up to this point implies that a blueprint cannot be devised. A community justice system is above everything else a *local* solution to *local* crime problems. A strategy that brings about community justice will necessarily grow out of a local assessment of strengths and impediments. In some areas, the initiative will come from citizens; elsewhere, justice officials will provide the guiding spark. The institutional design of community justice actions will be centered in traditional correctional procedures in some locales, and in law enforcement or adjudicatory practices in others. In other words, community justice implies only an activated community; the particular realization of community action will vary from place to place. There is no recipe for community justice, and to seek such a formula would be to waste opportunities for discovering creative new methods of achieving community justice.

Nevertheless, in this chapter we identify several domains of practice that need to be addressed in any attempt to move toward a more community-oriented justice system. These are: identifying communities, clarifying legal rights, fostering community development, decentralizing authority and accountability, mobilizing and representing communities, monitoring and supervising offenders in the community, and funding new practices.

Identifying Communities

Community justice typically emphasizes the local area as the unit of analysis. This approach undoubtedly engenders an appropriate sense of human proportion to criminal justice efforts. But in important ways, a focus on neighborhoods is unnecessarily narrow and evidences a reductionist conception of community. Three orthogonal dimensions ought to be considered when defining *community* with regard to community justice: geography, interdependency, and identity.

The geographic conception of community is rooted in intuitive understandings of community (e.g., as the small town) and in the human ecology of the Chicago School. Robert Park, for example, once wrote: "The essential characteristics of a community, so conceived, are those of: (1) a population, territorially organized, (2) more or less completely rooted in the soil it occupies, (3) its individual units living in a relationship of mutual interdependence that is symbiotic rather than societal" (Park 1936, p. 3). From the Chicago perspective, social relations have their origins in physical propinquity: To understand the metropolis, one must examine the "natural areas" that subdivide the city. Avery M. Guest (1984) associates the natural area concept with two geographically based factors: length of residence and number of local intimate ties. Much research supports the near association of geographic neighborhood with community. For example, Guest and Lee (1984) found that subjective definitions of community (by residents) are affected by the natural and the built environments (also see Taylor 1988).

These associations are fundamental to concepts of territoriality and surveillance in defensible space theory (Newman 1972); perceptions of social disorder (Skogan 1990; Wilson and Kelling 1982); and the foot and bicycle patrols of community policing (Peak and Glensor 1996). The geographic conception of community is advantageous to community justice because social relations are often more extensive and intensive with proximity, creating numerous opportunities for the exercise of informal social control. In addition, geography is (obviously) the most easily mapped of the three factors of community, facilitating empirical analysis and programmatic efforts to build community. Recent advances in Geographic Information Systems technology have greatly enhanced the potentiality of data collection at the local level.

The now well established idea of crime hot spots (Weisburd and Eck 1995) can be used to identify locations in which crime and related problems exist with the greatest density. These are the areas in which the negative effects of crime can be expected to be the most severe. The geography of crime is a relatively new area for scientific inquiry; but early studies indicate wide disparities in levels of crime across communities, and pockets of concentration in street crime. Using the type of geographic software that identifies places (such as MAPINFO) will enable community justice organizers to detect localities that stand to benefit most from concentrated efforts to prevent crime through environmentally specific approaches. The first step in a community justice rationale is to identify communities where the greatest payoff will occur in crime prevention efforts. Those are the communities suffering from the greatest crime and seeking to manage the greatest concentration of experienced offenders.

Geography has its limits, however. Unlike the early observations of the Chicago School, in which economy and geography were closely related (e.g., the concentric zones described in Burgess 1967), the two have become increasingly, though not entirely, detached as a result of technological advancement in communications and transportation (Hawley 1971). The same can be said of social relations. Familial links, friendship, and other social ties are now more diffused than concentrated. Barry Wellman and Barry Leighton (1979) have asserted that community is better described by social networks than by the determinism of space. Their research demonstrates the importance of intimate ties that extend well beyond neighborhood boundary lines.

As a second dimension of community, it is imperative to consider the interdependency of individuals. Individuals never exist in isolation (even when an individual is physically separated from others, his or her behavior follows from earlier socialization and social cognition); and if an individual's social ties are sparse in local geography, those ties are likely to be more intensive elsewhere. Interdependency refers both to affective attachments and to material investment. From this perspective, community may be viewed as strong where mutual dependence is high, and as weak where individuals are relatively independent. Such interdependence is made concrete in the political economy of a community as well as in its social institutions. To what extent do individuals make use of local institutions? Where do they work, shop, have bank accounts, and invest their civic energy? Who are their friends? Where do they find entertainment, legal advice, and educational training? The social networks created through social interactions are often stronger indicators of community than geography.

Since wealth is unevenly distributed across space, looking to the local area alone for evidence of community, and particularly communal obligation, precludes any coordination of resource exchange between rich and poor areas. The social isolation of urban ghettos is more important than their physical location (Wilson 1987). Nevertheless, suburban residents benefit greatly from the inner city, creating gross inequities as urban residents support services that suburbanites depend upon (Molotch 1976; Rusk 1995). Fostering interdependence between the class-divided areas of the metropolis may be the single most important action one could undertake toward eliminating ghetto crime.

Another dimension worthy of consideration is identity. Identity, too, does not necessarily conform to geography. Identity is a dimension of community that reflects the degree to which members share similar demographic traits: Solidarity is based on membership in the same church, race, profession, or other social organization or category. These status characteristics presuppose common values, attitudes, and beliefs. Communities of identity foster ties across space—a fact that is well illustrated when people from distant locales gather for some common purpose (e.g., the Million-Man March). Geography and identity, of course, often overlap, as they do in ethnic enclaves. But in these cases, shared identity may be a stronger factor than geography in sustaining the community (Firey 1945; Gans 1962; Suttles 1968).

Can the three dimensions of community—geography, interdependence, and identity—be enhanced, or can one compensate for another's deficit? Generally, community building strategies compensate for a weakness in one dimension by developing the others. Business Improvement Districts (BIDs), for example, increase community identity by making shared geography and economic interdependence salient. BIDs foster new conceptions of communal identity (businesses as active community members) and new normative standards for these actors (businesses have a responsibility for reducing social disorder). As another example, Neighborhood Watch programs and citizen patrols make use of identity born of shared concerns for neighborhood safety. This common ground helps overcome the anonymity of communities where individuals neither know nor depend on one another on a regular basis. However, as Wesley G. Skogan (1988, p. 47) has observed:

> Civilian patrols [are] most common in racially mixed areas of cities. Rather than drawing the community together, preservationist groups in these areas may selectively recruit members on the basis of their values and backgrounds, and their efforts—including crime prevention—may be divisive rather than integrative.

Unfortunately, the strong in-group identification that is sometimes used to get collective action off the ground may undermine the larger goals of community building and public safety if that identification invokes racial discord.

In history and in contemporary life, the concept of community has been closely tied to geography. But community justice can also explore and develop the other dimensions of community. Communities, bounded simply by geography, can easily become isolationist by their own design or can be cordoned off from the resources and opportunities enjoyed by their neighbors. Just as individuals are best understood as embedded within a larger social framework, so communities should be understood by the networks that extend beyond geographic boundaries. The crosscutting allegiances of community members to several geographic and extrageographic communities (Etzioni 1996b), and the nesting of communal identifications within ever larger frameworks (Hunter and Suttles 1972), provide a context for responsive relations across social as well as physical space.

Clarifying Legal Rights

The victims' rights movement reached something of a zenith when political leaders came together supporting a victims' rights amendment to the U.S. Constitution. This initiative would establish procedural rights for victims, assigning them a specific status in the formal justice system—the rights of notification, speed, and representation. Some critics have disputed the wisdom of this reform, arguing that elevating the status of the victim will handcuff prosecutors and weaken civil protections for accused persons. Nevertheless, this proposal symbolizes the centrality of victims in a reformed justice process.

The view of justice proposed here is very different from the procedural ideal of justice in traditional Western jurisprudence. In place of the adversarial contest between the state and an accused citizen, the idea of community justice concentrates on a problem-solving process designed to restore safety to the places where people live. Under such an ideal, rights are not procedural; instead, they are substantive. Where an adversarial ideal extends rights of due process, a problem-solving ideal extends rights of due consideration. The elements of due process are well known: timely notice, physical presence, counsel, permission to confront the other side, and an opportunity to be heard. What kinds of measures would rights to "due consideration" entail?

A right to due consideration based in problem-solving becomes an obligation to consider as important a range of needs and interests of victims, offenders, and the communities in which they live. In contrast to an adversarial ceremony in which strict rules apply to the admissibility of evidence and the weight it receives, "consideration" would permit parties to the process to offer whatever understandings they believed necessary to resolve the problem. The "problem" in terms of community justice is expressed as a series of questions and interests:

- What is needed to restore the victim?
- What is needed to ensure the community's future safety?
- What is needed to foster the offender's return to constructive community life?

In this context, *due consideration* means the full range of statements, claims, experiences, potentialities, and assurances that might help answer the core questions of community justice. Familiar elements of the evidentiary process, such as corroboration and cross-examination, do not adequately serve these ends. A process of adjudication of claims, facts, and inferences must be added in order to arrive at a resolution of the criminal event that allows the parties to proceed toward a new order of actions and responsibilities. Resolution will include elements such as treatment, restitution, community service, and public sanctions as evidence of a new commitment to live safely among neighbors. To establish this outcome, all parties involved must be willing to consider all possible responses that seem appropriate given the particular facts and circumstances of the case.

This does not mean an end to traditional procedural rights. Neither the victim nor the accused should be coerced into a problem-solving process they believe does not apply to them. Defendants who sincerely claim innocence must be able to force their accusers to prove them guilty. Victims should not be forced to interact with their admitted victimizers when this will only produce more pain and suffering on the victims' part. Communities should not be forced to consider embracing offenders who show no willingness to address the problems that make them dangerous to others. It may take repeated efforts on the part of community justice practitioners to pave the way for an interactive, problem-solving process.

In today's reality, however, full-blown trials are comparatively rare events. Most criminal cases are concluded when the offender enters a guilty plea. For the vast majority of offenders who admit their guilt, community justice activities could begin with the entry of a guilty plea. After the offender has publicly accepted responsibility for having committed the offense, a series of information-gathering activities can take place that are designed to answer these questions:

- What is the victim's loss, and how can that loss be compensated?
- What is the risk of reoffense, and how can that risk be managed and reduced?
- How can the community be made safe from crime, especially given this offender's presence?
- What actions on the part of the offender can publicly symbolize atonement for the crime?

Facts and opinions related to these questions are reviewed by the parties, and a plan that will meet the needs of the parties is proposed. If the plan is agreed to by victim, offender, and community, it takes the form of a written sentencing recommendation presented to the judge, submitted by the community justice panel. The panel's functioning would more closely resemble that of an administrative law tribunal than of a criminal court, and various ideas would be broadly explored for meeting the needs of the parties.

A similar process could follow a conviction at trial, but it would face two additional obstacles. First, the task of promoting confidence in the offender's sincerity is undermined by the trial, in which the offender's claim of innocence was found to be false. Second, the victim's belief that a safe and meaningful outcome to the crime is possible is made more problematic by the offender's forcing the system to prove its case. Thus, when a criminal trial results in a finding of guilt, a greater burden rests on the offender to find ways to convince a community justice panel that he or she feels a sense of personal responsibility and is prepared to make amends.

There will, of course, be cases when either the offender or the victim rejects the idea of a problem-solving process, just as there will be times when a post-conviction program cannot be devised that elicits enough confidence from community members that they can support it. In these cases, the traditional adversarial sentencing process can proceed as it normally would, without a recommendation from the community panel.

Likewise, there will be cases when the offender fails to conform his or her behavior to the plan. When there are new arrests, these can proceed by the same process as any other criminal complaint. When the problem is the offender's failure to carry out elements of the plan, the response can be a renewed effort to identify the obstacles to compliance (even if these are primarily the offender's resistance) and to articulate ways to overcome those obstacles.

Thus, community justice would not require replacing the existing justice system, nor would it invalidate any of the existing procedural rights of offenders and victims. Instead, a new process would be inserted that would, upon the establishment of guilt, attempt to broadly arrange a sanction that meets the needs of the parties to the criminal event.

Fostering Community Development

Community justice is an endeavor to embrace community development initiatives and move beyond the traditionally narrow mandate of law enforcement. But of the myriad possibilities for action, collaboration, and partnership, what should the substance of community justice activities include? Recent community justice initiatives appear to coalesce around three arenas: situational crime prevention, neighborhood reclamation, and citizen support services.

Situational crime prevention strategies have been widely discussed in recent criminological literature (Clarke 1995). There are particularized versions of this approach, but each is designed to attack specific crime problems through a problem identification/problem solving sequence that gathers information about precise crime problems—usually defined in terms of their precise location in time and space—and builds solutions based on the reduction of criminal opportunities. Much of the data used to analyze crime situations comes from the local police; but experts acknowledge that residents living near those crime problems can also be extremely helpful in developing intelligence about the crime as well as devising strategies for eliminating the crime. Situational crime prevention proceeds from expert leadership, and it is usually implemented by experts. Residents may play a role in these efforts, but it is generally quite limited.

That is not the case with neighborhood reclamation projects. These projects rebuild neighborhood structures that have deteriorated, such as dilapidated or abandoned buildings and disintegrating road surfaces. This type of work can be very useful for preventing crime. Unoccupied buildings become havens for illicit activities, and potholed streets are avoided by drivers, leaving them empty and inviting to illegal behavior. Most high-crime neighborhoods are also neglected neighborhoods, with decaying infrastructure that is in need of attention. Too often the political payoff for repairing such structures is very limited. Thus, in many of these areas, structures are left crumbling until they eventually fall. It often requires purposeful investments of time and priority for these problems to be overcome. A key assumption underlying the principle of stewardship, on which we commented at length in the preceding chapter, is that the maintenance of such basic infrastructure spills over into other social goods, such as safety.

Local human effort can be important to reclaiming physical aspects of neighborhoods, because hard labor is usually required. Numerous rebuilding groups heavily use volunteer labor because the costs of hired labor would be prohibitive. In high-crime neighborhoods, there is an untapped supply of potentially "free" labor that might be used to address these problems: offenders. Community justice models might attempt to employ this unused labor source to revitalize structures in their local areas, and this can be a way for the offenders to repay communities for their offenses, as well.

Citizen support services help citizens who are at risk to feel safer and obtain a higher quality of life while residing in these locales. Social groups at high risk include children (especially the children of lawbreakers), the elderly, and the disabled. Children can be supported through after-school programs, tutoring, mentoring, and recreational programs. The elderly also need various services, from transportation to and from medical and social services, to medical supervision and even social visits for conversation. The creation of these interdependencies helps establish the basis for mutuality that sustains community life.

Unlike crime prevention and reclamation projects, support services do not have an immediate payoff in controlling crime. The idea of strengthening communities through investing in the quality of life of its members is a long-range strategy. It seeks to address crime by addressing the malaise that cultivates crime; it fights the alienation and despair of the least vigorous citizens. It establishes a floor below which the quality of life will not descend. This fights crime by making the vulnerable less susceptible to the evils of crime.

Taken together, these three strategies—prevention, reclamation, and services—define a troika of targets for crime reduction that can be activated by communities. What role, if any, do offenders have in this strategy? As laborers and residents, offenders can fill some of the voids that others are unwilling to fill. But is this realistic? Some offenders plainly will not fit this agenda. Those who seek only to victimize their neighbors and who see them as opportunities for self-advancement—and many community members are like this, not only criminal offenders—will not take advantage of the chance to reinvest in community life. Others will. As a result, applicants for a community justice initiative will have to be screened. But the idea of offenders working to resurrect the very community that their crimes attacked is attractive.

Monitoring and Supervising Offenders in the Community

We should not be sanguine about offenders. Many reoffend, and often their crimes are serious. In fact, the biggest impediment to rational crime policy is the too-frequent public scandal of repeat offenders. Any program designed to improve the quality of life in the community must be concerned with community safety and must consider the threat presented to community safety by convicted serious offenders.

Community-based crime policy need not embrace dangerous offenders. Supporters of prison-based crime policy are fond of pointing out that people already known to the justice system commit most violent felonies. This is true. And it means that if the justice system were more effective with the people it encounters, great benefits in public safety might accrue. But the assumption that most offenders known to the justice system cannot be worked with in the community does not follow automatically, and indeed, it is plainly false. Most violent crime can be attributed to known offenders, but there are many more known offenders than there are violent crimes. Most known offenders never become violent offenders. The question is how to prevent crime by controlling violent offenders at the same time that we redirect the efforts of the nonviolent toward enhanced community life.

It is now possible to assess offender risk—not perfectly, but certainly usefully. Risk assessment has two components. First, what are the chances that a given offender will commit another crime? Second, what can be done to redirect the offender's behavior toward community development? These are important, even complicated questions, but they are not intractable. To find ways to benefit from offenders' work requires us to see them as potential resources, not as irremediable drains upon resources.

Offender work details tend not to be as efficient as labor provided by the private sector. Offenders are often less reliable workers; require more supervision, and a type of security not normally provided in the private sector; and their employment comes with risk management priorities that complicate the workplace. Therefore, it is seldom practical to use offender work details in projects that are bid out to private providers. But in most high-crime neighborhoods, there are numerous tasks needing attention for which there are no bids to be taken and no funds with which to purchase services. It seems an extremely desirable form of mutuality to invest in these uses of offender labor.

Decentralizing Authority and Accountability

When power is transferred from government to community, problems may occur at two margins. At one margin, there is the problem of mobilization when the community fails to take responsibility for the problems it is to solve (the next section discusses this). At the other margin, communities may take full responsibility, but in a sense, do too much. It is possible that communities will use means that conflict with broader values of the culture—for example, vigilantism or discrimination. When power is informal, how may actors (and communities) should be held accountable? This problem is especially acute for autonomous community crime prevention efforts because they lack the formal oversight of criminal justice agencies.

In New Haven, Connecticut, a late 1980s police crackdown on prostitution in the city's well-known red-light district had the unfortunate effect of displacing the sex trade to the surrounding residential neighborhoods. One of these was Edgewood Park, a racially and economically heterogeneous neighborhood. Prostitutes began their work in Edgewood early in the morning, targeting those heading to work, and continued through the day and into the night. Used condoms littered the playgrounds, and schoolchildren waited for buses adjacent to prostitutes waiting for johns. In response, community members organized a campaign to reduce prostitution (Bass 1992).

When neighbors saw a car circling the same block numerous times or picking up a prostitute, they would take down the license plate number and trace the registration through the Department of Motor Vehicles. They quickly discovered that most johns were not from Edgewood Park but came from other neighborhoods. They sent a letter to the car owner's address, advising the owner that the car had been seen "cruising" the neighborhood. The letter detailed the community's campaign against prostitution and urged the recipient to be careful about whom they lent the car to in the future. In this case, they were somewhat circumspect about directing blame. On the home front, however, the group posted flyers, noting the "john of the week" and carrying the john's name, address, and phone number, based on the information obtained from the DMV. After some johns complained that they were receiving anonymous, threatening phone calls, the group stopped including phone numbers on the flyers.

Although no formal study has been conducted, Edgewood's campaign appears to have worked. Daytime prostitution apparently disappeared after the campaign was initiated; and three years after the campaign began, prostitution was "basically gone from the area" (Winokur 1995). However successful, some have questioned the legitimacy of the approach. Lawsuits were filed by some johns against the members of the neighborhood association for harassment. In one case, the alleged john claimed his wife received the letter and left him. The plaintiff's attorney argued: "The harassment statute is certainly violated. They are inflicting wanton pain on people they know to be innocent in order to achieve what they consider a larger goal. I think that's a pretty fair definition of terrorism." Of course, the campaign leader disagreed: "The guy is patronizing a prostitute in my neighborhood. It's affecting my property value. What's the cause of his current problem? Visiting a prostitute in the first place, or having his wife find out about it?" (Bass 1992). Though several cases were filed, all were dismissed.

The Edgewood Neighborhood Association campaign is an example of informal control because the letters and flyers brought the johns' behavior to the attention of their family members and their community. The threat was not of formal sanctioning but of communal status loss. The marital breakup and harassment suits demonstrate the campaign's impact on the targeted individuals. This community action raises important questions regarding the application of informal control.

First, what should be the relationship between the community and the formal justice system? The Edgewood group operated completely autonomously. Obviously, this distance from a formal institution has implications for oversight. In other situations, autonomous community groups have been charged with racism (Skogan 1988) and vigilantism (Weisburd 1988). For example, all-Jewish citizen patrols in Brooklyn's Crown Heights have been known to target blacks, and in some cases, to exercise summary justice on the street (Mitchell 1992). Also, when community members involve themselves directly with criminals, they are placing themselves at risk, probably without the necessary preparation. What situations, if any, are inappropriate for citizen groups to handle? As yet there are no clearly delineated roles for community members.

Second, is this a viable method of sanctioning and deterrence? One of the intriguing decision points for the Edgewood Association involved determining where the flyers would be posted: only in Edgewood, or also near the residences of the targeted johns, who tended not to be locals? They believed that the impact would be stronger if they posted in both areas. In the end, they decided not to post flyers in johns' neighborhoods because this was believed to be overly punitive. The difference was subtle but important. Flyers in Edgewood were designed to be deterrents more than sanctions because they would be seen by other johns rather than by neighbors of the target. Flyers posted so that the johns' family and neighbors would see them were a significantly stronger exercise of informal sanctioning, perhaps effective as a special deterrent, but probably having little general deterrent effect, since johns came from so many different areas. The role of the community is often conceived of in all-or-nothing terms: They should or should not be involved in law enforcement. A far more sophisticated analysis is necessary to examine levels of involvement based on various characteristics of the situation (e.g., type of crime, risk, community capacity, and so on) and the types of sanctioning used. Part of the concern is uncertainty over the effects of normative sanctions. Days in jail are quantifiable, but the impact of a "Dear John" letter is unknown.

Third, to what extent does a community effort represent the entire community? Informal actions by the Edgewood Association were undertaken on behalf of the community. To what extent are they consistent with local normative standards? By definition, community actions are designed to tighten local standards and increase their enforcement. Community members are thereby claiming that what was once acceptable is no longer acceptable. But did they go through some democratic process that enabled community members to clarify their standards and identify appropriate methods of normative enforcement?

Fourth, are the rights of alleged offenders being violated? Clearly, this campaign targeted individuals who were not formally convicted of any offense. Yet they were definitely sanctioned. There was no due process, no opportunity to profess innocence, and no opportunity to contest the community's norms. It was certainly possible that a misread license plate would lead to the targeting of innocent people. Police need more justification than circling the neighborhood to arrest a john: Should community groups be held to a lesser standard? What other protections are necessary to shield the innocent from informal sanctions by the community?

Clearly, the presence of guiding local institutions with their own systems of accountability can help. The Edgewood Neighborhood Association depended primarily upon a local law firm and the leadership of an Orthodox Jewish congregation for its guidance.

In evaluating instances of community justice in the next chapter, we propose that our principles of community justice provide a powerful framework for knowing how beneficial the community justice program is for overall community quality of life. For example, the actions of residents in Edgewood raise questions about inclusion—just who is the community whose interests are at stake? We will return to our listing of principles and methodically show how they provide a structure by which community justice programs can be challenged to become stronger.

The criminal justice system has its formal power fairly consolidated and has traditionally emphasized a procedural model to ensure fairness. Community justice advocates decentralization of this power, in part to increase the system's legitimacy in the eyes of the public, but more importantly to increase the effectiveness of local collective action. In so doing, community justice raises the specter of Montana militias and the Ku Klux Klan. Community justice has yet to specify the framework for a community's accountability to broader standards of the culture.

Mobilizing and Representing the Community

The mantra of practitioners interested in community justice seems to be "We can't do it alone." When the responsibility for social control is shared with the community, we can be concerned about the community doing too much, exceeding the limits of their authority and contradicting overarching values. At the other extreme, it is possible, if not more likely, that the community will not fulfill its expected potential. What if the community fails to take responsibility and ends up doing less than government? In effect, what do we do when the community is invited but no one shows up? Moreover, how do we ensure that community groups and community leaders are fairly representing the "true" interests—or at least, the true diversity of interests—of the community?

Simply put, "Generating and maintaining participation is one of the major implementation difficulties for community crime prevention programs" (Bennett 1995, p. 74). How will we get the community to play an active role? Crime control is a public good. In principle, we would like to reduce crime rather than increase it, but we would also like to reduce the costs (time, effort, money) of fighting crime rather than increase them. The best strategy for individuals, therefore, is to free ride on the crime prevention efforts of others. Unfortunately, when we all depend on others to do the work, nothing gets done. Self-interest overwhelms the public good. The fundamental question is: How can we get people to participate in crime control activities when it is not in their immediate self-interest to do so?

People differ in their levels of trust, social values, and personal tastes. Some will be rallied by their optimism; others may hesitate, perhaps because of the overly optimistic propaganda of previous campaigns. Underlying this difference is uncertainty over the effectiveness of the effort. People will not join unless they are assured some probability of success, especially given the risks of participation. Safety in numbers is especially important when considering levels of distrust between many community members and police and when considering the risks of collective action, such as retaliation by drug dealers (Grinc 1994).

Many will join out of a deep sense of commitment to the community. For them, effectiveness is less important than the goal. Knowing that their cause is just is motivation enough. Some simply find participation interesting and enjoyable. For these people, it is less the goal or the assurance of success than the attractiveness of the means that inspires participation (Goldsmith 1998; Skogan 1988). Olson (1965) argued that collective action was unlikely unless participation offered something compelling in addition to the desired collective benefit. Consider the comment by an Orange Hat citizen patrol member of Washington, D.C.:

> "We enjoy it," says Patty Walker. "We may complain, oh it's cold out here or hot out here or I'm bored or I'd rather be doing something else, but I do think that we enjoy it. You talk, you see what's going on. In the course of all these years you've gotten to find out names and locations of everyone's children or grandchildren, how they're doing in school, where they're going to school. Things like that." (Goldsmith 1998, p. 58)

Mobilization is not completely dependent upon individual characteristics. In addition to trust, values, and tastes, the objective conditions under which collective action takes place may inspire or undermine it.

Some collective efforts require enormous commitments and provide little return. Robert C. Davis and Arthur J. Lurigio (1996) have observed that antidrug campaigns of the late 1980s and 1990s were far more successful than other, earlier crime prevention campaigns. This may be because drug sales take place in stable, visible settings, whereas burglaries and robberies can occur anywhere. Community surveillance is considerably easier in antidrug efforts because the targets are easily found. The Orange Hats, for instance, have targeted one street corner as the focal point of their efforts (Goldsmith 1998). Conducting cost/benefit analyses may resolve long-standing arguments about the likelihood of certain income groups to participate in crime prevention campaigns. Some have argued that those who need to organize the most are the least likely to do so

(Dubow and Podolefsky 1982; Skogan 1988). Yet antidrug efforts in disorganized communities do seem to occur when the potential benefits and the efficiency of crime prevention efforts sufficiently outweigh the costs.

Some communities are better organized than are others at the outset. They have strong local institutions (schools, churches, civic associations, and the like) and viable communication networks that quickly spread the word that a community campaign is under way. The predecessor to the Orange Hats Patrol, for example, was a Neighborhood Watch program organized in conjunction with the police, and this effort created a local network with a block captain (Goldsmith 1998). Community capacity is often dependent upon the social organization of communities (Chavis et al. 1993). To what extent do poverty, inequality, mobility, heterogeneity, urban density, family disruption and other macrolevel variables have an effect on the stake an individual has in the community? And to what extent does this stake, in turn, affect mobilization? Home owners, for example, are more likely to be mobilized than renters (Skogan 1988). Thus, the ratio of owners to renters, and similar macrolevel characteristics, may be important predictors of mobilization.

Even when mobilization is successful, it is important to consider who is being mobilized. Randolph M. Grinc's (1994) evaluation of a community policing program implies that many individuals and interests are typically underrepresented in crime prevention efforts. This may be a result of fear of retaliation by offenders or of the historically poor relationship between the community and the police. It may result from perceptions of low efficacy, in part because community members do not have clearly defined roles with regard to crime prevention and in part because of experience with prior, failed collective actions. Underrepresentation may also result from intergroup tension, manifest in the homogeneous and competitive organization of local groups in heterogeneous communities (Skogan 1988), and from intragroup conflicts that arise between leaders and group members (Grinc 1994).

In collaborations between law enforcement agencies and private citizens or community organizations, community agendas are often sidelined because of the clear power imbalances. Adam Crawford (1995, p. 114) argued that community representatives do not have the cultural capital (Bourdieu 1977) to compete with their formal criminal justice partners: "The resources, both human and material, available to the different agencies, their appeals to 'expertise' and their grasp of the technicist language in which much debate is couched leaves the community representatives in a relatively powerless position." Accordingly, various interests are excluded even in ostensibly democratic participation efforts. This may occur because of informal and biased leadership or advisory position selection processes that systematically exclude problematic individuals, groups, or perspectives. The result is not only a violation of democratic values but a failure to meet the needs of disadvantaged and marginalized groups whose views and concerns are excluded from the table. Such power processes may partly explain the persistence of crime in communities with few resources. Not only is it harder to compete for scarce development and public safety resources, but those that are delivered have so many strings attached that community empowerment is undermined.

Jeffrey M. Berry, Kent E. Portney, and Ken Thomson's (1993) study of citizen participation in city politics indicates that it is possible to garner significant and representative participation, but only with city-wide commitment to strong democracy. The latter is evidenced by the decentralization of power (including discretionary funding) to the structures of citizen participation; incentives for structural change in city administration; and clearly defined, nonpartisan, neighborhood associations that recruit citizens at the local level. Such efforts may reduce the informality and bias of current, piecemeal attempts to mobilize and equitably to represent communities and community members.

In the end, despite the difficulties of promoting citizen involvement in community justice, we have no choice but to do so. Communities struggling with crime problems are typically beset by crumbling institutional infrastructure. Formal social control systems enter these communities and fill an enormous void of purpose and potential. As long as the void remains, the formal systems of control will be the only basis for citizens' hope of relief from crime. Community justice strategies will require a kind of bootstrapping of resources, in the face of limited institutional strength. But with each newly established source of informal social controls, the community capacity will grow. As we have argued, these forms of control tend to be self-regenerating—one strong community group can plant a seed that grows into greater levels of mobilization. As these stronger community controls grow, they will tend to supplant the official agencies and develop their own agendas for improving community quality of life. The downward spiral of devastation can be changed into an upward cycle of empowerment.

Funding New Practices

There is sufficient money to fund the work of a community justice operation. A great deal of money is now spent on punishment—$31 billion in 1992 (United States Bureau of Justice Statistics 1997a). Moreover, a community justice initiative need not be costly, compared to contemporary expenditures. A few professional community workers can galvanize common efforts toward safer communities by building upon residents' strengths and focusing existing official agency efforts on strengthening the communities their clients live in. A community justice initiative can be paid for by diverting dollars from less-effective current expenditures to more-effective, community-oriented initiatives. The average prison commitment (of about two years) in the United States costs $40,000 in public funds. Each year, about 650,000 convicted offenders are incarcerated.[1] Redirection of just a handful of these decisions can alter the calculus of public protection.

The mathematics is particularly compelling at the community level. For example, in Washington, D.C.—an area much larger than a community— 5,700 residents are sentenced to prison in a given year (District of Columbia Department of Corrections 1997). At the average cost of $40,000 per sentence, a community that is willing to retain a mere five offenders in a given year has $200,000 to work with in improving its community safety. This is enough money to fully fund a small community development office. It seems plausible that there might be at least five offenders who could safely remain in the community instead of spending the two years in prison they would ordinarily serve.

There is much to be done in resource-poor, crime-ridden communities: There are buildings to be refurbished, roads to be repaved, elderly transported to day-living facilities, and so forth. Such communities cannot afford to purchase these services; they are filled with the destitute. By the same token, offenders—especially those wasting away in prison—are an untapped labor resource. Community organization initiatives could put offenders to work repairing the neighborhoods victimized by their crimes. The value of this work would be twofold: First, dollars that would be devoted only to the objective of removing offenders from their neighborhoods would be allowed to remain instead in those localities. Second, entrenched problems in those communities would be attacked through the labor of residents, who might thereby gain a greater sense of personal investment in community quality of life.

This scenario also envisages a professional group that identifies local problems requiring manpower—such as renovation of buildings or assistance to children and elderly residents—and mobilizes resources. A new, local agency devoted to addressing these problems would develop work and service projects that the local area needs and that can be provided by offenders. It would then assess applicant offenders to see what part, if any, they could have in community development. The agency's staff would then develop and manage the projects necessary to implement the vision of community justice.

There are many ways of implementing this approach. Community corrections acts have attempted—with some success—to achieve these aims.

---

[1]These data are based on Maguire and Pastore (1998a, b, c) and on Clear and Cole (1997).

Many attempts have been made to divert offenders from prison, and some have been successful. What makes our vision of community justice different? In most models of sentencing reform, offenders are treated as irrelevant at best, and as antithetical to community safety at worst. A community justice model recognizes reality: Offenders are community residents, and their capacity not only to live crime-free in communities but also to contribute to community life is central to the quality of life in a community. If offenders are filtered through incarceration only to return as confirmed antagonists to the communities from which they came, little progress is possible on the agenda of community safety, and ultimately, in quality of life. But if offenders can be redirected to *contribute* to community life—especially in the most deeply disadvantaged communities in America—then the calculus of community safety and quality of life is re-computed to include them as potential positive forces.

But this will require a fiscal realization of their contribution. And this fiscal reality relates to both the community and the victim—their fiscal interests—not just that of the offender. Imagine, for example, that

- the offender and victim each got the equivalent of a "voucher" that could be used to purchase a community justice process in place of the criminal justice process;
- the alternative process could be used *only* if both the offender and the victim purchased it (this would give them a coincidence of interests instead of adversarial interests); and
- a percentage of all moneys that would have been spent on the incarceration of the offender would remain in the community to be used as the community saw fit, on any community enhancement project.

Such measures would create incentives for all members to participate in a process of community recovery. They would also redirect investment in crime control toward community development. In the case of Washington, D.C., for example, a diversion of 50 percent of offenders from incarceration each year (roughly equivalent to the percentage of nonviolent offenders sentenced to prison) would net $114 million for community justice activities.

Defining Organizational Composition

The question arises whether existing criminal justice agencies can undertake these new responsibilities. The likely answer is that they cannot. A community justice strategy assumes cooperative problem solving in which each party treats the others' interests and needs with respect; the adversarial model calls for a strategic contest in which each side regards the others' perspectives as impediments to victory. The procedural rights of the constitution are meant to equalize the strengths of the parties to this contest, enabling each to maximally pursue its aims without regard to the other parties' aims. It is unrealistic to think that the traditional roles of defense and prosecution can be transformed from a combative norm to a cooperative one.

Moreover, the traditional model creates no specific role for the community. In most jurisdictions, elected prosecutors putatively represent the interests of the community, but this is patently a questionable assignment. Communities are often much smaller than the electoral jurisdictions that select prosecutors; and many communities feel they are not given equal priority in law enforcement. In the end, prosecutors have to take positions that support reelection, even if these positions are inconsistent with the views of some communities. The alienation that results between the community and the justice system is one of the problems that calls us to seek a deeper community focus in criminal justice.

A number of strategies might be used to develop community justice:

Local offices. Justice agencies can be located at the neighborhood level. This is already true of most police services—they are provided by precincts. But the idea recently has been extended to the creation of police "ministations," often located in storefronts or in public housing units. In the same fashion, prosecution, adjudication, and correctional services could be based in neighborhoods. Experiments with neighborhood justice services are currently under way in Portland, Oregon; Austin, Texas; and New York City. A truly local justice service operation would enable staff workers to get to know local residents and become not only acquainted with but also involved in local dynamics.

Functional integration. In today's justice system, there are firm distinctions between, say, police and probation officers, and prosecutors and victim advocates. At the local level, it will be appropriate for the roles to be more blended. The divisional structure of police, probation, and parole might be replaced by various crime prevention specialists who work equally with regular citizens and with those caught up in criminal events. Crime prevention workers would conduct victims' groups, work with offenders who are involved in risk management interventions, conduct offenders' groups, work with families of offenders and their neighbors, assist in the development of crime prevention strategies at the neighborhood level, and so on.

Information-based planning. Community justice needs to be proactive. It must use sophisticated mapping equipment to identify the location of crime problems in time and space. It must also place a premium on the communication of crime information with citizens so that the latter will provide feedback, further increasing the information bases for problem solving. Community justice services must also routinely evaluate their efforts and use the feedback to implement changes where necessary.

Local advisory boards. Local residents will be recruited to serve as advisers to the neighborhood-based justice operations. They will help set neighborhood justice policy, serve as important controls against excessively intrusive crime-prevention measures, and provide feedback on the results and the community reactions to crime prevention. These boards create a special type of accountability to the community.

Functional decisionmaking boards. It will be appropriate to have local residents meet to make certain types of decisions. For example, a group of residents trained for the task ought to approve the offenders' community plans (including risk management activities) as a part of the recovery process for offenders. In cases where offenders seek to remain in the community after serious crimes, these boards ought to be consulted. Likewise, boards of former victims can help advise a victim on the way to express their losses, and they can work with victims who are struggling with the community recovery process.

Use of volunteers and ex-offenders. Local residents should be encouraged, recruited, and trained for volunteer work with the various parties to a crime. They could serve as mentors for youth in trouble or for the children of residents who are in prison. They could help supervise community service activities of offenders, and could serve as partners to crime prevention professionals who are working on particular projects. In addition, former offenders are an untapped resource in the crime prevention arena. Ex-offenders are truly experts on crime in this location, and their expertise can be used to counteract crime after they have made a successful return to community life.

Local professionals. Finally, every effort should be made to have crime prevention specialists live in the areas they serve, including law enforcement officers, treatment specialists, and the like. This integrates the crime prevention actions into that local area far more effectively than merely by organizational policy. Several avenues can be used to achieve this end: Subsidies may be given for local housing; salary increments may be provided to those who live in the neighborhood where they work; and those who live away from the neighborhood might pay a tax. The intention of such practices is to truly localize the crime problem, including its professionals, and minimize the degree to which crime prevention is externally managed.

The limitations of existing agencies suggest the need for a new (and neutral) provider of community justice services. This is true for two reasons. First, to use existing agencies would require them to compromise their stance in relation to the adversarial process, and this they cannot reasonably be expected to do. Second, a new agency has more latitude to innovate in its approach to justice, and it can more directly align itself with the interests of local communities. Thus, a primary characteristic of community justice providers would be the ability to shed existing strategies in favor of linking their activities to local problems.

A community justice agency would operate with a professional shell and a volunteer core. The shell would include persons trained in criminal justice and prepared to work actively to recruit and involve community members in confronting quality-of-life problems. The core—the community's residents—would provide legitimacy to professional work by advising, approving, and giving direction to decisions about community justice.

Conclusion

This chapter has considered community justice strategically: How do we promote community justice activities in the face of the many impediments to change? There are, indeed, many impediments to the community justice ideal, ranging from problems in law to problems in mobilization and financing. Our discussion is not meant to suggest that change will be simple; but the strategies of community justice do include well developed and widely used approaches to organizational and community change. Community justice is not an idea without a track record, and we have identified some of the approaches to problem solving that have worked in particular settings.

Of all the strategies we describe, by far the most important (and in many ways the most difficult) is to mobilize community action in support of community justice. Given the currently widespread and deep-rooted alienation between and among community members, it seems far more likely that community members' energy will be expended in collective violence, demonstrations of public frustration, or expressions of private rage in public places. Citizens' frustration and anger with crime and disorder in their communities might easily take the form of vigilantism or out-group intolerance. How are these tendencies to be avoided and the community justice ideal, as we have described it, to be achieved? If community members see vigilantism as a form of community justice, then our advocacy of the community justice ideal will not lead to progress in social relations but to regress.

The next and final chapter is focused on this dilemma: How can we distinguish community justice as an ideal from other forms of collective action that although they might be useful, are not designed specifically to advance justice in the way we conceive of it? We return to our principled articulation of community justice, and we show how a series of programs now in operation can be assessed against the principles or criteria that we have outlined. Our hope is that these criteria will enable readers to assess for themselves the justice effects of particular community actions, and thus gain a deeper understanding of how communities can be revitalized by their pursuit of justice and a higher quality of life.

7

Evaluating
Community Justice
Initiatives

Numerous initiatives are being advanced under the banner of community justice. But do they promote the community justice ideal, as we have described it? What are the standards for evaluating community justice in practice?

We have argued in favor of developing a broad vision of community justice that advances a set of principles applicable both to criminal incidents and to criminogenic neighborhood conditions. These principles establish a lofty standard to which community justice initiatives can aspire. We recognize this is a challenging portrait of the community justice ideal, but we also realize how easily well-intended reforms in justice practices can be co-opted or distorted. Unintended consequences are an inherent danger of any social change, and this possibility certainly faces our new model of community justice. In this concluding chapter, we consider the criteria for community justice initiatives in more detail by inspecting some current examples of community justice initiatives. Our purpose here is not to systematically evaluate particular programs but to make our abstract concepts of community justice more concrete and to illustrate the unique challenges of evaluating community justice initiatives.

The goal of community justice is to expand the criminal justice system's capacity as a vehicle of justice beyond its crime control function (Moore 1997). It is not enough simply to pursue the "bad guys"—to "trail 'em, nail 'em, jail 'em." That singular pursuit is insufficient, in large part because it fails on its own terms, but also because we want more from our justice system than mere adversarial victories. When citizens abdicate responsibility for social control to the criminal justice system, they weaken their capacity for exerting informal control. As they become dependent on the system, citizens also become distanced from it, which ultimately reduces the system's legitimacy (Tyler 1990). In a community justice model, crime control and the production of justice are interdependent.

Community justice reconciles crime control and justice concerns by fo-cusing on the broader goal of enhancing the quality of community life. Its advocates embrace the position that crime is an outcome of numerous, overlapping social processes. They believe that "crime prevention results from the web of institutional settings of human development and daily life. These institutions include communities, families, schools, labor mar-kets and places, as well as the legal institutions of policing and criminal justice" (Sherman 1997a). To address crime, fear, and disorder, we must also address the quality of community life. Our strategy for doing so rests on three foundations: neighborhood conditions, such as crime and disor-der rates; aggregate individual competencies that enable individuals to contribute successfully to the common good as well as to their own wel-fare; and the subjective experience of community that reflects the sym-bolic and affective links between individuals and the collectivity.

In Chapters 4 and 5, we advanced seven principles of democratic and egalitarian community justice. These will serve as our guideposts in the assessment of community justice initiatives. In this chapter, we consider some current initiatives in light of these principles, illustrating the extent to which the principles can be operationalized in particular programs and how these programs are aimed at fulfilling the community justice ideal. We are under no illusion that these programs are the perfect manifesta-tion of community justice or that they are guaranteed to succeed. We also recognize at the outset how much extraordinary effort, vision, and com-mitment have gone into making these programs happen. Criticism is a far easier task than social change; so although we inspect these programs critically, we hope our remarks will not discourage. The very existence of these innovative initiatives enables us to deepen our thinking about com-munity justice, and we recognize with appreciation the contribution these programs have made to the community justice agenda, regardless of any shortcomings we may see in them. In traveling from theory to action, no program remains perfect. The difficulties encountered by real programs can provide valuable lessons for thinking about and planning future com-munity justice efforts. We conclude the chapter with a discussion of the state of the art in evaluating community-oriented initiatives.

Democratic Principles

In Chapter 4, we defined a community justice perspective that is respon-sive to criminal incidents. We described the rights and responsibilities of various stakeholders: offenders, victims, onlookers, community institu-tional representatives, and criminal justice practitioners. Our view is that all parties have unique and important roles to play in the pursuit of a just resolution to criminal incidents. This democratic outlook emphasizes

civic participation in the criminal justice process according to three overarching principles: norm affirmation, restoration, and public safety.

Norm Affirmation

When a community responds to a criminal incident, it seeks to restore
credibility to the community's conception of the moral order by reaffirming that individuals are accountable for their violations of community
life. The belief that responses to crime must dramatically and publicly
confirm that offenders are not free to violate the rights of another in the
pursuit of their own ends goes back to Kant. Durkheim thought it a fundamental aspect of social organization that

> When crimes occur which violate the norms of social life, these norms are
> weakened and shown to be less than universal in their binding force. The ef-
> fect, however, of the upswelling of a collective passionate reaction to such
> crimes is to give a powerful demonstration of the real force which supports
> the norms, and thereby reaffirms them in the consciousness of individual
> members. (Garland 1990, p. 33)

A fundamental principle of democratic community justice is the reaffir-
mation of standards that have been brought into dispute by the criminal
incident. Norm affirmation is more than an intuitive recognition of right
from wrong; it is a conscious process that articulates behavioral standards
and provides justification for them. Representatives of the community are
in a position to state what the standards have been. Victims and onlookers, who suffer the consequences of the crime, are in the best position to
represent the primary justification for the norm. In their communication
of the harm wrought by the offense, they plainly illustrate the consequences of the crimes. To affirm norms, community justice replaces the
cold procedural pomp and circumstance of the criminal courtroom with
an interactive process involving victims, offenders, and their communities. The purpose of this new process is to allow offenders to tell their
own story, and having heard the stories of the victim and community, to
take responsibility for the conduct and its results for everyone concerned.
In this way, the offender has the opportunity to join the others in affirming the collective normative standards of community life.

An interest in affirming norms can have undesirable side effects. Most
prominent among these is public hostility to the offender—a kind of quiet
vigilantism. In the quest to affirm normative standards of conduct, an
overzealous intolerance can develop as a substitute for affirmative acts.
We see evidence of this today in neighborhood persecution of former sex
offenders, demonstrations that harass residents of suspected crack
houses, placement of signs in the front yards of convicted drunk drivers,

and the all-too-common hostility toward homosexuals. In the desire to affirm common norms, the community runs the risk of crossing the line into retributive vigilantism. It is important that we clearly identify the difference between the appropriate community desire to affirm its norms and wrongful community conduct against offending cocitizens.

Vermont's Community Reparative Boards

An award-winning probation program in Vermont illustrates the appropriate affirmation of community norms.[1] In 1994, the Vermont Department of Corrections faced contradictory demands. Vermont had seen a rise in crime, which gave rise to a call for more certain and longer sentences, and consequently, a mounting demand for prison space that far exceeded capacity. At the same time, there was a strong public desire for tax relief. The department was expected somehow to expand its capacity to manage offenders at the same time as it moderated its drain on state revenues. Faced with this pragmatic dilemma, the department was forced to ask: Is it possible to adequately sanction offenders without increasing prison capacity? Is there an alternative to incarceration that can ensure public safety, meet the needs and concerns of victims and the public, and deliver a strong message to offenders that their criminal behavior is unacceptable?

The department approached its dilemma by doing a series of customer satisfaction studies that included focus groups and surveys. What they learned about the public's expectations for the sanctioning of offenders has been described in Chapter 4. This information led them to establish a dual-track system of sanctioning. For high-risk offenders and those convicted of violent offenses, incarceration was identified as the sanction of first choice. Community service projects undertaken by inmates would be used to pay some of the offenders' debts to society, but protection of society would be the primary concern in handling these offenders.

To fill the space between incarceration and doing nothing at all, the department created the Community Reparative Boards Program for nonviolent offenders, a community-based restorative justice program (Dooley 1995). By 1999, more than 40 boards had been formed in townships across the state. Offenders convicted of misdemeanors or nonviolent felonies are sentenced to "reparative probation." A condition of this probation is that the offender meet with a community board composed of volunteers, to negotiate a reparative agreement. This process builds community by creating a vital niche for citizen participation in the criminal justice system.

---

[1]This initiative, like others discussed in this chapter, may reflect more than one principle; but to clarify and exemplify the particular principle, we focus on how each initiative embodies that principle—here, that of norm affirmation.

The board's task is not to determine guilt, which has already been established in court, but to develop an agreement that specifies how the offender will make reparation to the victim and the community.

Upon an individual's conviction of a minor offense—for example, a burglary or drunk driving—the judge will sentence the offender to probation with the condition that he or she appears before the local reparative board. The board convenes with the offender and the victim (if the victim so wishes) and attempts to work out a solution to the problem created by the offense. First, the group seeks ways of demonstrating to the offender the consequences of the crime on the victim and the community. This may entail asking the offender to listen to the victim's account, to the reactions of victims of similar offenses, and/or to other members of the community. It might mean asking the offender to write an essay describing the harm that was done. Second, the board seeks to identify ways the offender can repair the damage. Restitution to the victim, community service, and a letter of apology may be negotiated. Third, the board works with the offender to find a strategy to reduce the likelihood of reoffending. This might include a wide variety of educational and counseling opportunities. After these three solutions are negotiated, the offender signs an agreement and is given three months to comply.

In essence, it is an approach that mobilizes community members to respond to crime in their midst by enabling them to clarify and enforce appropriate standards of behavior. When the sanctioning process is moved from the courtroom to the informal setting of the community boardroom, offenders are forced to confront their community peers directly. The harmful consequences of the crime are made plain, and the community representatives are given a strong voice in the process of communicating normative standards. Community justice initiatives seek to affirm local standards of behavior; accordingly, the reparative boards are given a fair degree of autonomy and discretion in what is to be communicated.

The Vermont Reparative Boards are an attempt to give a role to the community in many aspects of the sanctioning process, and especially to provide community members a forum for affirming local norms of conduct. How might we know if this approach reflects a community justice ideal, and what might tell us if the community response has shifted beyond affirmation into a problematic form of intolerance? Questions to confirm the active presence of a community justice ideal might be:

- Do community members know about and generally agree with the work of the board?
- In the process of affirming normative values of the community, do both the victim and the offender feel that their stories have a chance to be told and that their opportunity to speak is honored?

- Do offenders and victims perceive the board's process more as a legitimate part of the community's self-maintenance or as an extension of the formal criminal justice system?
- Do offenders have a better understanding of the wrong they have done, and do victims have a stronger sense that the offender has realized the wrongfulness of the conduct?

Questions to confirm the absence of inappropriate vigilantism might be:

- Do community boards define their success in terms of the offender's eventual, successful reintegration into normal life in this community?
- Do boards take specific steps to avoid words and actions that would humiliate offenders?
- Are boards willing to consider the special circumstances of the offender that might provide some understanding about the offense?
- Do differences between boards' articulation of normative standards reflect important differences in the communities they represent, and not just differences in the membership of the boards?

Comment

The Vermont program has won numerous awards, and it is currently being evaluated on a number of criteria. The questions we have posed show one of the main differences between a community justice initiative and the traditional justice approaches it seeks to replace: the community's (and victim's) knowledge, support, and involvement in the program is a central aim of its design. The Vermont program, like most community justice initiatives, must select a sample of citizens to represent the citizenry generally. How well do they do so? How well is the work of the board communicated to community members who might otherwise not know about it? And what do these people think when they hear about the board?

Another set of questions has to do with the attitudes of the boards in their work. Do they reject offenders as anathema to the community, or do they cultivate a sense that the offender "belongs" to the board and its community? To the extent that boards are able to deal with offenders in a way that respects their citizenship, it will be aiming toward the goals of the community justice ideal. But whenever a group of citizens is designated with "special" power to deal with others, there is a potential for disregard of offenders as citizens. How the Vermont boards individually respond to this challenge will have a great deal to say about their relationship to broader issues of justice.

Restoration

Restoration as a principle of sanctioning has gained much attention recently (Bazemore and Umbreit 1994; Braithwaite 1997; Galaway and Hudson 1996; Sherman and Strang 1997; Van Ness and Strong 1997). In essence, this principle counters retributive sanctioning that punishes offenders without holding them specifically accountable for making amends to victims and the community at large. The idea underlying the pursuit of restoration is that crime has wrought harm that must be rectified, preferably through restoration (Clear 1994). The determining goal of restorative justice is to repair the damage done by the offense rather than to inflict proportionate harm on the offender (Bazemore and Umbreit 1995). In the words of Martin Wright, restorative justice

> would have a single primary aim: to restore (or improve) the condition of the victim, where there are individual victims, as far as possible. This would be done by the community, through victim support; by the offender, through reparation; and by the state, through criminal injuries compensation for crimes of violence. Ideally there would also be a safety-net compensation scheme for the most disadvantaged victims of crimes against property. (1992, p. 528)

The role and responsibilities of stakeholders emerge from the offender's obligation to make reparations. Victims are obligated to specify the nature of the harm and their own view of what would be necessary to achieve restoration. The community is obligated to make its own effort to facilitate restoration of the victim—in part directly, by providing victim services, and in part indirectly, by providing opportunities for offender reparation.

The pursuit of restoration raises questions of equity. Offenders who have greater personal resources of money and skills are better situated to take restorative action. Victims who because of their particular vulnerabilities suffer greater loss from crime may be less capable of being restored; victims who harbor resentments about the crime may forbid the offender from attempting restoration. To some extent, restoration depends upon personal capacities; and as capacities vary, the potential for inequitable treatment grows.

Family Group Conferences in Australia

In New South Wales, Australia, a unique community policing initiative created a mechanism for community participation and problem solving in the criminal justice system. The model is predicated on holding juvenile offenders accountable for their crimes, and at the same time, on increasing their social ties to the local community. It seeks to restore offenders to satisfactory community life. The basic model of the family group conference originated in New Zealand (Maxwell and Morris 1994) and increasingly is used in the United States (Immarigeon 1996; McCold and Stahr 1996). It is a diversionary program most often used with youthful offenders arrested for relatively minor crimes. A major experiment is currently being undertaken with juvenile offenders and drunk drivers in Australia (Sherman and Strang 1997), following on the heels of a positively evaluated juvenile conferencing project (Moore and O'Connell 1994).

The Australian model employs police officers as facilitators of a conference between victims, offenders, and onlookers (typically, supporters of the victim and offender). The explicit goals of a family group conference are to ensure that the offender understands the seriousness of the crime and takes responsibility for making amends; to provide a forum for the victim's participation in the sanctioning process and in obtaining recompense; to provide a meaningful role for police and other community institutions in facilitating the justice process; and to provide opportunities for rehabilitation and community service. Unlike Vermont's reparative boards, the emphasis in family group conferences is on victim-offender mediation and problem solving rather than on the affirmation of local norms.

The police facilitator arranges the conference by inviting stakeholders to the table. This typically includes the victim, the offender, and five or more supporters of each. Participation is voluntary; where offenders or victims choose not to participate, the case is referred back to the courts for traditional sentencing. The object of the conference is both educative, in its discourse over the nature and ramifications of the incident, and problem solving, in negotiating an agreement for reparations.

> The conference begins with statements by the offenders about what they did, followed by statements by the victims about the harm the crime caused, both material and psychological. Supporters of both are then asked to discuss the crime, its impact, and the best way to repair the harm it has caused. The police officer facilitating the conference, who has no role in determining the outcome, asks the victims if they have any recommendations about appropriate punishment or restitution. This can include cash payments or services by the offenders. The officer then states the emerging consensus, and asks the offenders whether they will agree to the terms. (Strang and Sherman 1997)

Preliminary evaluation results (Sherman and Strang 1997; Strang and Sherman 1997) of the drunk driver/juvenile offender conferences find that conferencing (over formal court processing) increases the likelihood of offenders expressing remorse and shame, offering apology, and eliciting forgiveness by victims. Conferencing helps victims feel safer and more involved in the sanctioning process. Compliance by offenders in honoring reparative agreements has been found to be high, both in absolute terms and relative to court-ordered restitution (McCold and Stahr 1996; Moore and O'Connell 1994; Sherman and Strang 1997).

Questions we might ask to confirm the active presence here of a community justice ideal include:

- Do victims receive restitution in the form of services or goods? Are they "healed" by the process?
- Are victims satisfied with the process—both with their own role in it and with the justice outcomes for offenders?
- Do offenders feel well positioned to make amends for their crimes and to accept a role as full members of the community after the process?
- Do onlookers feel that justice was done?

Questions we might ask to confirm equity in justice:

- Are there policies in place that afford an equal capacity for restoration among offenders who lack personal resources?
- Do poorer and less capable offenders feel as satisfied with the process as those better situated to make reparation?
- Is there a special effort made to work with victims who are resistant to the process?

Comment

Listening to the offender, and asking that the offender listen to those affected by the crime, is the most profound centerpiece of community justice. But offenders vary in their ability to engage in introspection and self-evaluation, to feel and to articulate remorse. They also differ in the resources they can bring to bear on restoring the victim or the community; and some of this difference is due to long-standing social inequalities of our cities. It is incumbent upon those interested in just communities to work especially hard to find ways in which disadvantaged offenders can become restorers of their victims and of themselves.

The alternative is to strengthen inequality—and this is incompatible with the values of community justice. This dilemma is inherent in "conferencing" models. When the offender seems incapable of acting as a full player in the conference, the community is especially liable for its broader agenda of justice. How can the person's limited resources be turned into a positive attribute for community life? As community members are committed to this result, they advance a broader conception of justice within the places where they live.

Public Safety

The third principle of a community justice approach to criminal incidents is public safety—the assurance that the offender will not cause additional harm to community members. This is particularly important for the victim's healing and the reducing of fear of crime in the community. The quality of community life is, in part, predicated on the confidence its members have in moving through public spaces and safely engaging other community members. Conviction of an offense undoubtedly makes people suspicious of the offender's future intentions. A community-oriented response to a criminal incident must address stakeholders' concerns about the offender's potential recidivism and the victim's acute need to be insulated from revictimization. Moreover, an active campaign must be undertaken to reassure the community of its safety, through concrete steps to enhance formal and informal controls.

It is incumbent on the offender in some way to demonstrate a commitment not to reoffend. Winning the trust of other stakeholders is a supreme challenge for an offender, and it is inevitably a prerequisite of the offender's full reintegration. Victims and other affected members of the community have a responsibility to conduct self-examination to determine the conditions that would reduce their fear without necessitating their withdrawal from community life. A first response of communal institutions in a community justice model is to secure the safety of victims, particularly those at risk of repeat victimization (Farrell 1995). Moreover, the community is responsible for providing supervision of offenders until they have won back the community's trust. Incarceration is only one means of supervision; here we are particularly concerned with formal and informal mechanisms of supervision in the community. But winning back the public trust is likely to be impossible for many offenders, if they are left to their own devices. Most will need services to help overcome social deficits, from drug addiction to school failure to job unpreparedness.

The concern for public safety might appear to excuse an unwillingness to take risks. But if a community is to provide a realistic opportunity for the offender to be restored, it must be willing to risk reoffense, at least to a degree. A risk-free community is not feasible. Therefore, the community is confronted by two questions: How does the community define its reasonable risks, and how will the community minimize problems stemming from those risks? A legitimate concern for public safety becomes an illegitimate concern for order when the community is intolerant of reasonable circumstances under which identified offenders might return to community life.

Boston's Operation Ceasefire

Because violent crime is not evenly distributed across the geographic and social landscape, we know that some individuals are at greater risk for violence than others. Areas hard hit by violent crime typically also harbor youth gang activity. David M. Kennedy (1997), the director of Operation Ceasefire in Boston along with Anne M. Piehl and Anthony A. Braga, found that most juvenile homicides in Boston (generally gang-related) were committed by offenders already well known to various authorities—because they had been in court before, schools had cautionary data on them, or they or their families had been recipients of various social services. In other words, few serious offenders come before the court without bringing an extensive paper trail with them. The goal of Operation Ceasefire, which began in Boston in March 1996, is not to suppress gang membership or activity but to end gang violence. The strategy makes use of data widely available to the criminal justice system; in particular, the facts that a few offenders account for a substantial proportion of all crime, and that these offenders are often concentrated in geographic space. These factors suggest that public safety can be increased substantially by focusing institutional resolve on gang offenders.

Two basic strategies underlie Operation Ceasefire. First, interagency collaboration helps authorities to identify individuals and gangs at risk for violence. Partner agencies include the Boston Police Department; the Bureau of Alcohol, Tobacco, and Firearms; the United States Attorney for the Commonwealth of Massachusetts; the Suffolk County District Attorney; the Massachusetts Department of Probation; City of Boston youth outreach workers; the Massachusetts Department of Parole; and the City of Boston school police. For these agencies to meet regularly on a strategic basis and to share information was critical to the identification of gang members who would be targeted, increasing the effectiveness of investigation and aiding in the development of a repertoire of appropriate interventions and sanctions. Moreover, the agencies have worked together to strengthen the tone of seriousness regarding the intervention. The coordinated effort has enabled the project to focus its intervention strategy on the most violence-prone areas.

Second, the operation is based on increasing deterrence effects through swift and certain sanctioning, overcoming traditional weaknesses in these critical domains. These objectives are achieved through a variety of means. When a violent act is committed, the various agencies can, at their discretion, not only arrest suspects but also shut down drug markets, enforce probation restrictions, make disorder arrests, deal more strictly with cases in adjudication, deploy federal enforcement power, and so on.

> In essence, the authorities' message to the gang members was: we know who you are; we know what you're doing; we cannot stop all your offending all the time, which you know and we know, but it's a new day where violence is concerned; violence will simply not be tolerated in Boston any longer; we're doing this in large part to protect you; here's how *we're* going to do business from now on; what happens subsequently is up to you; and go home and tell your friends. (Kennedy 1997, p. 466)

The purpose is to deliver to gang members a new set of expectations regarding their violent behavior. Where gang members seek rehabilitative services, the project assists them. But where they persist in violent activity, the coordinated efforts of the agencies provide a variety of undesirable sanctions that will be exerted until the violence stops.

The Ceasefire strategy appears to have been quite successful: Its implementation coincides with a dramatic drop in Boston gang violence (Kennedy 1997). The success of the strategy is predicated on the capacity of the system to keep track of the activities of individuals at great risk for offending. The intervention, however, requires substantial interagency coordination and institutional resolve. The criminal justice system typically ignores supervision in the community only to punish offenders severely after the fact; Operation Ceasefire points to the real possibility of prevention through deterrence. The strategy is unique in making use of the aggressive enforcement powers of the criminal justice system, but applying them as a preventive strategy. By focusing on patterns of violence in the community and the communication of enforcement standards, the project facilitates the creation of a new normative environment in the community.

Questions we might ask in this case to confirm the active presence of a community justice ideal include:

- Is the intervention consistent with what we know about risk and risk management?
- Is the basis for the risk assessment shared with the offender, victim, and community, and does each have an opportunity to influence the risk assessment by pointing out factors that may not have been taken into account?
- Is the community informed of the intervention that will be used to control or reduce the risk, and do community members express confidence in and approval of the techniques?
- Do offenders have choices available that enable them to take personal action that would lead to a reduction in their risk?

Questions we might ask in order to confirm an appropriate level of risk control include:

- Must factors in addition to the offender's risk (such as the unwillingness to cooperate with risk control programs, or new offending behavior) be present in order to justify the removal of the offender due to the level of risk?
- Is the community willing to experiment with a number of alternative approaches to dealing with the offender's risk, other than simple removal and incarceration?
- Are risk management programs tailored to the specific circumstances of the offender rather than applied across the board to all offenders?

Comment

Is the Boston project a type of "tough love," or is it merely toughness? There are few targets of community justice for whom more is at stake than gang members who have demonstrated their capacity for violence. The Boston program illustrates the link between the idea of norm affirmation and public safety: Certain acts will not be tolerated. Inherent in the Boston approach is the belief that potential offenders are capable of choosing to avoid violence, and that when they make that choice the appropriate response is to provide them with some of the freedoms that ordinary citizens enjoy.

Our images of gang members distort how we understand a program such as this one. But the Boston program is not merely a tough response to gang behavior. Emphasis is placed on the services—treatment, training, and other forms of prosocial supports—that are available to gang members for the asking. The question is whether gang members are able to benefit from the approach by achieving better life chances and a higher level of justice in their communities.

Egalitarian Principles

In Chapter 5, we advanced four principles that frame a community justice approach to criminogenic neighborhood conditions. These principles expand the community justice model from the particular milieu of criminal justice to a broader context of social conditions that place individuals at risk for a number of social problems, such as drug abuse, unemployment, school failure, and teenage and out-of-wedlock childbearing. Our aim is to broaden the community justice approach beyond "reaction" to proactive and preventive measures. The four principles are meant to orient community justice approaches toward egalitarian concerns for equality, inclusion, reciprocity, and stewardship.

Equality

The pursuit of social equality is grounded in the moral concern that opportunity not be unevenly distributed across society. Researchers have expressed particular concern for the inequalities that result from racial segregation (Massey and Denton 1993) and concentrated poverty (Sampson and Wilson 1995). Communities hard hit by crime are nearly always communities that suffer extreme levels of poverty and disorganization, and these communities are most likely to lack the resources to take on their crime problems. A community justice approach to inequality begins by considering a community's capacity for responding to crime, and the institutional resources it has available to provide directly for the community welfare. The aim is to increase the community's capacity to leverage extralocal resources in its own behalf (Bursik and Grasmick 1993) so as to enhance its indigenous resources.

The question is very much like that posed by Amartya Sen (1985) in his classic critique of Rawls's ideal of social justice. He pointed out that true inequality is not produced by unequal distribution of resources but by unequal capacities to take advantage of a given level of resources. Our use of the word *equality* has this same intention: We mean to redistribute criminal justice resources so that the community justice ideal is possible in areas suffering from high levels of crime.

From a capacity-building perspective, the approach should not bypass local institutions in the delivery of extralocal resources to individuals. Nor should incentives be created for individuals to leave their troubled neighborhoods. Either of these strategies may provide real benefits for individuals (Rosenbaum 1995), but they do little to improve the neighborhood. Most importantly, we cannot ignore the resource needs of poor communities on the false premise that communities develop only through their own organization. We must not try, to use Lawrence W. Sherman's (1997a) metaphor, to "empower" drowning neighborhoods by offering them the chance to design their own life-preservers with little or nothing in the way of extralocal resources.

The Community Building Initiative by LISC

A good example of a program that adheres to the equality principle is the Community Building Initiative (Chavis et al. 1997). This project is sponsored by the Local Initiatives Support Corporation (LISC), which was established by the Ford Foundation to facilitate the development of Community Development Corporations (CDCs). CDCs are neighborhood organizations generally set up to revitalize urban neighborhoods by renovating housing and by pursuing other strategies to address local social problems. CDCs engender change by (1) property management strategies that affect, through selection and eviction, the composition of tenants in a property; (2) tenant and community organizing, affecting the way community members relate to one another; (3) social service delivery, working directly with individuals and families to overcome problems and develop competencies; and (4) advocacy, affecting the relationships of the neighborhood to external actors (Sullivan 1993).

The Community Building Initiative provides funding, training, and other capacity-building support to CDCs in a number of U.S. cities. The project is meant to assist CDCs in their efforts to engage residents in neighborhood development activities and to create linkages between the CDCs and public and private institutions capable of supporting the development of local housing and other community facility development projects. The premise of the initiative is

> that comprehensive community development can take place only in the hands of the community residents. Only the residents themselves can determine their needs, and how to go about improving the physical, social, and economic conditions of their neighborhoods. The program, therefore, promotes resident-driven approaches and empowers residents to collaborate among themselves to strengthen their community capacity. (Chavis et al. 1997, p. 1)

However, this premise does not ignore the need for external linkages, since community capacity in many neighborhoods is greatly underdeveloped and in need of substantial external support. Thus self-development is linked to external resources by the work of the initiative.

The Community Building Initiative brings technical assistance to local CDCs, promotes collaboration among CDCs, and fosters connections between CDCs and public agencies and private investors. As a result, CDCs develop action plans and engage community residents, local social service providers, and outside collaborators in community building. Specific activities can vary greatly depending on the local will. For example, David M. Chavis and his colleagues (1997) describe a number of projects, such as organizing block or tenant associations, creating community leadership development programs, organizing to close drug houses, developing community gardens, and developing programs to involve parents in schools. The initiative on which they report helped foster linkages to external organizations through CDC outreach by bringing health care services to the local neighborhood through partnerships with area hospitals and universities. There were also efforts to bring criminal justice resources from the city government through partnerships with various criminal justice agencies.

Community justice efforts to increase social equality through capacity building raise a number of evaluative questions. Questions to confirm the active presence of a community justice ideal in community development initiatives include:

- Does the community justice strategy contain initiatives for the transfer of resources from extralocal sectors to the community at risk?
- Is there within the initiative an explicit strategy for confronting the problem of crime in the community?
- Is the core of the initiative designed to help neighborhood economic conditions improve, not simply to fight crime?
- Does the initiative organize local residents?

Questions to confirm the capacity building nature of the community justice initiative might include:

- Do initiatives strengthen the ability of community organizations and local agencies to obtain their own resources?
- Are partnerships and coalitions formed to help establish priorities and increase the chances of success?
- Are community actions developed by local residents and do they center around residents' needs, as they express them?

Inclusion

The principle of inclusion asserts that communal membership is not cheaply bought or sold. Much of the pressure for longer prison sentences is predicated on a "kinds-of-people" perspective on crime: The world can be cleanly divided into good guys and bad, and the sooner the bad are removed from the public domain, the better. A community justice approach favors public safety, but rejects the simplistic claim that removal of the "bad guys" is the best strategy for solving community safety problems. Offenders are potential resources on which communities can draw to strengthen their self-regulation. The goal is not to remove as many residents as possible but to find a way to include as many as possible in efforts to improve community quality of life and public safety.

The principle of inclusion sensitizes us to the special problem of stigmatization and exclusion, which initiate a process that often leads to the formation of oppositional subcultures (Braithwaite 1989). The effectiveness of offender reintegration is an important litmus test of a community justice initiative: In seeking to include all members, is the community justice practice ignoring the needs and interests of most residents in a sense of safety and in public order? The problem is not one of balancing competing interests against each other but of integrating them: How can we sustain an ethic of inclusion of the aberrant at the same time that we recognize and affirm the value of public order?

The Drug Court Movement

Another significant effort toward community justice is the formation of drug courts to facilitate the treatment of substance abusers (General Accounting Office 1997; Roberts et al. 1997). Given the close linkage between substance abuse and crime (Belenko and Dumanovsky 1993), and the minimal effect of incarceration without treatment on reducing substance abuse (Office of Justice Programs 1995), drug courts were conceived of as a way of providing treatment while keeping nonviolent offenders in the community. For this reason the drug court movement has not focused on violent offenders or drug dealers but on offenders (typically charged with felonies) who have been identified as having substance abuse problems.

Drug courts are an important example of the inclusion principle because they indicate a shift in perspective that accepts substance abusers as troubled members of the community in need of help rather than social misfits in need of exile through incarceration. Drug courts also represent a systematic change in the criminal justice system. As of March 1997, there were 161 drug courts operating nationally (General Accounting Office 1997).

Drug courts manage the process of offender reintegration in several ways (National Institute of Justice 1995). First, drug courts specialize in the particular legal and social concerns of drug offenders. Second, the courts foster collaboration between criminal justice agencies, treatment agencies, and community organizations. For example, the Jefferson County Juvenile Drug Court in Birmingham, Alabama, is a collaboration between the Jefferson County Family Court and the Birmingham Treatment Alternatives to Street Crime Program (Roberts et al. 1997). The primary treatment component of the court involves outpatient services administered through the Drug-Free Program at the University of Alabama. Third, the drug courts' specialization not only enables education and training of judges, prosecutors, defenders, and other criminal justice practitioners in substance abuse and treatment modalities but also the education and training of treatment providers in criminal justice procedures and concerns. This enhances the working relationship between agencies of sanction and rehabilitation. Fourth, drug courts foster the centralization of case management and follow-up with offenders, facilitating rational sanctioning and treatment procedures of supervision and evaluation. For example, in the Dade County Drug Court, "The judge works with the prosecutor, defender, and drug treatment specialists as a team to select the appropriate treatment approach, monitor progress in the courtroom, and help overcome problems (for example housing and employment) that may hinder treatment progress" (National Institute of Justice 1995).

Questions we might ask to confirm the implementation of the principle of inclusion are:

- To what extent do community justice initiatives have procedures designed to attend to both reintegration and public safety?
- Is there a priority given to reducing risk by fostering legitimate social ties?
- How do these programs avoid labeling or stigmatizing offenders?
- To what extent do programs depend on community participation and consensus as opposed to professional services?
- Are the offender and the victim reasonably confident of the prospects of their returning to a more normal level of functioning within the community when the process is completed?

Mutuality

Would that the world was made of altruists. But many of us, perhaps most, are dedicated to our own self-advancement and give only secondary regard to the consequences of our pursuits for others. As an ethical minimum, community justice stands for peaceful coexistence of self-interested actors, and more importantly, cooperation in pursuing mutually beneficial ends. On the one hand, this entails incentives for prosocial behaviors, exemplified by community service, joining a community crime prevention campaign, socializing and supervising youth, and so on. On the other hand, the mutuality principle endorses disincentives for antisocial behavior: holding offenders accountable for the damage they have caused, increasing the risks of criminal detection, making criminal targets less vulnerable, and reducing the rewards of criminal behavior.

The mutuality principle helps counteract the rational incentives that underlie much criminal activity, particularly the perception by offenders that no one cares enough to intervene. In the words of Ralph B. Taylor and Adele V. Harrell (1996, p. 2), "Offenders often operate in a rational fashion; they prefer to commit crimes that require the least effort, provide the highest benefits, and pose the lowest risks." Even a modicum of mutual care will deter a significant level of crime. The best approaches alter criminal incentives without increasing coercion in society; freedom is preserved, but the attractiveness of criminality is diminished.

Some forms of mutual assistance must concern us, however. If there is little more than a restructuring of the physical environment of crime, then people have become tangential to crime control. And whenever some members of the community band together to oppose crime, the possibility arises of heavy-handed responses that violate other principles, such as inclusion and restoration.

CPTED and BIDs

Crime Prevention Through Environment Design (CPTED) is based on the observation that certain characteristics of places facilitate crime. Many types of places do not seem to be criminogenic, whereas other places are frequent sites of crime, such as convenience stores or taverns (Eck 1997). Taylor and Harrell (1996) identify four CPTED strategies that alter the criminal incentive structure in physical settings. First, by changing housing design or block layout, criminal targets may become less vulnerable. For example, replacing densely settled public housing projects that foster anonymity with smaller dwellings may increase informal control as residents more easily detect intruders (Newman and Franck 1982). Second, shifting land use and circulation patterns may alter routine contacts between potential offenders and targets. For example, altering street patterns with barriers may reduce the flow of drug dealers and buyers on a block. Third, employing territorial or boundary-setting markers such as picket fences and making aesthetic improvements may indicate the vigilance and commitment of residents to protecting their neighborhood, increasing a sense of community and dissuading criminal activity. Fourth, and related to territorial boundary-setting, reducing physical disorder by removing abandoned cars, planting gardens in vacant lots, removing graffiti, and painting murals may also send a message to offenders about the level of social control in the area. Taylor and Harrell (1996) have observed that territorial marking is primarily a matter of individual initiative in private areas, whereas reduction of physical disorder generally involves collective action and the efforts of public agencies to assist in the improvement of public spaces.

A good example of the mutuality principle in action was the 1995 renovation of Bryant Park in midtown Manhattan (MacDonald 1996). Prior to the renovation, the park was a well-known haven for drug dealers; robberies, assaults, and shootings were common there. Today, the tree-lined open space is crowded with picnickers and Frisbee-throwers. The park's transformation is the result of a substantial beautification and maintenance project that combined landscaping, sanitation, and security. In essence, park planners availed themselves of a variety of CPTED strategies that made the park attractive to community members in general but not conducive to criminal activity.

Bryant Park exemplifies the mutuality principle for a second reason that goes beyond its physical transformation. Its reclamation is the result of an increasingly common partnership of proximate commercial establishments known as Business Improvement Districts (BIDs). In New York, the Bryant Park BID levied taxes on local businesses and corporations and used the funds to enhance public spaces, reducing disorder and—from the perspective of the merchant—increasing the commercial viability of the area. Under New York law, the BIDs are formed voluntarily by agreement of local businesses; however, after their formation, compliance with the taxation becomes mandatory—"mutual coercion, mutually agreed upon," in Garrett Hardin's (1968) words.[2] BIDs are a structural mechanism for enjoining private interests to secure public goods. The mechanism relies on shared self-interest: The businesses have an economic incentive to make neighborhood improvements they know the city cannot afford (or will not otherwise commit to). Both CPTED strategies and BIDs are predicated on altering the criminal incentive structure—that is, making crime less rewarding to the rational actor.

Mutuality carries with it the potential for practices of exclusion. BIDs may come together to arrange for troublesome neighbors to be arrested or evicted. For example, Manhattan's Midtown Community Court provides a large number of services for offenders; but if it did not do so, a local court would merely arrest outsiders and sanction them. Mutuality need not give rise to an interest group cabal; at its best, it brings about a broad coalition of interests that encourages adherence also to the other principles of community justice.

Questions to confirm mutuality in the community justice ideal include:

- Does the justice program provide incentives to increase the cooperation of self-interested actors?
- Are joint actions taken that identify, respond to, and effectively alter physical and environmental incentives for crime?
- Are positive incentives provided for informal monitoring and sanctioning by community members?
- Are shared identity, common interests, and a shared stake used to promote solidarity in the provision of public safety and other collective goods?

Questions to demonstrate that mutuality is broad based rather than narrowly self-interested include:

- Are there procedures to prevent overreliance on market-style incentives that undermine norms of altruistic community service?

---

[2]Another New York BID, the Grand Central Partnership, was a primary community group behind the Midtown Community Court.

- Are there mechanisms in place for reconciling the uneasy relationship between egoistic coordination and communitarian action?

Stewardship

It would be a mistake to view community justice mutuality as merely an assemblage of structural incentives to reduce free riding. Stewardship is a principle that raises the standard for moral action, calling upon citizens to view themselves as responsible for the welfare of the larger community, in response not only to their own immediate interests but also to the needs and interests of others, particularly those who are disadvantaged or vulnerable. Stewardship represents an essential feature of democracy; that citizens cannot abdicate their public responsibilities without risking disorder at one extreme or the usurpation of power by the state at the other (Wrong 1994).

Stewardship is the community justice principle that advocates civic participation at all levels of the criminal justice process (except in committing the crimes, of course). Who is to be the "community" in community justice, if not its residents? The goal is not simply to enhance the legitimacy of the system in the eyes of the public, but more fundamentally to promote democratic citizenship. Community members have an implicit responsibility for obeying the law, socializing youth to do so, monitoring compliance, and participating in organized prevention and sanctioning activities. Above all, community members are obligated to oversee the process, ensuring its fairness and relevance to the normative codes of the community.

Stewardship is also a resource-building idea. The goods that serve the collective community are well maintained and strengthened by their oversight, and the resulting benefits are shared among the members of the community. Structures are maintained in good working order; public places are kept clean, attractive, and accessible. The community acts as manager of its living space. And benefits accrue from living in a clean, well-functioning local area. When public goods are shepherded, their value increases. There is then a chance that some minority will profit from this result. Stewardship of public goods should not be achieved to benefit the few but should have as its objective a broad collective benefit.

Austin's Community Justice Council

Under the leadership of District Attorney Ronnie Earle, Travis County, Texas—which includes the state capital, Austin—has become a major site of community justice initiatives. One of the most important innovations has been the creation of a democratic decisionmaking structure that facilitates the collaboration of criminal justice system agencies, citizens, and the private sector. The goals of this structure are:

> (1) to develop and maintain collaborative and cooperative relationships among and between entities of government, (2) to establish partnerships among coordinated government entities and private enterprise, and (3) to create opportunities for citizen interaction and involvement with each other, private enterprise, and government entities to address issues of crime and related social function. (Earle 1996, p. 7)

The county's community justice system centers on the activities of the Community Justice Council, a decisionmaking body composed of ten elected officials, including prosecutors, legislators, city council and school board members, and judges. The Council is responsible for developing community justice plans for Austin and Travis County. The Council is closely linked to and advised by the Community Justice Task Force, which has fifteen appointed officials, including the Chief of the Austin Police Department, the Superintendent of Austin's school system, and the directors of the Juvenile and Adult Probation Departments. Finally, the Council is advised by the Neighborhood Protection Action Committee, which includes twenty-five citizen activists selected for representation by local neighborhoods.

The formal coordination of criminal justice agencies, social service agencies, and community groups enables the council to devise plans that are comprehensive and that serve the needs and interests of local communities. For example, one of the major efforts of the Council has been the creation of the Community Justice Center, which is a community correctional facility located in a troubled neighborhood and built on community justice principles. The collective work in developing this center ranged from site selection and facility design to the composition of programs and services aimed at offender reintegration.

The strength of the Community Justice Council is that it provides an organizational structure for citizens to exercise a voice in criminal justice planning. This is an opportunity not merely to sound an opinion in a neighborhood meeting but to work collaboratively and substantively with representatives from numerous public agencies in the production of policy and programs. Moreover, the Council is guided by a philosophical mission that invites participants to reflect on the wider goals of criminal justice and to seek means of accomplishing them. In this sense, the Council cultivates stewardship as it displaces consideration of narrow, short-term interests in favor of the general, long-term welfare of the community.

Questions we might ask in order to confirm stewardship in the community justice practice include:

- Does the community justice strategy stem from an ethic of volunteerism?
- Is stewardship undertaken as a collaborative process, with broad-based representation from the community?
- Are there specific elements of community justice that tend to renovate and maintain public goods, such as housing and parks?
- Do offenders have opportunities to develop community goods by devoting their labor and other capacities to the public benefit?
- Do offenders work together with other residents in the tasks of stewardship?
- Do citizens not involved directly in the community justice process know about ways in which community justice benefits their living space?

Questions to confirm broad benefits from stewardship of community goods include:

- Are the public resources that benefit from public stewardship producing private gain?
- Are citizens not involved in community justice benefiting from the stewardship of public resources of justice?

Conclusion

Community justice initiatives have a number of features that link the arenas of community building and criminal justice. As we argued in Chapter 1, community justice is a local phenomenon, emphasizing the relations between individuals at the neighborhood level, whether through community justice councils or a focus on gang activity in a local hot spot (like the Operation Ceasefire initiative in Boston). Community justice pays attention to local concerns and priorities for improving the quality of community life. Community justice also has a problem-solving orientation, particularly with regard to disorder as an antecedent to serious crime. Problem solving encompasses both short-term, immediate community concerns and an orientation toward long-term issues requiring extensive planning and resource mobilization: Bryant Park is transformed almost overnight into an attractive urban escape; and the LISC helps develop community capacity for long-term problem solving. Community justice decentralizes authority and accountability, encouraging line workers to take the initiative in solving community problems and in bringing citizens into the justice process. Family group conferences, often facilitated by police officers, offer new roles and expectations for line workers who engage stakeholders in an emotional setting with a high degree of individual discretion. Finally, community justice prioritizes citizens' inclusion in the justice process as advisers, stakeholders, collaborators, and partners with unique functions. Reparative boards empower citizens, victims, and onlookers by providing a forum in which all are respectfully included, and by holding them all accountable for problem solving, reparation, and norm affirmation.

These aspects of community justice initiatives help distinguish them from traditional practices and may prove to be their strongest assets. Lisbeth B. Schorr (1997) has asserted that the strongest community initiatives share certain features in common: They are in and of the community; they have long-term, preventive orientations; and they are flexible and continue to evolve over time. However, these laudable features pose significant challenges to evaluators who are trying to assess the effectiveness of the initiatives. Perhaps in part for this reason, much of community justice practice has been disconnected from research that is aimed at evaluation and generalization. We must ask how communities might become involved in ways that enhance their understanding of successes and failures, so that these communities and others can learn and grow in the practice of justice. In principle, no one is against strategies aimed at helping people identify what works best. In practice, however, such discoveries rarely occur. It is important to consider why. We will advance only one issue here, following closely the recent insights of Susan Bennett (1995). Essentially, Bennett argues that many evaluators fail to identify important organizational successes, and impose constraints that undermine the effectiveness of the community organizations in achieving their goals.

Since Robert F. Bales's (1950) pioneering work on group dynamics, the tension between process and product has been seen as central to group functioning. Evaluations of community-level efforts to prevent crime tend to emphasize the product orientation without much regard to process. Bringing process back into the evaluation of community justice efforts is essential to understanding collective actions for crime prevention. Where the ideals of evaluative research conflict with the ideals of community organizing, we are likely to find either unsatisfactory designs with strong results or good designs with weak results. We therefore offer a series of questions that might be used to evaluate the processes of community justice proposals and initiatives in practice.

Evaluators favor clearly defined, rationally conceived, data-driven program designs, and implementation that carefully proceeds according to plan. Predesigned programs are favored because these details are worked out ahead of time. Though such programs are an evaluator's dream, they might easily be derailed because they fail to consider local problems and citizen preferences with regard to approach. Without explicit attention to the process of community inclusion in decisionmaking, such programs often undermine the opportunity for consensus formation that undergirds mobilization. In contrast to predesigned programs, a process-driven evaluation explicitly avoids clearly stated goals and means in order to maximize consensus amidst diversity of opinion. Moreover, process-driven designs are likely to be quite flexible, changing course in response to changing local conditions: from bad weather, to the emergence of new problems, to the sudden availability of resources. Consider the example given by Bennett (1995, p. 79):

> One community organization, for instance, originally targeted underage drinking in local parks in its antidrug work plan. By the time the work plan was approved and the program started, fall had arrived and residents were no longer concerned about drinking in the parks. This issue was replaced with others of more immediate importance, and by the next spring, residents' concerns about youth activities had evolved beyond park drinking.

A second contrast between product and process is illuminated by evaluators' needs for decontextualized programs with clear beginnings, middles, and ends, constructed as if the community did not exist before and will not after. Communities will continue to exist and therefore will build into program designs goals that are only indirectly related to the identified problem but that directly affect the community's ability to organize in the future. Evaluators would prefer that the community exert all of its influence in resolving the immediate problem, exercising its power to the fullest extent in order to maximize the effect on the dependent variable. Communities, however, often need to reserve (and accumulate) some of their power. For example, some time is dedicated to leadership development and to building relationships between local organizations. A single product focus that fails to attend to long-term needs may undermine organizational capacity as narrow interests compete in zero-sum games.

Evaluators love a paper trail. Data need organization, and organization requires bureaucracy. Organizations typically need more resources than their members can provide, and this also requires bureaucracy. However, formalization generally distances organizations from their membership. As Bennett (1995, p. 79) noted:

> One community organization, for example, needed to develop collaborative relationships with city and state agencies to work on its goals of increasing employment and housing opportunities. This focus reduced its contacts within the neighborhoods, alienating at least some of the members and reducing attendance at the organization's annual meeting.

The prerequisites for traditional program evaluation fail to account for the social learning process that is vital to the long-term success of community organizations. The organizations' process orientation requires flexible designs that change as the organization becomes skilled at mobilizing participants, collaborating with other organizations and agencies, and developing new strategies to deal with new problem definitions. Imposing stringent requirements for the conduct of evaluations may undermine the social learning process of the community organization and reduce its effectiveness in dealing with local problems.

It is difficult to reconcile the requirements of proper evaluation and the process needs of organizations for several reasons. First, evaluations might be too narrow in scope. The inclusion of process indicators in their design will add to the list of measurable variables without discounting product variables (Bazemore 1997). Sometimes this is done to divert attention from weak outcomes; but the intent should be to recognize the inevitability of process and to account for it accordingly. Second, the failure to explicitly acknowledge process might undermine product outcomes because programs with a product evaluation bias tend to short-circuit the social learning process. To discover how programs can be evaluated without undermining processes is an enormous challenge for community justice.

In the end, evaluation is purposive. We seek to learn whether a given program worked so as to decide what we should do in the future. Evaluation is not undertaken to give someone a grade and be done with it; the task is to sustain meaningful action. We want to know whether we are headed in an appropriate, meaningful direction so as to decide whether to continue. We evaluate not because we are interested in the past but because we are devoted to the future.

There is every reason to think that community justice is an idea that will gain wider acceptance and broader application in the near future. This book offers a number of guidelines that we hope will be helpful for designing meaningful and ambitious community justice programs that will succeed. Through mutual support, we believe that all communities in America can experience a level of justice far greater and more satisfying than what most currently enjoy.

References

Adler, Jacob. 1991. *The Urgings of Conscience*. Philadelphia: Temple University Press.

Alder, Christine, and Joy Wundersitz, eds. 1994. *Family Conferencing and Juvenile Justice*. Canberra: Australian Institute of Criminology.

American Probation and Parole Association. 1996. "Restoring Hope Through Community Partnerships: The Real Deal in Crime Control." *Perspectives* 20:40–42.

Anderson, David C. 1996. "In New York City, a 'Community Court' and a New Legal Culture." February. Publication no. 158613. Washington, DC: National Institute of Justice.

Anderson, Elijah. 1990. *Streetwise: Race, Class, and Change in an Urban Community*. Chicago: University of Chicago Press.

Anderson, Susan M., Inga Reznick, and Serena Chen. In press. "The Self in Relation to Others: Motivational and Cognitive Underpinnings." In *The Self Across Psychology: Self-Recognition, Self-Awareness, and the Self-Concept*, eds. J. G. Snodgrass and R. L. Thompson. New York: New York Academy of Science.

Andrews, Don, and James Bonta. 1994. *The Psychology of Criminal Conduct*. Cincinnati, OH: Anderson.

_____. 1996. *The Level of Service Inventory—Revised*. Toronto: Multi-Health Systems.

Axelrod, Robert. 1984. *The Evolution of Cooperation*. New York: Basic Books.

Bales, Robert F. 1950. *Interaction Process Analysis: A Method for the Study of Small Groups*. Cambridge, MA: Addison-Wesley.

Barber, Benjamin. 1984. *Strong Democracy*. Berkeley, CA: University of California Press.

_____. 1995. *Jihad vs. McWorld*. New York: Times Books.

Bass, Carole. 1992. "Colleagues Go to the Mat Over Campaign to Out 'Johns'." *Connecticut Law Tribune*, April 20, p.4.

Baumgartner, M. P. 1988. *The Moral Order of a Suburb*. New York: Oxford University Press.

Bazemore, Gordon. 1997. "Evaluating Community Youth Sanctioning Models: Neighborhood Dimensions and Beyond." Paper presented at the National Institute of Justice Annual Conference on Criminal Justice Research and Evaluation, Washington, D.C.

Bazemore, Gordon, and Dennis Maloney. 1994. "Rehabilitating Community Service: Toward Restorative Service Sanctions in a Balanced Justice System." *Federal Probation* 58:24–34.

Bazemore, Gordon, and Mark S. Umbreit. 1994. "Balanced and Restorative Justice." U.S. Department of Justice, Office of Juvenile Justice and Delinquency Prevention.

_____. 1995. "Rethinking the Sanctioning Function in Juvenile Court: Retributive or Restorative Responses to Youth Crime." *Crime & Delinquency* 41:296–316.

Belenko, Steven, and Tamara Dumanovsky. 1993. "Special Drug Courts." November. NCJ 144531. Washington, DC: National Institute of Justice.

Bellah, Robert N., Richard Madsen, William M. Sullivan, Ann Swidler, and Steven M. Tipton. 1985. *Habits of the Heart: Individualism and Commitment in American Life*. Berkeley: University of California Press.

_____. 1991. *The Good Society*. Berkeley: University of California Press.

Bennett, Susan. 1995. "Community Organizations and Crime." *Annals of the American Academy of Political and Social Science* 539:73–84.

Bennett, William J., John J. DiIulio, and John P. Walters. 1996. *Body Count*. New York: Simon and Schuster.

Berry, Jeffrey M., Kent E. Portney, and Ken Thomson. 1993. *The Rebirth of Urban Democracy*. Washington, DC: Brookings.

Blau, Peter M. 1977. *Inequality and Heterogeneity: A Primitive Theory of Social Structure*. New York: Free Press.

Block, Richard. 1979. "Community, Environment and Violent Crime." *Criminology* 17:46–57.

Blumstein, Alfred. 1995. "Violence by Young People: Why the Deadly Nexus." *NIJ Journal* 229 (August):2–9.

Boland, Barbara. 1998. "Community Prosecution: Portland's Experience." Pp. 253–277 in *Community Justice: An Emerging Field*, ed. David R. Karp. Lanham, MD: Rowman and Littlefield.

Bourdieu, Pierre. 1977. "Cultural Reproduction and Social Reproduction." Pp. 496–521 in *Power and Ideology in Education*, eds. Jerome Karabel and A. H. Halsey. New York: Oxford University Press.

Braithwaite, John. 1979. *Inequality, Crime, and Public Policy*. London: Routledge and Kegan Paul.

_____. 1989. *Crime, Shame, and Reintegration*. Cambridge: Cambridge University Press.

_____. 1997. "One Future Direction: Restorative Justice." Paper presented at the Second National Outlook Symposium: Violent Crime, Property Crime and Public Policy, in Canberra, Australia.

Braithwaite, John, and Stephen Mugford. 1994. "Conditions of Successful Reintegration Ceremonies." *British Journal of Criminology* 34:139–171.

Bratton, William J. 1995. "Explaining the Drop in Urban Crime." Paper presented at the annual meeting of the American Society of Criminology, in Boston, in November.

Brewer, Marilyn B., and Roderick M. Kramer. 1986. "Choice Behavior in Social Dilemmas: Effects of Social Identity, Group Size, and Decision Framing." *Journal of Personality and Social Psychology* 50:543–549.

Brodsky, Stanley. 1975. *Families and Friends of Men in Prison*. Lexington, MA: Lexington Books.

Buerger, Michael. 1994. "A Tale of Two Targets: Limitations of Community Anti-crime Actions." *Crime & Delinquency* 40:411–436.

Burgess, Ernest W. 1967. "The Growth of the City: An Introduction to a Research Project." Pp. 47–62 in *The City*, eds. Robert Park and Ernest W. Burgess. Chicago: University of Chicago Press.

Bursik, Robert. 1986. "Ecological Stability and the Dynamics of Delinquency." Pp. 35–66 in *Communities and Crime*, eds. Albert J. Reiss and Michael Tonry. Chicago: University of Chicago Press.

Bursik, Robert J., Jr. 1988. "Social Disorganization and Theories of Crime and Delinquency: Problems and Prospects." *Criminology* 26:519–551.

Bursik, Robert J., and Harold G. Grasmick. 1993. *Neighborhoods and Crime: The Dimensions of Effective Community Control*. New York: Lexington Books.

Caporael, Linnda R., Robyn M. Dawes, John M. Orbell, and Alphons J. C. van de Kragt. 1989. "Selfishness Examined: Cooperation in the Absence of Egoistic Incentives." *Behavioral and Brain Sciences* 12:683–739.

Carlson, Bonnie, and Neil Cerveera. 1992. *Inmates and Their Wives*. Westport, CT: Greenwood Press.

Chavis, David M., Kien Lee, and Suzanne Merchlinsky. 1997. "National Cross-Site Evaluation of the Community Building Initiative." Bethesda, MD: Cosmos.

Chavis, David M., Paul W. Speer, Ira Resnick, and Allison Zippay. 1993. "Building Community Capacity to Address Alcohol and Drug Abuse: Getting to the Heart of the Problem." Pp. 251–284 in *Drugs and the Community*, eds. Robert C. Davis, Arthur J. Lurigio, and Dennis P. Rosenbaum. Springfield, IL: Charles C. Thomas.

Christie, Nils. 1977. "Conflict as Property." *British Journal of Criminology* 17:1–14.

Clarke, Ronald V. 1995. "Situational Crime Prevention." Pp. 91–150 in *Building a Safer Society: Strategic Approaches to Crime Prevention*, eds. Michael Tonry and David P. Farrington. Chicago: University of Chicago Press.

Clear, Todd R. 1994. *Harm in American Penology*. Albany, NY: State University of New York (SUNY) Press.

Clear, Todd R., and George F. Cole. 1997. *American Corrections*. 5th ed. Belmont, CA: Wadsworth.

Clear, Todd R., and Dina Rose. 1996. "A Thug in Jail Can't Shoot Your Sister: Exploring the Unanticipated Consequences of Incarceration." Paper presented at the annual meeting of the American Sociological Association, in New York, in August.

Clines, Francis X. 1992. "Ex-Inmates Urge Return to Areas of Crime to Help." *New York Times*, Dec. 23, Late Edition–Final, p. A1, col. 1.

Cohen, Lawrence, and Marcus Felson. 1979. "Social Change and Crime Rate Trends: A Routine Activity Approach." *American Sociological Review* 44:588–608.

Coleman, James. 1990. *Foundations of Social Theory*. Cambridge, MA: Harvard University Press.

Connell, James P., Anne C. Kubisch, Lisbeth B. Schorr, and Carol H. Weiss, eds. 1995. *New Approaches to Evaluating Community Initiatives*. Washington, DC: Aspen Institute.

Corbett, Ronald P., Bernard L. Fitzgerald, and James Jordan. 1996. "Operation Night Light: An Emerging Model for Police-Probation Partnership." Pp.

105–115 in *Invitation to Change: Better Government Competition on Public Safety*, eds. Linda Brown and Kathryn Ciffolillo. Boston: Pioneer Institute for Public Policy Research.

Cornish, Derek B., and Ronald V. Clarke. 1986. *The Reasoning Criminal*. New York: Springer-Verlag.

Corsaro, William A., and Donna Eder. 1994. "Development and Socialization of Children and Adolescents." Pp. 421–451 in *Sociological Perspectives on Social Psychology*, eds. Karen S. Cook, Gary A. Fine, and James House. Boston: Allyn and Bacon.

Cragg, Wesley. 1992. *The Practice of Punishment*. New York: Routledge.

Crawford, Adam. 1995. "Appeals to Community and Crime Prevention." *Crime, Law, and Social Change* 22:97–126.

Crutchfield, Robert. 1997. "Labor Markets, Employment, and Crime." Washington, DC: U.S. Department of Justice.

Cunningham, William C., John J. Strauchs, and Clifford W. Van Meter. 1991. "Private Security: Patterns and Trends." Washington, DC: U.S. Department of Justice.

Davis, Robert C., and Arthur J. Lurigio. 1996. *Fighting Back: Neighborhood Antidrug Strategies*. Thousand Oaks, CA: Sage Publications.

Dawes, Robyn M., Alphons J. C. van de Kragt, and John M. Orbell. 1990. "Cooperation for the Benefit of Us—Not Me, or My Conscience." Pp. 97–111 in *Beyond Self-Interest*, ed. Jane J. Mansbridge. Chicago: University of Chicago Press.

———. 1988. "Not Me or Thee But We: The Importance of Group Identity in Eliciting Cooperation in Dilemma Situations: Experimental Manipulations." *Acta Psychologica* 68:83–97.

Deutsch, Morton. 1975. "Equity, Equality, and Need: What Determines Which Value Will Be Used as the Basis of Distributive Justice?" *Journal of Social Issues* 31:137–149.

DiIulio, John J., and Beth Z. Palubinsky. 1997. "How Philadelphia Salvages Teen Criminals." *City Journal*, Summer: 23–40.

District of Columbia Department of Corrections. 1997. Washington, D.C.: Office of Planning and Program Development.

Dooley, Michael. 1996. "Restorative Justice in Vermont: A Work in Progress." March. Washington, DC: National Institute of Corrections.

Dubow, Fred, and Aaron Podolefsky. 1982. "Citizen Participation in Community Crime Participation." *Human Organization* 41:307–314.

Duffee, David E. 1997. "Working with Communities." Pp. 85–95 in *Community Policing in a Rural Setting*, eds. Quint C. Thurman and Edmund F. McGarrell. Cincinnati, OH: Anderson.

Dunford, Franklyn W., and Delbert S. Elliott. 1984. "Identifying Career Offenders Using Self-Reported Data." *Journal of Research in Crime and Delinquency* 21:57–82.

Dworkin, Ronald. 1984. "Liberalism." Pp. 60–79 in *Liberalism and Its Critics*, ed. Michael J. Sandel. New York: New York University Press.

Earle, Ronald. 1996. "Community Justice: The Austin Experience." *Texas Probation* 11:6–11.

Eck, John. 1997. "Preventing Crime at Places." In *Preventing Crime: What Works, What Doesn't, What's Promising: A Report to the United States Congress*, eds.

Lawrence W. Sherman, Denise Gottfredson, Doris MacKenzie, John Eck, Peter Reuter, and Shawn Bushway. College Park, MD: University of Maryland, Department of Criminology and Criminal Justice.

Ekblom, Paul. 1995. "Less Crime, by Design." *Annals of the American Academy of Political and Social Science* 539:114–129.

Elias, Robert. 1983. *Victims of the System.* New Brunswick, NJ: Transaction.

_____. 1986. *The Politics of Victimization: Victims, Victimology, and Human Rights.* New York: Oxford University Press.

Elliott, Delbert S., Amanda Elliott, Robert Sampson, David Huizinga, William Julius Wilson, and Bruce Rankin. 1996. "The Effects of Neighborhood Disadvantage on Adolescent Development." *Journal of Research in Crime and Delinquency* 33:389–427.

Etzioni, Amitai. 1993. *The Spirit of Community.* New York: Crown.

_____. 1996a. "The Responsive Community: A Communitarian Perspective." *American Sociological Review* 61:1–11.

_____. 1996b. *The New Golden Rule.* New York: Basic Books.

Farley, Reynolds, Howard Schuman, Suzanne Bianchi, Diane Colasanto, and Shirley Hatchett. 1978. "'Chocolate City, Vanilla Suburbs': Will the Trend Toward Racially Separate Communities Continue?" *Social Science Research* 7:319–344.

Farrell, Graham. 1995. "Preventing Repeat Victimization." Pp. 469–534 in *Building a Safer Society: Strategic Approaches to Crime Prevention,* eds. Michael Tonry and David P. Farrington. Chicago: University of Chicago Press.

Felson, Marcus. 1996. "Those Who Doscourage Crime." Pp. 53–66 in *Crime and Place: Crime Prevention Studies,* eds. John E. Eck and David Weisburd. Albany, NY: Harrow and Heston.

Finckenauer, James O. 1982. *Scared Straight: The Panacea Phenomenon.* Englewood Cliffs, NJ: Prentice-Hall.

Firey, William. 1945. "Sentiment and Symbolism as Ecological Variables." *American Sociological Review* 10:140–148.

Fischer, Claude S., Michael Hout, Martin Sanchez Jankowski, Samuel R. Lucas, Ann Swidler, and Kim Voss. 1996. *Inequality by Design.* Princeton, NJ: Princeton University Press.

Fishkin, James S. 1992. *Democracy and Deliberation: New Directions for Democratic Reform.* New Haven, CT: Yale University Press.

Fishman, Laura. 1990. *Woman at the Wall.* Albany: SUNY Press.

Fleishman, John A. 1980. "Collective Action as Helping Behavior: Effects of Responsibility Diffusion on Contributions to a Public Good." *Journal of Personality and Social Psychology* 38:629–637.

Freeman, Richard B. 1992. "Crime and Unemployment of Disadvantaged Youth." in *Drugs, Crime, and Social Isolation: Barriers to Urban Opportunity,* eds. Adele Harrell and George Peterson. Washington, DC: Urban Institute.

Fukuyama, Francis. 1995. *Trust: The Social Virtues and the Creation of Prosperity.* New York: Free Press.

Gabel, Stewart. 1992. "Children of Incarcerated and Criminal Parents: Adjustment, Behavior, and Prognosis." *Bulletin of American Academic Psychiatry Law* 20:33–45.

Galaway, Burt, and Joe Hudson, eds. 1996. *Restorative Justice: International Perspectives*. Monsey, NY: Criminal Justice Press.

Gans, Herbert. 1962. *The Urban Villagers: Group and Class in the Life of Italian Americans*. New York: Free Press.

Garland, David. 1990. *Punishment and Modern Society*. Chicago: University of Chicago Press.

General Accounting Office. 1997. "Drug Courts: Overview of Growth, Characteristics, and Results." July. GAO/GGD–97–106. Washington, DC: General Accounting Office.

Gilligan, Carol. 1982. *In a Different Voice: Psychological Theory and Women's Development*. Cambridge, MA: Harvard University Press.

Glendon, Mary Ann. 1991. *Rights Talk: The Impoverishment of Political Discourse*. New York: Free Press.

Goldsmith-Hirsch, Suzanne. 1998. "The Takoma Orange Hats: Fighting Crime and Building Community in Washington, D.C." Pp. 47–79 in *Community Justice: An Emerging Field*, ed. D. R. Karp. Lanham, MD: Rowman and Littlefield.

Goldstein, Herman. 1976. *Policing in a Free Society*. Cambridge, MA: Bainger.

———. 1990. *Problem-Oriented Policing*. New York: McGraw-Hill.

Gorczyk, John. 1996. "The Vermont Reparative Justice Model." Paper presented at the Conference on Restorative Justice, National Institute of Justice, Washington, D.C.

Gottfredson, Denise. 1997. "School-Based Crime Prevention." In *Preventing Crime: What Works, What Doesn't, What's Promising: A Report to the United States Congress*, eds. Lawrence W. Sherman, Denise Gottfredson, Doris MacKenzie, John Eck, Peter Reuter, and Shawn Bushway. College Park, MD: University of Maryland, Department of Criminology and Criminal Justice.

Gottfredson, Michael J., and Travis Hirschi. 1990. *A General Theory of Crime*. Stanford: Stanford University Press.

Greenberg, Stephanie W., and William M. Rohe. 1986. "Informal Social Control and Crime Prevention in Modern Urban Neighborhoods." Pp. 79–118 in *Urban Neighborhoods: Research and Policy*, ed. Ralph B. Taylor. New York: Praeger.

Greene, Jack R., and Edward McLaughlin. 1993. "Facilitating Communities Through Police Work: Drug Problem Solving and Neighborhood Involvement in Philadelphia." Pp. 141–161 in *Drugs and the Community*, eds. Robert C. Davis, Arthur J. Lurigio, and Dennis P. Rosenbaum. Springfield, IL: Charles C. Thomas.

Grinc, Randolph M. 1994. "'Angels in Marble': Problems in Stimulating Community Involvement in Community Policing." *Crime & Delinquency* 40:437–468.

Grogger, Jeffrey. 1995. "The Effect of Arrests on the Employment and Earnings of Young Men." *Quarterly Journal of Economics* 110:51–71.

Guest, Avery M. 1984. "Robert Park and the Natural Area: A Sentimental Review." *Sociology and Social Research* 68:1–21.

Guest, Avery M., and Barrett A. Lee. 1984. "How Urbanites Define Their Neighborhoods." *Populations and Environment* 7:33–57.

Gutmann, Amy, and Dennis Thompson. 1996. *Democracy and Disagreement*. Cambridge: Harvard.

Hagan, John. 1993. "The Social Embeddedness of Crime and Unemployment." *Criminology* 31:465–492.

_____. 1996. "The Next Generation: Children of Prisoners." Pp. 22–39 in *The Unintended Consequences of Incarceration.* New York: Vera Institute of Justice.

Hardin, Garrett. 1968. "The Tragedy of the Commons." *Science* 162:1243–1248.

Hart, H.L.A. 1963. *Law, Liberty and Morality.* New York: Vintage.

Hawley, Amos. 1971. *Urban Society: An Ecological Approach.* New York: Ronald.

Hechter, Michael. 1987. *Principles of Group Solidarity.* Berkeley: University of California Press.

Hillery, George A. 1955. "Definitions of Community: Areas of Agreement." *Rural Sociology* 20:779–791.

Hirschi, Travis. 1969. *Causes of Delinquency.* Berkeley: University of California Press.

Hochschild, Arlie R. 1997. *Time Bind: When Work Becomes Home and Home Becomes Work.* New York: Metropolitan Books.

Hope, Timothy. 1991. "Construction of Community Safety and Disorder." Paper presented at the annual meeting of the American Society of Criminology, in San Francisco.

Hudson, Joe, Allison Morris, Gabrielle Maxwell, and Burt Galaway, eds. 1996. *Family Group Conferences.* Monsey, NY: Criminal Justice Press.

Huizinga, David, and Delbert S. Elliott. 1987. "Juvenile Offenders: Prevalence, Offender Incidence, and Arrest Rates by Race." *Crime and Delinquency* 33:208–210.

Hunter, Albert J., and Gerald D. Suttles. 1972. "The Expanding Community of Limited Liability." Pp. 44–81 in *The Social Construction of Communities,* ed. Gerald D. Suttles. Chicago: University of Chicago Press.

Immarigeon, Russ. 1996. "Family Group Conferences in Canada and the United States: An Overview." Pp. 167–179 in *Family Group Conferences,* eds. Joe Hudson, Allison Morris, Gabrielle Maxwell, and Burt Galaway. Monsey, NY: Criminal Justice Press.

Jargowsky, Paul A. 1997. *Poverty and Place: Ghettos, Barrios, and the American City.* New York: Russell Sage Foundation.

Kahan, Dan M. 1996. "What Do Alternative Sanctions Mean?" *University of Chicago Law Review* 63:591–653.

Karp, David R., ed. 1998a. *Community Justice: An Emerging Field.* Lanham, MD: Rowman and Littlefield.

_____. 1998b. "Judicial and Judicious Use of Shame Penalties." *Crime and Delinquency* 44:277–294.

Karp, David R., and Clark L. Gaulding. 1995. "Motivational Underpinnings of Command-and-Control, Market-Based, and Voluntarist Environmental Policies." *Human Relations* 48:439–465.

Kasarda, John. 1989. "Urban Industrial Transition and the Underclass." *Annals of the American Academy of Political and Social Science* 501:26–47.

Kelling, George. 1992. "Measuring What Matters: A New Way of Thinking About Crime and Public Order." *City Journal,* Spring: 21–33.

Kelling, George L., and Catherine M. Coles. 1996. *Fixing Broken Windows.* New York: Free Press.

Kennedy, David M. 1996. "Neighborhood Revitalization: Lessons from Savannah and Baltimore." *National Institute of Justice Journal,* August:13–17.

_____. 1997. "Pulling Levers: Chronic Offenders, High-Crime Settings, and a Theory of Prevention." *Valparaiso University Law Review* 31:449–484.

Kerr, Norbert L. 1989. "Illusions of Efficacy: The Effects of Group Size on Perceived Efficacy in Social Dilemmas." *Journal of Experimental Social Psychology* 25:287–313.

_____. 1993. "Efficacy as a Causal and Moderating Variable in Social Dilemmas." Pp. 59–80 in *Social Dilemmas: Theoretical Issues and Research Findings,* eds. W.B.G. Liebrand, D. M. Messick, and H.A.M. Wilke. New York: Pergamon.

King, Anthony E. O. 1993. "The Impact of Incarceration on African American Families: Implications for Practice." *Journal of Contemporary Human Service:* vol. 75, no. 3:145–153.

Klandermans, Bert. 1984. "Mobilization and Participation: Social-Psychological Expansions of Resource Mobilization Theory." *American Sociological Review* 49:583–600.

Kohlberg, Lawrence. 1968. "Moral Development." In *International Encyclopedia of the Social Sciences,* ed. David L. Sills. New York: Macmillan.

Kohn, Melvin L., and K. M. Slomczynski. 1990. *Social Structure and Self-Direction.* Oxford: Basil Blackwell.

Kornhauser, Ruth Rosner. 1978. *Social Sources of Delinquency: An Appraisal of Analytic Models.* Chicago: University of Chicago Press.

Kramer, Roderick M., and Marilyn B. Brewer. 1986. "Social Group Identitiy and the Emergence of Cooperation in Resource Conservation Dilemmas." Pp. 205–234 in *Experimental Social Dilemmas,* eds. Henke A. M. Wilke, David M. Messick, and Christel G. Rutte. Frankfurt: Verlag Peter Lang.

Kuhn, M. H., and R. McPartland. 1954. "An Empirical Investigation of Self Attitudes." *American Sociological Review* 19:68–76.

Lewis, Dan A., and Greta Salem. 1986. *Fear of Crime: Incivility and the Production of a Social Problem.* New Brunswick, NJ: Transaction.

Lewis, Oscar. 1968. "The Culture of Poverty." In *On Understanding Poverty: Perspectives from the Social Sciences,* ed. Daniel P. Moynihan. New York: Basic Books.

Logan, John R., and Harvey L. Molotch. 1987. *Urban Fortunes: The Political Economy of Place.* Berkeley: University of California Press.

Lowstein, A. 1986. "Temporary Single Parenthood: The Case of Prisoners' Families." *Family Relations* 35:79–85.

Luce, R. D., and H. Raiffa. 1957. *Games and Decisions.* New York: Wiley.

Lukes, Steven. 1973. *Individualism.* Oxford: Basil Blackwell.

Lynch, James. 1995. "Crime in International Perspective." Pp. 11–38 in *Crime,* eds. James Q. Wilson and Joan Petersilia. San Francisco, CA: Institute for Contemporary Studies.

Lynch, Michael, and William J. Sabol. 1992. "Macro-Social Changes and their Implications for Prison Reform: the Underclass and the Composition of Prison Populations." Paper presented at the annual meeting of the American Society of Criminology, in New Orleans.

Lyon, Larry. 1987. *The Community in Urban Society.* Chicago: Dorsey Press.

MacDonald, Heather. 1996. "BIDs Really Work." *City Journal* 6:29–42.

Maguire, Kathleen, and Ann L. Pastore, eds. 1998a. Table 5.19. *Sourcebook of Criminal Justice Statistics*. Available on line: http://www.albany.edu/sourcebook.[4/9/99]
_____. 1998b. Table 5.45. *Sourcebook of Criminal Justice Statistics*. Available on line: http://www.albany.edu/sourcebook.[4/9/99]
_____. 1998c. Table 5.48. Sourcebook of Criminal Justice Statistics. Available on line: http://www.albany.edu/sourcebook.[4/9/99]

Marx, Gary. 1989. "Commentary: Some Trends and Issues in Citizen Involvement in the Law Enforcement Process." *Crime & Delinquency* 35:500–519.

Massey, Douglas S., and Nancy A. Denton. 1993. *American Apartheid*. Cambridge: Harvard University Press.

Mauer, Mark. 1995. *African American Males and the Criminal Justice System, 1995*. Washington, DC: Sentencing Project.

Maxwell, Gabrielle, and Allison Morris. 1994. "The New Zealand Model of Family Group Conferences." Pp. 15–44 in *Family Conferencing and Juvenile Justice*, eds. Christine Alder and Joy Wundersitz. Canberra: Australian Institute of Criminology.

McCold, Paul, and John Stahr. 1996. "Bethlehem Police Family Group Conferencing Project." Paper presented at the annual meeting of the American Society of Criminology, in Chicago, in November.

McMillan, David W., and David M. Chavis. 1986. "Sense of Community: A Definition and Theory." *Journal of Community Psychology* 14:6–23.

Mead, George H. 1956. P. 226 in *On Social Psychology*, ed. Anselm Strauss. Chicago: University of Chicago Press.

Merton, Robert K. 1938. "Social Structure and Anomie." *American Sociological Review* 3:672–682.
_____. 1957. *Social Theory and Social Structure*. Glencoe, IL: Free Press.

Miethe, Terance D. 1995. "Fear and Withdrawal from Urban Life." *Annals of the American Academy of Political and Social Science* 539:14–27.

Miller, Ted R., Mark A. Cohen, and Brian Wiersma. 1996. "Victim Costs and Consequences: A New Look." Washington, DC: National Institute of Justice.

Mitchell, Alison. 1992. "In an Often Violent City, A Not-So-Simple Beating." *New York Times*, Dec. 6. 1992, Late Edition–Final, Section 1, p. 51, col. 1.

Molotch, Harvey. 1976. "The City as a Growth Machine." *American Journal of Sociology* 82:309–330.

Moore, David B., and Terry A. O'Connell. 1994. "Family Conferencing in Wagga Wagga: A Communitarian Model of Justice." Pp. 45–86 in *Family Conferencing and Juvenile Justice*, eds. Christine Alder and Joy Wundersitz. Canberra: Australian Institute of Criminology.

Moore, Mark H. 1997. "The Legitimation of Criminal Justice Policies and Practices." Paper presented at conference "Perspectives on Crime and Justice," National Institute of Justice, Washington, D.C.

Morris, Norval, and Michael Tonry. 1990. *Between Probation and Parole: Intermediate Punishments in a Rational Sentencing System*. New York: Oxford University Press.

Moynihan, Daniel P. 1969. *Maximum Feasible Misunderstanding: Community Action in the War on Poverty*. New York: Free Press.

Murphy, Jeffrie, and Jeanne Hampton. 1988. *Forgiveness and Mercy*. New York: Cambridge University Press.

National Institute of Justice. 1995. "The Drug Court Movement." *National Institute of Justice Update.* July. Washington, DC: Department of Justice.

National Institute of Justice. 1996. *National Institute of Justice Journal.* August. Washington, DC: NIJ.

New York Times. 1996. "Philadelphia Feels Effects of Inquiry." *New York Times,* March 24, p. A35.

Newman, Oscar. 1972. *Defensible Space.* New York: Macmillan.

Newman, Oscar, and Karen Franck. 1982. "The Effects of Building Size on Personal Crime and Fear of Crime." *Population and Environment* 5:203–220.

Nisbet, Robert. 1953. *The Quest for Community.* Oxford: Oxford University Press.

Office of Justice Programs. 1995. "Drug Courts Program Office Fact Sheet." Washington, DC: Department of Justice.

Olson, Mancur. 1965. *The Logic of Collective Action.* Cambridge: Harvard University Press.

Park, Robert E. 1936. "Human Ecology." *American Journal of Sociology* 17:1–15.

Peak, Kenneth J., and Ronald W. Glensor. 1996. *Community Policing and Problem Solving.* Upper Saddle River, NJ: Prentice Hall.

Piliavin, Jane, and Hong-Wen Charng. 1990. "Altruism: A Review of Recent Theory and Research." *Annual Review of Sociology* 16:27–67.

Pithers, William D. 1987. *Relapse Prevention of Sexual Aggression.* South Burlington: Vermont Department of Corrections.

Police Executive Research Forum. 1995. "Community Policing." Washington, DC: Department of Justice.

Popenoe, David. 1988. *Disturbing the Nest: Family Change and Decline in Modern Societies.* New York: Aldine de Gruyter.

Pruitt, Dean G., and Melvin J. Kimmel. 1977. "Twenty Years of Experimental Gaming: Critique, Synthesis, and Suggestions for the Future." *Annual Review of Psychology* 28:363–392.

Putnam, Robert. 1995. "Bowling Alone: America's Declining Social Capital." *Journal of Democracy* 6:64–78.

Quinn, Thomas. 1996. "Restorative Justice." Paper presented at the Conference on Restorative Justice, National Institute of Justice, Washington, D.C.

Rand, Michael R., James P. Lynch, and David Cantor. 1997. "Criminal Victimization, 1973–95." Washington, DC: Department of Justice.

Rawls, John. 1971. *A Theory of Justice.* Cambridge, MA: Belknap.

Ritzer, George. 1993. *The McDonaldization of Society : An Investigation into the Changing Character of Contemporary Social Life.* Newbury Park, CA: Pine Forge Press.

Roberts, Marilyn, Caroline Brophy, and Jennifer Cooper. 1997. "The Juvenile Drug Court Movement." Washington, DC: U.S. Department of Justice.

Rosenbaum, Dennis P. 1988. "Community Crime Prevention: A Review and Synthesis of the Literature." *Justice Quarterly* 5:323–395.

_____. 1993. "Civil Liberties and Aggressive Enforcement: Balancing the Rights of Individuals and Society in the Drug War." Pp. 55–82 in *Drugs and the Community,* eds. Robert C. Davis, Arthur J. Lurigio, and Dennis P. Rosenbaum. Springfield, IL: Charles C. Thomas.

Rosenbaum, James E. 1995. "Changing the Geography of Opportunity by Expanding Residential Choice: Lessons from the Gautreaux Program." *Housing Policy Debate* 6:231–269.

Rottman, David B. 1996. "Community Courts: Prospects and Limits." *National Institute of Justice Journal*, August:46–51.

Rusk, David. 1995. *Cities Without Suburbs*. Washington, DC: Woodrow Wilson Center Press.

Sagy, Shifra, Eliahu Stern, and Shaul Krakover. 1996. "Macro- and Microlevel Factors Related to Sense of Community: The Case of Temporary Neighborhoods in Israel." *American Journal of Community Psychology* 24:657–676.

Sampson, Robert J. 1987. "Communities and Crime." Pp. 91–114 in *Positive Criminology*, eds. Michael R. Gottfredson and Travis Hirschi. Beverly Hills, CA: Sage.

_____. 1995. "The Community." Pp. 193–216 in *Crime*, eds. James Q. Wilson and Joan Petersilia. San Francisco, CA: Institute for Contemporary Studies.

Sampson, Robert J., and John Laub. 1993. *Crime in the Making: Pathways and Turning Points Through Life*. Cambridge: Harvard University.

Sampson, Robert J., and Janet L. Lauritson. 1994. "Violent Victimization and Offending: Individual-, Situational-, and Community-Level Risk Factors." Pp. 1–114 in *Understanding and Preventing Violence*, eds. Albert J. Reiss and Jeffrey A. Roth. Washington, DC: National Academy Press.

Sampson, Robert J., and William Julius Wilson. 1995. "Toward a Theory of Race, Crime, and Urban Inequality." Pp. 37–54 in *Crime and Inequality*, eds. John Hagan and Ruth D. Peterson. Stanford, CA: Stanford University Press.

Scheff, Thomas. 1996. "Crime, Shame, and Community: Mediation Against Violence." Unpublished manuscript.

Schorr, Lisbeth B. 1997. *Common Purpose: Strengthening Families and Neighborhoods to Rebuild America*. New York: Doubleday.

Schwartz, Shalom H. 1992. "Universals in the Content and Structure of Values: Theoretical Advances and Empirical Tests in 20 Countries." *Advances in Experimental Social Psychology* 25:1–65.

Selznick, Philip. 1992. *The Moral Commonwealth*. Berkeley: University of California Press.

_____. 1996. "Social Justice: A Communitarian Perspective." *Responsive Community* 6:13–25.

Sen, Amartya K. 1978. "Rational Fools: A Critique of the Behavioral Foundations of Economic Theory." Pp. 317–344 in *Scientific Models and Men*, ed. H. Harris. Oxford: Oxford University Press.

_____. 1985. *Commodities and Capabilities*. Amsterdam: North-Holland Press.

Sentencing Project. 1997. "Facts About Prisons and Prisoners." Washington, DC: Sentencing Project.

Shaw, Clifford R., and Henry D. McKay. 1942. *Juvenile Delinquency in Urban Areas*. Chicago: University of Chicago Press.

Sherman, Lawrence W. 1997a. "Thinking About Crime Prevention." In *Preventing Crime: What Works, What Doesn't, What's Promising: A Report to the United States Congress*, eds. Lawrence W. Sherman, Denise Gottfredson, Doris MacKenzie, John Eck, Peter Reuter, and Shawn Bushway. College Park, MD: University of Maryland, Department of Criminology and Criminal Justice.

_____. 1997b. "Family-Based Crime Prevention." In *Preventing Crime: What Works, What Doesn't, What's Promising: A Report to the United States Congress*, eds. Lawrence W. Sherman, Denise Gottfredson, Doris MacKenzie, John Eck, Peter Reuter, and Shawn Bushway. College Park, MD: University of Maryland, Department of Criminology and Criminal Justice.

Sherman, Lawrence W., Denise Gottfredson, Doris MacKenzie, John Eck, Peter Reuter, and Shawn Bushway, eds. 1997. *Preventing Crime: What Works, What Doesn't, What's Promising: A Report to the United States Congress*. College Park, MD: University of Maryland, Department of Criminology and Criminal Justice.

Sherman, Lawrence W., and Heather Strang. 1997. "The Right Kind of Shame for Crime Prevention." Press release.

Skogan, Wesley G. 1988. "Community Organizations and Crime." Pp. 39–78 in *Crime and Justice: A Review of the Research*, eds. Michael Tonry and Norval Morris. Chicago: University of Chicago.

_____. 1990. *Disorder and Decline: Crime and the Spiral of Decay in American Neighborhoods*. New York: Free Press.

_____. 1997. *Community Policing, Chicago Style*. New York: Oxford University Press.

Skolnick, Jerome H., and David H. Bayley. 1986. *The New Blue Line: Police Innovation in Six American Cities*. New York: Free Press.

Smith, Adam. 1966 (1759). *The Theory of Moral Sentiments*. New York: Kelley.

Smith, Margaret, and Todd R. Clear. 1995. "Fathers in Prison: Interim Report." Rutgers University School of Criminal Justice, Edna McConnell Clark Foundation.

Sparrow, Malcolm K., Mark H. Moore, and David M. Kennedy. 1990. *Beyond 911: A New Era for Policing*. New York: Basic Books.

Stern, D. N. 1985. *The Interpersonal World of the Infant*. New York: Basic Books.

Stone, Christopher. 1996. "Community Defense and the Challenge of Community Justice." *National Institute of Justice Journal*, August:41–45.

Strang, Heather, and Lawrence W. Sherman. 1997. "The Victim's Perspective." Press release.

Stuart, Barry. 1996. "Circle Sentencing: Turning Swords into Ploughshares." Pp. 193–206 in *Restorative Justice: International Perspectives*, eds. Burt Galaway and Joe Hudson. Monsey, NY: Criminal Justice Press.

Sullivan, Mercer. 1989. *Getting Paid: Youth, Crime, and Work in the Inner City*. Ithaca, NY: Cornell University Press.

_____. 1993. *More Than Housing: How Community Development Corporations Go About Changing Lives and Neighborhoods*. New York: New School for Social Research, Community Development Research Center.

Sullivan, William, and David R. Karp. 1997. "The Civil Society Debate." Report to the Smith Richardson Foundation.

Suttles, Gerald D. 1968. *The Social Order of the Slum*. Chicago: University of Chicago Press.

Sykes, Gresham M., and David Matza. 1957. "Techniques of Neutralization: A Theory of Delinquency." *American Sociological Review* 22:665–670.

Taylor, Ralph B. 1988. *Human Territorial Functioning*. Cambridge: Cambridge University Press.

_____. 1995. "The Impact of Crime on Communities." *Annals of the American Academy of Political and Social Science* 539:28–45.

_____. 1997. "Crime, Grime, and Responses to Crime: Relative Impacts of Neighborhood Structure, Crime, and Physical Deterioration on Residents and Business Personnel in the Twin Cities." In *Community Crime Prevention at a Crossroads*, ed. Steven P. Lab. Cincinnati, OH: Anderson.

Taylor, Ralph B., and Jeanette Covington. 1988. "Neighborhood Changes in Ecology and Violence." *Criminology* 26:553–589.

Taylor, Ralph B., and Adele V. Harrell. 1996. "Physical Environment and Crime." National Institute of Justice.

Tittle, Charles R., W. J. Villemez, and D. A. Smith. 1978. "The Myth of Social Class and Criminality: An Empirical Assessment of the Empirical Evidence." *American Sociological Review* 43:643–656.

Tocqueville, Alexis de. 1945 (1840). *Democracy in America.* New York: Vintage.

Travis, Jeremy. 1996. "Introduction." *NIJ Journal* 31:637–655.

Triandis, Harry C., Christopher McCusker, and C. Harry Hui. 1990. "Multimethod Probes of Individualism and Collectivism." *Journal of Personality and Social Psychology* 59:1006–1020.

Trojanowicz, Robert, and Bonnie Bucqueroux. 1990. *Community Policing: A Contemporary Perspective.* Cincinnati, OH: Anderson.

Tyler, Tom R. 1990. *Why People Obey the Law.* New Haven: Yale University Press.

Umbreit, Mark S. 1994. *Victim Meets Offender: The Impact of Restorative Justice and Mediation.* Monsey, NY: Criminal Justice Press.

Umbreit, Mark S., and Robert B. Coates. 1993. "Cross-Site Analysis of Victim-Offender Mediation in Four States." *Crime & Delinquency* 39:565–585.

United States Bureau of Justice Statistics. 1995. "Prisoners in 1994." Washington, DC: U.S. Department of Justice.

_____. 1997a. "Justice Expenditure and Employment Extracts, 1992." Washington, DC: U.S. Department of Justice.

_____. 1997b. "Criminal Victimization in the United States, 1994." Washington, DC: U.S. Department of Justice.

Van Ness, Daniel, and Karen Heetderks Strong. 1997. *Restoring Justice.* Cincinnati, OH: Anderson.

Weisburd, David. 1988. "Vigilantism as Community Social Control: Developing a Quantitative Criminological Model." *Journal of Quantitative Criminology* 4:137–153.

Weisburd, David, and John Eck, eds. 1995. *Crime and Place.* New York: Harrow and Heston.

Wellman, Barry, and Barry Leighton. 1979. "Networks, Neighborhoods, and Communities: Approaches to the Study of the Community Question." *Urban Affairs Quarterly* 14:363–390.

Widom, Cathy Spatz. 1994. "Childhood Victimization and Risk for Adolescent Problem Behaviors." Pp. 127–164 in *Adolescent Problem Behaviors*, eds. M. E. Lamb and R. Ketterlinus. New York: Earlbaum.

Wilkins, Leslie. 1964. *Social Deviance.* London: Tavistock.

Williams, E. J. 1996. "Enforcing Social Responsibility and the Expanding Domain of the Police: Notes from the Portland Experience." *Crime & Delinquency* 42:309–323.

Wilson, James Q. 1993. *The Moral Sense.* New York: Free Press.

Wilson, James Q., and Richard J. Herrnstein. 1985. *Crime and Human Nature.* New York: Simon and Schuster.

Wilson, James Q., and George L. Kelling. 1982. "Broken Windows." *Atlantic Monthly,* March:29–38.

Wilson, William J. 1987. *The Truly Disadvantaged.* Chicago: University of Chicago Press.

_____. 1996. *When Work Disappears.* New York: Alfred A. Knopf.

Winokur, Cheryl. 1995. "He's the Neighborhood Watcher." *Connecticut Law Tribune,* July 3, p. 14.

Wirth, Louis. 1938. "Urbanism as a Way of Life." *American Journal of Sociology* 44:8–20.

Wolfe, Alan. 1989. *Whose Keeper? Social Science and Moral Obligation.* Berkeley: University of California Press.

Wolfgang, Marvin E., Robert M. Figlio, and Thorsten Sellin. 1972. *Delinquency in a Birth Cohort.* Chicago: University of Chicago.

Working Group on Restorative Justice. 1996. "Community Justice Principles: Report of the Working Group." Washington, DC: Department of Justice.

Wright, Martin. 1992. "Victim-Offender Mediation as a Step Towards a Restorative System of Justice." Pp. 559–567 in *Restorative Justice on Trial,* eds. H. Messmer and H.-U. Otto. Netherlands: Kluwer.

Wrong, Dennis. 1994. *The Problem of Order.* Cambridge, MA: Harvard University Press.

Yamagishi, Toshio. 1994. "Social Dilemmas." Pp. 311–334 in *Sociological Perspectives on Social Psychology,* eds. Karen S. Cook, Gary A. Fine, and James House. Boston: Allyn and Bacon.

Zehr, Howard. 1990. *Change Lenses.* Scottdale, PA: Herald Press.

Index

INSTRUCTIONS FOR USING NURSES' GUIDE TO THE INTERNET SOFTWARE

To help you use *Computers in Nursing's Nurses' Guide to the Internet* as efficiently as possible, we have provided the links from the book as a simple HTML file. Using the file on the enclosed floppy disk, you can easily locate all the sites and services mentioned in the book simply by clicking. This file will work with any web browser.

To use the enclosed disk on a Microsoft Windows system:

1. Follow the normal steps to run the web-browsing software you would like to use.
2. Insert the enclosed floppy disk into your disk drive.
3. Select "Open" or "Open File in Browser" from the File menu. (The exact name of this command may vary slightly depending on the browser you're using.)
4. Type **A:\ngi.htm**
5. Use the alphabetical menu at the top of the screen and the scrollbars to locate the entry or entries you are interested in. Click on the entry title to go to that resource. For e-mail and mailing list addresses, click on the address to compose and send mail. (If you are subscribing to a mailing list, carefully note the subscription instructions.)

To use the enclosed disk on a Macintosh system:

1. If you use Macintosh system version 7.0 or higher, you can mount and read the enclosed DOS-formatted disk just as you would a standard Macintosh-formatted disk.
2. Follow the normal steps to run the web-browsing software you would like to use.
3. Insert the enclosed floppy disk into your disk drive.
4. Select "Open" or "Open File in Browser" from the File menu. (The exact name of this command may vary slightly depending on the browser you're using.)
5. Click on the "Desktop" button.
6. Double-click on the icon for the floppy disk you inserted. (If you can't see it in the window immediately, use the scrollbar to locate it.)
7. Double-click on the file "ngi.htm."
8. Use the alphabetical menu at the top of the screen and the scrollbars to locate the entry or entries you are interested in. Click on the entry title to go to that resource. For e-mail and mailing list addresses, click on the address to compose and send mail. (If you are subscribing to a mailing list, carefully note the subscription instructions.)